Faraway Places

**Your Source for
Picture Books
That Fly Children
to 82 Countries**

Catherine Blakemore

A-PP
Adams-Pomeroy Press
Albany, Wisconsin

T 90020

Published by: A-PP   Adams-Pomeroy Press
                            P.O. Box 189
                            Albany, Wisconsin 53502
Copyright © 2002 by Catherine Blakemore. All rights reserved.

Every effort has been undertaken to ensure the accuracy and completeness of the information in this book. However, this book is intended as only a general guide to picture books that introduce young children to other countries. The author and Adams-Pomeroy Press assume neither liability nor responsibility for any errors, omissions, inconsistency, or loss or damages caused by the information in this book.

Printed in the United States of America
First Printing 2002

Cover by Robert Howard

Publisher's Cataloging-in-Publication
(Provided by Quality Books, Inc.)

Blakemore, Catherine.
   Faraway places : your source for picture books that
fly children to 82 countries / Catherine Blakemore. --
1st ed.
    p. cm.
   Includes bibliographical references and index.
   LCCN 2001132599
   ISBN 0-9661009-2-1

   1. Picture books for children--Educational aspects--
United States--Bibliography. 2. Travel--Juvenile
literature--Bibliography. 3. Voyages and travels--
Juvenile literature--Bibliography. 4. Picture books for
children--United States--Bibliography. 5. Children's
literature, American--Bibliography. 6. Pluralism
(Social sciences)--Juvenile literature--Bibliography.
7. Ethnic groups in literature--Bibliography. 8. Folk
literature--Bibliography. I. Title.

LB1044.9P49.B53 2001   371.33
                       QBI01-700747

The author gratefully acknowledges the following for permission to reprint previously published material:

EAGLE. Text Copyright © 1994 Judy Allen. Illustrations © 1994 Tudor Humphries. Reproduced by permission of the publisher Candlewick Press, Inc., Cambridge, MA, on behalf of Walker Books Ltd., London.

Excerpt from A JUST FOR A DAY BOOK: JAGUAR IN THE RAINFOREST by JOANNE RYDER. TEXT COPYRIGHT (c) 1996 BY JOANNE RYDER. Used by permission of HarperCollins Publishers.

Excerpt from *Abuela's Weave* by Omar S. Castañeda. Reprinted with permission of LEE & LOW BOOKS Inc., New York.

Excerpt from AN ISLAND CHRISTMAS. Copyright (c) 1996 by Lynn Joseph. Reprinted by permission of Clarion Books/Houghton Mifflin. All rights reserved.

Excerpt from BIG BOY by Tololwa M. Mollel. Text copyright (c) 1995 by Tololwa M. Mollel. Reprinted by permission of Clarion Books/Houghton Mifflin. All rights reserved.

Excerpt from CALL ME AHNIGHITO by PAM CONRAD. TEXT COPYRIGHT (c) 1995 BY PAM CONRAD. Used by permission of HarperCollins Publishers.

Excerpt from *Caravan* by Lawrence McKay, Jr. Reprinted with permission of LEE & LOW BOOKS Inc., New York.

Excerpt from *Chaska and the Golden Doll*, copyright © 1994 by Ellen Alexander, reprinted by permission of Arcade Publishing, New York, New York.

Excerpt from CHUBBO'S POOL. Copyright (c) 1996 by Betsy Lewin. Reprinted by permission of Clarion Books/Houghton Mifflin Company. All rights reserved.

Excerpt from *Elinda Who Danced in the Sky*, adapted by Lynn Moroney. Reprinted with the permission of the publisher, Children's Book Press, San Francisco, CA.

Excerpt from ENCOUNTER, copyright © 1992 by Jane Yolen, reprinted by permission of Harcourt, Inc.

Excerpt from FORTY FORTUNES: A TALE OF IRAN by Aaron Shepard. Text copyright (c) 1999 by Aaron Shepard. Reprinted by permission of Clarion Books/Houghton Mifflin. All rights reserved.

Excerpt from *Judge Rabbit and the Tree Spirit*, told by Lina Mao Wall and adapted by Cathy Spagnoli. Reprinted with the permission of the publisher, Children's Book Press, San Francisco, CA.

Excerpt from *Leaving for America*, written by Roslyn Bresnick-Perry. Reprinted with the permission of the publisher, Children's Book Press, San Francisco, CA.

Contents

Acknowledgments   xi

THE BENEFITS OF PICTURE BOOK TRAVEL   1

THE TRAVELERS   7

THE TRAVEL GUIDES   11

THE PICTURE BOOKS   15

THE DESTINATIONS   19

AFRICA   21

Benin • Botswana • Cameroon • Democratic
Republic of the Congo • Egypt • Ethiopia •
Gambia • Ghana • Kenya • Lesotho • Liberia •
Malawi • Mali • Morocco • Namibia • Nigeria •
Rwanda • South Africa • Tanzania • Zimbabwe

ASIA   71

Afghanistan • Armenia • Cambodia • China •
India • Indonesia • Iran • Iraq • Israel • Japan •
Jordan • Kazakhstan • Laos • Mongolia • North
Korea • Palestine • Philippines • South Korea •
Sri Lanka • Thailand • Turkey • Tuva • Vietnam

AUSTRALIA AND OCEANIA   165

Australia • Fiji

EUROPE   179

Austria • Belarus • Denmark • England • Estonia
• France • Germany • Greece • Hungary • Ireland
• Italy • Lithuania • Netherlands • Norway •
Poland • Romania • Russia • Scotland • Spain •
Sweden • Switzerland • Ukraine • United
Kingdom • Wales

NORTH AMERICA   345

Bahamas • Canada • Costa Rica • Cuba •
Dominican Republic • El Salvador • Greenland •
Guatemala • Haiti • Jamaica • Martinique •
Mexico • Montserrat • Nicaragua • Panama •
Saint Lucia • Trinidad and Tobago • Turks and
Caicos Islands

SOUTH AMERICA   403

Brazil • Chile • Ecuador • French Guiana • Peru •
Venezuela

Resources   415
Destination Index   418
Author Index   424
Title Index   442

Acknowledgments

The writing of *Faraway Places* has been enjoyable because of the wealth of picture books I have had the pleasure of reading, and rewarding because *Faraway Places* provides a means for introducing young children to their global neighbors.

Although I am solely responsible for the book's contents, I am indebted to the many persons who have helped make *Faraway Places* a reality.

First, I would like to mention those whose reviews of picture books furnished me with references to the more than 1,500 books that I considered.

I would also like to thank the staff of Albany, Wisconsin's tiny Albany Public Library: Hilary Bauman, Mark Brunner, Rosie Hart, and Rosalie Ness. Always resourceful and supportive, they devoted hours to securing the picture books I requested. In addition, Sandi Erickson of the Lakewood Library, Lakewood, Colorado helped me during the earlier stages of my research.

Additional thanks to Hilary Bauman, Elizabeth Blakemore, John Corry, Sharon Cybart, Nancy Mellott, Noreen Rueckert, Cris Valenti, Merry Valentin, Rochelle VanDusen, and Gail Van Hove, who reviewed my initial manuscript. I greatly appreciate their suggestions, comments, and insights, many of which have been incorporated into the book.

In creating *Faraway Places* I was fortunate to discover the skills of Andrew Oliver, who provided valuable advice during the later stages of the book's preparation, and of Robert Howard, whose cover design speaks for itself. I am also deeply indebted to Mary Brinkopf, whose proofreading resulted in numerous corrections and editorial changes; Elizabeth Blakemore, who served throughout as an invaluable adviser and sounding board; and David Prentice, who makes Vaughan Printing the ideal choice for printing my books. They once again provided their expertise, and I wish to thank them for their contributions.

Finally, my thanks to you, the readers, for guiding your young travelers as they experience the joys of visiting faraway places.

"Learning is growing out into the world or worlds around us."
—Holt. *What Do I Do Monday?*

The Benefits of Picture Book Travel

To live as caring, knowledgeable, and responsible citizens of the twenty-first century, children must become aware of and attuned to the peoples of other countries and to the cultural customs and values of the overwhelming majority of Americans whose heritage lies in those countries.

Only a few might argue with this thesis, but many may question why such an awareness should begin in early childhood, in the years from three to eight. Can't the introduction of faraway places be postponed? How can it even be accomplished since the opportunity to go abroad is not available to most youngsters?

The answer to these questions lies in the wealth of picture books that can "fly" children to distant lands and in the varied and compelling reasons to take advantage of them. These reasons may be divided into four categories: affirming identity, accepting and treasuring differences, developing intellectual abilities, and meeting specific needs.

Affirming Identity

Young children are involved in discovering and being pleased with their identity, a task crucial to their success in school and throughout life.

- Establishing identity can be of special significance to minority children, who all too often will experience prejudice because of their skin color or ethnic group. It is important that before receiving these negative inputs children have positive feelings about themselves. It is in the more sheltered early years that parents, relatives, and other adults can help children to recognize in what respects they may differ from others and to help them take pride in these differences and who they are. One way in which children can have their identity affirmed is through stories about people who look like they do. Books set in those foreign countries that have persons of the same or similar ethnicities aid children in meeting this need.

- All children's identities are enhanced when they have pride in their heritage. With the exception of Native Americans, American children have roots in other countries. When their parents or other nearby relatives have immigrated to the United States, they have heard firsthand accounts of life in these other lands. However, many small children do not live in extended families with relatives whose stories and recollections could give them a sense of their cultural background. They can feel a better sense of who they are when they are introduced to books set in the country or countries of their heritage.

Accepting and Treasuring Differences

- Picture books set in other countries introduce children to a variety of people, often of a different appearance, to whom they can relate. They learn that children in these places share the same experiences (such as being part of a family, obtaining and eating food, playing, going to school) and the same emotions (such as longing to be big, jealousy of siblings and friends), but in completely different environments. Indeed, they may find that the differences make the stories and settings more interesting. As they identify with the characters and settings in the stories and illustrations, they easily adopt a positive view of differences.

- By introducing these picture books at an early age, teachers, parents, and other adults can exercise choice over the books introduced. They can omit portions they find inappropriate, especially for the very young; explain and answer questions about the stories and the settings; reinforce the positive characteristics of the books; and use the books as a means of fostering understanding and tolerance. At this age children turn to adults rather than peers as their models, thereby providing a window of opportunity that will not be available if this introduction is delayed.

- Children who have learned to accept differences have no reason to fear persons who differ from them as they have already encountered similar-appearing persons in books. Chances are they will not only be accepting of and open to those of other cultures, but also more apt to seek their friendship.

- Children who have pride and security in their own identity, as discussed in the preceding section, should feel less need to affirm it at the expense of others.

- Children who have knowledge and positive feelings about peoples of other cultures are better equipped to reject negative stereotypes and attitudes.
- Culturally-aware and informed children are better prepared for the future of our country, which is becoming increasingly diverse.
- Early interest in the world around them may spur some of these children to pursue this interest through careers in the international sphere whether it be in working abroad for a business, the government, or a nonprofit organization; as translators, as international journalists, lawyers, or computer consultants; or in any of the international careers which may emerge in this new century.
- As more young children adopt tolerance and acceptance as a way of living, there is hope that as adults they will live as informed, caring citizens in a more equitable, peaceful world.

Developing Intellectual Abilities

- Children learn through relating new information to their existing knowledge. As they absorb initial impressions about the world around them, their knowledge base grows so that a much wider range of learning is relevant to them. As adults we experience this every day. For instance, if we are conversant with the latest developments in astronomy, a new discovery is both meaningful and exciting to us, whereas if we are not into astronomy, it is just an item that we come across and then quickly forget. The wider the breadth of children's early learning, the more easily they will grasp new concepts and information.

- Closely related is the development of children's reading skills. As beginning readers they focus on decoding words they encounter, but as they advance into more complex post-second grade reading, understanding plays a crucial role. Further, when children understand what they read, they are more likely to become motivated readers (Hirsch, 1987, pp. 27-28).

- Children learn about the world through exposure to a variety of experiences and media. Picture book stories and illustrations can initiate, reinforce, and expand this learning.

- The satisfaction and excitement which young children gain from early exposure to other countries hopefully will not be turned off by any less-than-stimulating school lectures, textbooks, or videos. At any rate, the children will not be dependent on later academic instruction to turn it on.

Meeting Specific Needs

- Grandmother and Grandfather are going on a Caribbean cruise. Daddy is being stationed in Germany. Mommy is going on a business trip to Brazil. Best friend Brisa has gone to spend the summer with relatives in Mexico. Picture books about these faraway places will enable children to share in their travels and to be less confused and more comfortable with their loved ones' absence.

- The family is going overseas for a vacation or is being

transferred to another country. The children will be leaving their "here" to go "somewhere else", some place unknown where things will be unfamiliar and perhaps scary. Picture books about the new country can enable the children to visualize this unknown place. The characters in the stories provide a personal link to the country. After all, if Abdul and Ali live in Morocco, it can't be all that bad. Picture books can help reduce fears and stimulate curiosity about the new "here".

Since it is so important that other countries be introduced to young children, it is especially fortunate that the picture books that can do so are easily available. All the picture books described in this book were listed as in print in R. R. Bowker's *Children's Books in Print 2000* or were published in 1999 or 2000. Compared to the cost of actual travel, they are available for a pittance to schools, child care centers, and parents. Further, thanks to this nation's public library systems and interlibrary loans, they are also available free for the asking. With only a little effort by adults, all children can discover for themselves the rewards of traveling.

"The child's mind between three and six can not only see by intelligence the relations between things, but it has the higher power still of mentally imagining those things that are not directly visible....Yet, when all are agreed that the child loves to imagine, why do we give him only fairy tales and toys on which to practice this gift? If a child can imagine a fairy and fairy land, it will not be difficult for him to imagine America."
—Montessori. *The Absorbent Mind.*

The Travelers

The travelers are those young children who fly via picture books to countries around the world. For the most part they range in age from three to eight, but they may be older or as young as two. Academically, they would generally be preschoolers, kindergartners, or first or second graders.

These children live primarily in the here and now, in their immediate environments: their homes, their neighborhoods, their child care settings, and their schools—and, for some, a slightly broader environment of grandparents' homes and vacation spots. Their physical "stomping grounds" are quite restricted, but they are born travelers. They are all blessed with two invaluable traits: insatiable curiosity and boundless imagination that enable them to transcend their environments and experience a broader world.

Young children are curious about everything they encounter. Their refrains of "What?" and then "Why?" lead to an amazing array of increasingly ingenious questions. Budding scientists, they scrutinize every new object or piece of information, absorbing every observation and in the process modifying their earlier knowledge and concepts to accommodate them. It is these children's curiosity that fuels their intellectual development.

Coupled with this font of curiosity is an equally astounding imagination. Young children are not only curious about the firefighter and the teacher; they assume their identities. They are not only curious about the racing car and the train; they become these vehicles. And, when they have listened to a story, looked at a picture book, watched a TV program, a movie, or a video; or played a computer game, their imaginations allow them to identify with characters they have never actually met. City toddlers "moo" like cows and "baa" like sheep. Depending on the popular figures of the day, they become Superman or Shaq. They even assume the identities of historical personages such as Pocahantas or those who live in foreign countries such as Madeline (France). Further, they give their dolls and stuffed animals distinct personalities. Whether personally or through their toys, they not only imitate the actions of those they have observed, but also create new imaginative scenarios.

As noted above by Italian educator Maria Montessori, it is this mental imagining that enables young children to imagine foreign countries. Even though they have only an incipient concept of space (here, there, far away), so long as the stories and illustrations relate to what the children have experienced either personally or through the media or earlier books, the stories should attract the interest of these curious youngsters. Thus, picture books generally feature animals, including those who are anthropomorphic, children, families, and/or vehicles. They are set in homes, schools, and markets. They depict situations that are experienced by children worldwide, but in varying settings.

Take the book *Koala Lou* by Mem Fox, which is set in Australia. Although they may never have seen a koala, even the youngest children relate to animals. Even if they have no younger siblings, they have experienced jealousy. Although they may never have lost a tree-climbing race, they have experienced failure and feared the loss of their mother's love. Thus, they relate to the book and experience Australia as the land of koalas and gum trees.

Just as each tourist in a tour group takes away different impressions of the spots visited, so each child will take away something different from each picture book. Fortunately, learning about a country need not be done in a particular sequence so that picture books are accessible to both the novice and the experienced child traveler. The illustrations and often the text (sometimes with modification) will appeal to three-year-olds as well as to those who are older and can experience the book at a higher developmental level. For instance, some children will note the presence of animals other than koalas in *Koala Lou* and may want to find out more about them.

If, after enjoying *Koala Lou*, the young travelers are then introduced to the same author's *Possum Magic*, they have the opportunity, depending on their age and book experience, to learn that the Australian bush also contains possums, wombats, snakes, kangaroos, and dingoes; that people live in Australia; and that there are places called Adelaide, Melbourne, Sydney, Brisbane, and Tasmania. This book even contains a map of Australia that traces the journey of the two possums, with illustrations of the food they ate marking each location.

The more children learn more about each country and about different countries, the more perceptive travelers they become. The world is, in a very literal sense, at their fingertips. They use their fingers to turn the pages that will fly them to distant lands.

"Without the help of adults, a baby or small child has no chance at all of discovering books...."
—Butler. *Babies Need Books.*

The Travel Guides

The travel guides are those persons who introduce the picture books to young travelers. They may be parents, teachers, child care providers, librarians, grandparents, uncles, aunts, other adults, and/or older children.

The Itineraries

Just as professional travel guides set up itineraries for their clients, so too these travel guides help in selecting the countries and places visited and stimulate the potential travelers' interest. Just as professional guides respond to the wishes of their clients, so too these guides listen carefully to the voices of their young travelers. These voices may be communicated verbally or perceived by adults who are aware of the children's interests, their environments, and their developmental levels. To illustrate:
- When, whether in the library, in the classroom, or at home, children show interest in a picture book set in a different country, that book can be the springboard for additional "travel" in that location.
- When children like a particular ethnic food or restaurant; enjoy a TV program or movie about or set in another country; admire a team or an athlete from

another nation (e.g., the Toronto Maple Leafs, Sammy Sosa); or watch zoo animals from a specific locale (e.g., kangaroos), this interest can be built upon through picture books set in that country.

- As pointed out earlier, it is especially valuable to select countries of the children's and their friends' ethnic origins as well as of the places they visit.
- After looking at the picture books available about various countries, adults can choose the countries for which there are books at the children's age/ability level.
- If a school uses a storybook curriculum, the country can be chosen on the basis of the availability of picture books which best lend themselves to activities appealing to these particular students. If a class follows a multicultural curriculum, countries can be selected that reflect the ethnic diversity of the class. If the school curriculum is based upon a theme (e.g., folktales), the teachers can select those countries of interest for which folktales are available.
- When teachers wish to present an in-depth look at one country, they can choose a country for which there are picture books from several regions as well as of different genres. Here again, the children's interests and developmental levels should play a determining role in the choice.

The Visits

What roles should the travel guides play during the trips themselves? Once again it is helpful to look at the roles of professional travel guides, whether they are directing a six-week bus tour around Europe or guiding visitors through a tourist attraction. The guides present information about the site, answer the group's questions, point out items to look at or look for, give visitors time to explore for themselves, and converse individually with those tourists who have individual questions or prefer walking next to the guide.

So too do the roles of the picture book guides vary. Depending on the age of the children, their experience with books, and the size of the group, differing strategies are used. To mention but a few, the guides may point to or ask the child or children to point to different items in the illustrations; simplify the text; read the book exactly as it is written again, again, and again; point out or ask about ways in which there are similarities and/or differences in the foreign country; offer explanations or elaboration; leave out words, particularly repeated words and expressions, and wait for the children to furnish them; sit with the children and read the book together; help young readers with difficult words; let children look at, pretend read, or read the book on their own; listen to the children read or pretend read; discuss the book with the children during and/or after the reading; and explore with them possibilities for using different activities and media to reinforce or expand upon the text.

As with professional guides, the storybook guides need to be attuned to their clients: pursuing tangents children suggest and being aware when the children are tired or their interest wanes. In short, the guide is observer, facilitator, and participant, with the exact blend varying according to the children, the situation, and the moment.

Training

If you feel that you need assistance in becoming a travel guide, help lies only as far away as your library. If you want information about the types of books and reading experiences appropriate for the different younger ages, you might want to read, among other books, *Babies Need Books* (Butler) or *The New Read-Aloud Handbook* (Trelease). If you need help in expanding upon the book experience, there are once again a number of resources. You might especially want to look at the periodical, *Bookbag*, or the book, *Open Books: Literature in the Curriculum, Kindergarten through Grade 2* (Hurst).

But, what do you really need to be a great travel guide? The answer: a love of children, a responsiveness to children, a love of books, a genuine interest in and respect for the cultures visited, some creativity, enthusiasm, and above all, the commitment to make the shared journey an enjoyable one.

In short, you're already well qualified for the job. Don't keep your young travelers waiting!

"It is story that focuses our attention, helps us make sense out of the world around us."
—Trelease. *The Read-Aloud Handbook.*

The Picture Books

An amazing story was related in the January 1977 issue of *Learning*. At a dinner when *Paddle-to-the-Sea* was mentioned, six of the eight adults present enthusiastically recalled details of this picture book which they had read some thirty years before (Borton, p. 26). Presumably this book, which is still in print and described under "Canada", is still making a lasting impression on young children as are many of the other books described. When one realizes that for many adults Spain is associated with Ferdinand the Bull and Italy with Strega Nona, the impact of picture books on geographical awareness cannot be underestimated.

Picture books are those books in which illustrations and text combine to present a story or a descriptive presentation. The pictures play an integral role in the book, whether they are full- or double-page color paintings or smaller pictures complementing the text in a reader. The pictures generally appear on at least every other page.

For purposes of this book, the illustrations are artist-created, and books with photographs are excluded. Likewise, board books, pop-up books, big books, books with audio cassettes, books written in foreign languages (other than bilingual English/—), and teacher edition books are not included.

The age ranges indicated for a particular book in book reviews often vary widely. Thus, specific ages are not noted in *Faraway Places* although in some cases age levels are mentioned. Where it is noted that the picture book should interest even the youngest children, the book will generally be of interest to children in the entire three-to-eight age range. Picture books indicated for older or the oldest children will usually appeal only to those in first and/or second grade, but, in some instances where the subject is of particular interest or the children have become "book-wise", the books may also appeal to those who are younger. It should be remembered that picture books read to a group of children often need to be simpler because of more distractions, difficulties in viewing the illustrations, and, often, differing developmental levels.

The picture books described in *Faraway Places* should be available for purchase as well as through libraries. The bibliography at the end of each country lists the books alphabetically by author, with the earliest available published edition of each book listed first (*Children's Books in Print 2000*). The most commonly used accent marks are included.

The picture books described are set in or are folktales from a specific country or one specific country and the United States. In rare instances, where several countries are shown but the setting of one country predominates, the book is included. Books set only in regions such as the Caribbean, Eastern Europe, or Africa are not covered.

The picture books embrace a variety of genres. Books describing religious figures, e.g., Joan of Arc and Saint Francis, as well as those presenting religious celebrations reflecting various cultures are included. Bible stories are not. For some countries there is a predominance of folktales. For others the picture books are more balanced in the genres represented.

However, whatever their genre, the picture books presented here will fly small children to other countries and introduce them to the diverse peoples and places of their world.

"Great wide, beautiful, wonderful world...."
—Rands, William Brighty [Matthew Browne].
The Child's World.

The Destinations

The picture book destinations, the countries, are divided by continent. Children may visit twenty countries in Africa, twenty in Asia, two in Australia and Oceania, twenty-one in Europe, fourteen in North America, and five in South America.

Russia, which could be included under both Europe and Asia, is listed under Europe. There are picture book descriptions not only for the United Kingdom, but also for the specific destinations: England, Scotland, and Wales. The British crown colonies of Montserrat and the Turks and Caicos Islands are listed separately under North America. Likewise, Greenland, a self-governing entity of Denmark, and Martinique, an overseas department of France, are listed under North America. Another French overseas department, French Guiana, is listed under South America. The United States and its territories and possessions are not covered.

For each continent the countries are presented in alphabetical order. The top listing for a country shows the name by which it is commonly known, with, in some cases, alternate names and/or former names following in parentheses. The country's official name, if different, appears on the next line. For each country the official name is underlined. Geographical information has been secured primarily from *Merriam Webster's Geographical Dictionary, Third Edition*, and an older, but detailed atlas, *Hamond World Atlas, Classics Edition. Merriam Webster's Biographical Dictionary* has been helpful in providing historical information.

For those countries for which there are at least ten picture books there is a further division by administrative region as well as by the following general categories: Alphabet, counting, and word books; Celebrations; Fables, fairy tales, folktales, legends, myths, and proverbs (including original works); Historical figures; Nonfiction; Poetry and songs; and Stories. With the exception of books that relate to historical figures, books that have a specific location are described under location rather than under genre.

The picture book descriptions and bibliographic references follow. The world awaits its youngest travelers. Bon voyage!

Afri

<u>Africa</u>

"Market day was also a time for visiting."
—Cowen-Fletcher. *It Takes a Village.*

Benin
(formerly Dahomey)

Jane Cowen-Fletcher's *It Takes a Village* tells of young Yemi who loses her little brother at the marketplace and then discovers that five different vendors have taken care of him.

In *Only One Cowry*, which is retold by Phillis Gershator, a tightfisted king wishes to find a bride costing only one cowry shell. By astute trading, a young man converts the shell into gifts fit for a chief. When the chief's daughter discovers that the king was willing to part with only one cowry, she too displays her cleverness by inveigling the unsuspecting king into providing her with a feast, palm wine, a wardrobe, and jewelry.

Books

Cowen-Fletcher, Jane. *It Takes a Village.* Illustrated by author. New York: Scholastic, 1994.

Gershator, Phillis, reteller. *Only One Cowry: A Dahomean Tale.* Illustrated by David Soman. New York: Orchard Books, 2000.

"He heard rustling grass and the footsteps of zebras and warthogs coming to drink and wallow in the mud at the edge of the pool."
—Lewin. *Chubbo's Pool.*

Botswana
(formerly Bechuanaland)

Even very young children should relate to Betsy Lewin's *Chubbo's Pool*, the story of a hippopotamus who won't share—until "his" pool becomes a mud wallow and his friends come to his rescue.

Book

Lewin, Betsy. *Chubbo's Pool.* Illustrated by author. New York: Clarion Books, 1996; 1998, paperback.

"We planted yams and corn and tobacco and the finest coffee grown in the Cameroons."
—Grifalconi. *The Village of Round and Square Houses.*

Cameroon

Full-page and double-page oil paintings illustrate Katrin Hyman Tchana and Louise Tchana Pami's story, *Oh, No, Toto!*, about a very young child, the ever-hungry Toto. Taking Toto to market when buying ingredients for the dinner's egussi soup proves to be a disaster, with Toto knocking over a pile of puffpuffs, grabbing a hard-boiled egg, falling into palm oil, and eating a woman's plate of food. Finally, Big Mami gets Toto home—and then he eats all the egussi soup.

The remote village of Tos, next to the almost extinct volcanic Naka Mountain, comes to life in the illustrations of Ann Grifalconi's *The Village of Round and Square Houses*. A young girl listens to her grandmother's story that explains why in this village men live in square houses and the women and children in round ones.

Madoulina, by Joël Eboueme Bognomo, is set in Yaoundé, the capitol of Cameroon. Eight-year-old Madoulina cannot go to school since she must earn money for her family by selling fritters. However, thanks to her younger brother's teacher, Madoulina returns to school—and the fritters are sold.

The first fortune-teller in *The Fortune-Tellers*, by Lloyd Alexander, tells a carpenter about his future and then disappears. Mistaken for the fortune-teller, the carpenter assumes his identity and, dispensing the same fortune to one and all, fulfills the real fortune-teller's predictions.

In Tololwa M. Mollel's *The King and the Tortoise* the tortoise displays his cleverness, not by carrying out the king's impossible demand, but by making an equally impossible demand of the king.

Gollo and the Lion, by Éric Oyono, tells of a lion, who, cleverly deceiving Gollo's sister, swallows her. Heeding the advice of a soothsayer, Gollo dries up the land's water, thereby enabling him to enlist the other animals' support in making the lion cough up his sister. It is a sparrow hawk who restores the water in this folktale, which is brightly illustrated with pictures of Cameroon's diverse animal population.

Books

Alexander, Lloyd. *The Fortune-Tellers*. Illustrated by Trina Schart Hyman. New York: Dutton Children's Books, 1992, paperback; Viking Penguin, 1997, paperback; Puffin, 1997.

Bognomo, Joël Eboueme. *Madoulina: A Girl Who Wanted to Go to School: A Story from West Africa*. Illustrated by author. Honesdale, PA: Boyds Mills Press, 1999.

Grifalconi, Ann. *The Village of Round and Square Houses*. Illustrated by author. New York: Little, Brown and Company, 1986.

Mollel, Tololwa M. *The King and the Tortoise*. Illustrated by Kathy Blankley. New York: Clarion Books, 1993.

Oyono, Éric. *Gollo and the Lion*. Illustrated by Laurent Corvaisier. New York: Hyperion Books for Children, 1995.

Tchana, Katrin Hyman, and Louise Tchana Pami. *Oh, No, Toto!* Illustrated by Colin Bootman. New York: Scholastic, 1997.

"And Nzambi went back into her hut to think about how many stripes she wanted to put on the Zebra she would make that day."
—Knutson. *Why the Crab Has No Head.*

Democratic Republic of the Congo (formerly Zaire, Congo, Belgian Congo)

In Sanna Stanley's *Monkey Sunday*, Luzolo, the pastor's daughter, does her best to show her father that she can sit still in the church service, despite the intrusion of chickens, goats, pigs, and a banana peel-throwing monkey.

Barbara Knutson's retelling of a Bakongo folktale, *Why the Crab Has No Head*, shows how the crab's boasting about the head he is to receive so displeases Nzambi Mpungu, who makes all of the animals, that she gives him no head at all.

Books

Knutson, Barbara, reteller. *Why the Crab Has No Head: An African Tale*. Illustrated by reteller. Minneapolis: Carolrhoda Picture Books, 1988.

Stanley, Sanna. *Monkey Sunday: A Story from a Congolese Village*. Illustrated by author. New York: Farrar, Straus & Giroux, 1998.

"Far back in time, in a land where kings were once called pharoahs and the great river is still called the Nile, a boy in a tiny village by the banks of this river was very sad."
—Oppenheim. *The Hundredth Name.*

Egypt (formerly United Arab Republic)
Arab Republic of Egypt

Specific Locations

Cairo

In *The Day of Ahmed's Secret*, by Florence Parry Heide and Judith Heide Gilliland, young Ahmed spends his day traveling around Cairo on a donkey cart, delivering heavy bottles of butane gas to his regular customers—and all the time looking forward to the evening when he will reveal his secret to his family.

General

Fables, fairy tales, folktales, legends, myths, and proverbs (including original works)

In Shirley Climo's *The Egyptian Cinderella* the Greek slave Rhodopis is poorly treated by her master's servants, but is given a beautiful pair of slippers by her master. When a falcon picks up one of her slippers and drops it in the Pharaoh Amasis's lap, as in the more traditional Cinderella story, Amasis searches Egypt for the owner of the slipper and chooses Rhodopis as his queen.

Gift of the Nile, retold by Jan W. Mike, tells how a friendship between the Pharaoh Senefru and the girl Mutemwia grows until the Pharaoh realizes that Mutemwia needs both his friendship and her freedom.

The Winged Cat, by Deborah Nourse Lattimore, is a story for the oldest children as it presents the Egyptian views of death, the judgment rendered in the Netherworld, and hieroglyphics which readers can interpret. In this tale the servant Merit, together with the soul of a sacred cat, and the High Priest travel to the Netherworld to determine which one is telling the truth.

Historical figures

Robert Sabuda's *Tutankhamen's Gift* tells of the pharoah's youngest son, who loves to watch the workmen at the temples. When at the age of ten Tutankhamen succeeds his older brother, who has destroyed many of the temples, the boy pharaoh restores them to the people and to the gods.

Nonfiction

Egyptian Gods and Goddesses, by Henry Barker, is a reader for older children which presents some of the ancient Egyptian gods and goddesses of life and death and introduces mummies and tombs.

Aliki's *Mummies Made in Egypt* should appeal to those oldest children who are interested in discovering the reason that the ancient Egyptians wished to preserve their dead and the detailed presentation, both through text and illustrations, of the processes of embalming and coffin and tomb making.

Stories

Four books are set in ancient Egypt.

In Roy Gerrard's *Croco'nile* a little boy who becomes a sculptor and his sister who becomes an artist work on a pyramid, prepare a special gift for the queen, and, after being kidnapped, are saved by their crocodile friend. The oldest children may enjoy decoding the book's hieroglyphic messages using the key on the back cover.

Children may also decode hieroglyphics in Jill Paton Walsh's *Pepi and the Secret Names,* which is a book for older children. Pepi helps his father paint and carve pictures on the tomb of Prince Dhutmose by guessing the secret names of such animals as a lion and a crocodile and then taking them to the tomb to pose for his father. When Pepi meets Prince Dhutmose, he discovers that the tabby cat who has been showing up in the tomb—and in the pictures— is, in fact, the prince's treasured cat, Lady Tmiao.

Andrew Clements's *Temple Cat* relates the story of another cat, one who is lord of a temple. Frustrated because servants care for his every need and allow him no freedom, the cat escapes and finds happiness with a fisherman's family where he enjoys the life of a typical cat.

Inspired by hieroglyphics showing the plans for a polar bear burial vault, JoAnn Adinolfi's *The Egyptian Polar Bear,* tells of the polar bear who, transported to Egypt on an iceberg, becomes the young king's royal playmate.

Another book dealing with Egyptian hieroglyphs is James Rumford's *Seeker of Knowledge*, a biography of the Frenchman Jean-François Champollion. It is included under France.

The Hundredth Name, by Shulamith Levey Oppenheim, is set in the Egypt of long ago, but after the time of the pharaohs. Worried because his favorite camel Qadiim and all the other camels seem so sad, seven-year-old Salah prays to Allah to tell the camel his hundredth name, a name which no human knows. In the morning Qadiim's whole demeanor has changed; he has assumed the wise and proud look of today's camels.

Three stories, all by Tomie dePaola, relate the humorous adventures of the crocodile Bill and the bird Pete, Bill's toothbrush and friend.

In *Bill and Pete*, Pete rescues Bill from the man who is taking him to Cairo to become a suitcase, and then Bill scares the bad man into abandoning his trade.

The bad man appears again in *Bill and Pete Go Down the Nile*. On a field trip with their school class, Bill and Pete prevent him from stealing the Sacred Eye of Isis.

It is the bad man's brother with whom Bill and Pete contend in *Bill and Pete to the Rescue*. Following the villain and his kidnapped animals, including Bill's crocodile cousin, the two heroes take a ship to Louisiana where they not only rescue the animals, but also discover Bill's long lost father.

Detective Seymour Sleuth and his photographer are joined by Professor Slagbottom in solving the case of the stolen stone chicken in Doug Cushman's *The Mystery of*

King Karfu. Older children can participate with Seymour Sleuth in figuring out the clues and then, once the stone chicken is found, in using the key to the secret code to discover both the location of King Karfu's treasure and his secret recipe. The book is illustrated with pages of the detective's journal/scrapbook.

Mary Matthews's *Magid Fasts for Ramadan* is a book for older children with a longer text and full-page watercolors. Even though he is a child, seven year old Magid secretly tries to fast for the Muslim month of Ramadan. He discovers how difficult it is and that it is better to be honest.

Books

Adinolfi, JoAnn. *The Egyptian Polar Bear*. Illustrated by author. Boston: Houghton Mifflin Company, 1994.

Aliki. *Mummies Made in Egypt*. Illustrated by author. New York: T Y Crowell Junior Books, 1979; Harper Trophy, 1985, paperback.

Barker, Henry. *Egyptian Gods and Goddesses*. (All Aboard Reading Series) Illustrated by Jeff Crosby. New York: Grossett & Dunlap, 1999.

Clements, Andrew. *Temple Cat*. Illustrated by Kate Kiesler. New York: Clarion Books, l996.

Climo, Shirley. *The Egyptian Cinderella*. Illustrated by Ruth Heller. New York: T Y Crowell Junior Books, 1989; Harper Trophy, 1992, paperback.

Cushman, Doug. *The Mystery of King Karfu*. Illustrated by author. New York: HarperCollins Children's Books, 1996.

dePaola, Tomie. *Bill and Pete*. Illustrated by author. New York: Paperstar, 1996, paperback.

dePaola, Tomie. *Bill and Pete Go Down the Nile.* Illustrated by author. New York: G. P. Putnam's Sons, 1987; Paperstar, 1996, paperback.

dePaola, Tomie. *Bill and Pete to the Rescue.* Illustrated by author. New York: G. P. Putnam's Sons, 1998.

Gerrard, Roy. *Croco'nile.* Illustrated by author. New York: Farrar, Straus & Giroux, 1994.

Heide, Florence Parry, and Judith Heide Gilliland. *The Day of Ahmed's Secret.* Illustrated by Ted Lewin. New York: Mulberry Books, 1995, paperback.

Lattimore, Deborah Nourse. *The Winged Cat: A Tale of Ancient Egypt.* Illustrated by author. New York: HarperCollins Children's Books, 1992; Harper Trophy, 1995, paperback.

Matthews, Mary. *Magid Fasts for Ramadan.* Illustrated by E. B. Lewis. New York: Clarion Books, 1996.

Mike, Jan M., reteller. *Gift of the Nile: An Ancient Egyptian Legend.* (Legends of the World) Illustrated by Charles Reasoner. Mahwah, NJ: Troll Communications, 1996, paperback; 1997.

Oppenheim, Shulamith Levey. *The Hundredth Name.* Illustrated by Michael Hays. Honesdale, PA: Boyds Mills Press, 1997, paperback.

Sabuda, Robert. *Tutankhamen's Gift.* Illustrated by author. New York: Atheneum Books for Young Readers, 1994; Aladdin Paperbacks, 1997.

Walsh, Jill Paton. *Pepi and the Secret Names.* Illustrated by Fiona French. New York: Lothrop, Lee & Shepard Books, 1995.

"Once, in the mountains of Ethiopia lived an orphan girl named Tshai...."
—Araujo. *The Perfect Orange.*

Ethiopia (Abyssinia)

Four of the books are set in Ethiopia's mountains.

In Nancy Raines Day's *The Lion's Whiskers*, which is for older children, the young boy Abebe will not warm up to his stepmother. Heeding a medicine man's advice, the stepmother wins the trust of a lion from whom she plucks three whiskers. When she shows similar patience with Abebe, she wins him over.

A different twist is given to the story in Jane Kurtz's *Pulling the Lion's Tail*, which is also for older children. In this case Almaz finds it difficult to get her new stepmother's attention. It is Almaz who heeds her grandfather's advice and patiently gains a lion's trust so that she is able to pull hair from its tail. In the process she learns that it is only by patiently approaching her shy stepmother that she can receive her affection.

A second book by Kurtz, *Fire on the Mountain*, retells the story of the vain and deceitful rich man who learns that being warmed by the sight of a distant fire is not the same as experiencing its heat and of the boy who receives the money and cows that were promised him.

The Perfect Orange, by Frank P. Araujo, retells the folktale of the generous girl who, asking nothing in return, takes a perfect orange to her ruler and is given a reward.

When the greedy hyena seeks an even greater reward, he receives instead the perfect orange.

A book for older children set in Addis Ababa, *Only a Pigeon*, by Jane and Christopher Kurtz, tells of Ohduahlem, who spends his mornings in school, his afternoons shining shoes, and the rest of his time caring for his homing pigeons: protecting them, and, in a game, risking his favorite pigeon in the hope that it will return home and bring his competitor's pigeon with it.

In Jane Kurtz's *Faraway Home* Desta, an American, is afraid when she learns that her father will be traveling to Ethiopia to visit his sick mother. Ethiopia is far away and perhaps he will not return. However, after her father tells her of his life there as a boy, Desta comes to accept his going.

Books

Araujo, Frank P. *The Perfect Orange: A Tale from Ethiopia.* (Toucan Tales Series) Illustrated by Xiao Jun Li. Windsor, CA: Rayve Productions, 1994.

Day, Nancy Raines. *The Lion's Whiskers: An Ethiopian Folktale.* Illustrated by Ann Grifalconi. New York: Scholastic, 1995.

Kurtz, Jane. *Faraway Home.* Illustrated by E. B. Lewis. San Diego: Gulliver Books, 2000.

Kurtz, Jane. *Fire on the Mountain.* Illustrated by E. B. Lewis. New York: Simon & Schuster Children's Publishing, 1998.

Kurtz, Jane. *Pulling the Lion's Tail.* Illustrated by Floyd Cooper. New York: Simon & Schuster Books for Young Readers, 1995; 1995, paperback.

Kurtz, Jane, and Christopher Kurtz. *Only a Pigeon.* Illustrated by E. B. Lewis. New York: Simon & Schuster Children's Publishing, 1997.

"There were sheep wandering along the roadside and people selling watermelons under the trees."
—Hoffman. *Boundless Grace.*

Gambia (The Gambia)
Republic of the Gambia

Mary Hoffman's *Boundless Grace* tells of an American girl who with her grandmother travels to Gambia to visit her father and his family. It is difficult for Grace to adjust, but she comes to accept her new family and enjoys her experiences in Gambia.

Book

Hoffman, Mary. *Boundless Grace.* Illustrated by Caroline Binch. New York: Dial Books for Young Readers, 1995, paperback.

"Long ago in Africa, long before there were stories on earth, there lived a Spider named Ananse."
—Chocolate. *Spider and the Sky God.*

<u>Ghana</u> (formerly Gold Coast)

General

Fables, fairy tales, folktales, legends, myths, and proverbs (including original works)

All but one of the books set in Ghana are folktales, with eleven of them featuring the trickster Anansi (Ananse, Anancy). Anansi stories set in Africa, even if Ghana is not explicitly mentioned, are described here.

Three of these tales are retold by Eric A. Kimmel and feature bright, humorous illustrations.

In *Anansi and the Talking Melon*, the spider Anansi pierces one of Elephant's melons and, climbing in, gets so fat eating that he can't get out. He then enjoys convincing Elephant and other animals that the melon talks.

Anansi and the Moss-Covered Rock tells how Anansi tricks the other animals so that he can steal their food—until Little Bush Deer turns the tables on him.

It is Turtle who tricks Anansi in *Anansi Goes Fishing*. Anansi does the work and Turtle eats the fish. However, Anansi and other spiders do learn how to weave spider webs.

Verna Aardema relates three of the Ashanti people's Anansi tales.

Her *Anansi Finds a Fool* is a different version of Kimmel's *Anansi Goes Fishing*. In this case both Anansi and Bonsu are men (instead of a spider and a turtle), and a python and a crocodile are included in the story. As in the other version, it is Bonsu who tricks the lazy Anansi and dines on the fish.

Ananse is also a man in *Oh, Kojo! How Could You!* Kojo buys an apparently worthless dog and a worthless cat from Ananse, but the dove he purchases brings him a magic ring and good fortune. When Ananse gets hold of the ring, it is the cat, not the dog, who reclaims it and so, as a reward, cats sleep inside with their food served in a dish.

The third Aardema book, *Anansi Does the Impossible*, explains the origin of the Anansi tales. Thanks to the advice of his wife, the spider Anansi is able to pay the price which the Sky God demands for his stories: a python, a fairy, and forty-seven hornets.

A slightly different version of this tale is related in *Spider and the Sky God*, which is retold by Deborah M. Newton Chocolate. In this book, the Sky God also demands a leopard and the payment is brought to the sky via spider web.

The Caldecott Medal winner, *A Story, A Story*, which is retold and illustrated by Gail E. Haley, relates a third version of this story. There is no wife in this tale in which the spider man, who is old, uses his own ingenuity to capture a leopard, hornets, and a fairy and then takes them to the Sky God.

In *Anansi the Spider*, adapted by Gerald McDermott, each of Anansi's six sons uses his special talent to rescue their father from his troubles. Since Anansi cannot decide which of the sons should be rewarded with the globe of light he has discovered, the Sky God places the globe in the sky where we know it as the moon.

Ananse's Feast, retold by Tololwa M. Mollel, relates how the spider repeatedly sends the turtle back to the river to wash his hands and, in his absence, consumes the entire feast. However, when the turtle invites Ananse to a feast, the spider is likewise unable to partake as he floats up and out of the turtle's underwater home.

In *Don't Leave an Elephant To Go and Chase a Bird*, which is retold by James Berry, Anancy makes a series of trades, until his greediness distracts him from claiming a young elephant—and he ends up with nothing.

Anansi also appears, although not as the main character, in *The Royal Drum*, which is retold by Mary Dixon Lake. All the animals but the monkey cooperate in making a drum for sending messages. Therefore, the monkey, as the laziest animal, is assigned the onerous task of transporting the drum to the palace. The use of rebus characters in this book enables emergent readers to participate in the reading.

In Jessica Souhami's *The Leopard's Drum*, it is the soft-shelled tortoise who succeeds in taking the leopard's drum to the Sky God. As a reward, she receives a protective hard shell.

The version of the folktale retold by Ruby Dee in *Tower to Heaven* originates in Ghana. When the Sky God goes way up into the sky to avoid being hit by the pestle of a talkative old woman, the village builds a tower of mortars so that they can speak to him again. However, they lack the one mortar they need to reach heaven.

Even the chief is in a panic when inanimate objects and animals start talking in Angela Shelf Medearis's amusing *Too Much Talk*.

Nonfiction

Chocolate's *Kente Colors* brings to life the distinctive colors and designs of the Ashanti and Ewe's Kente cloth. The striking double-page paintings representing the colors portray Ghana and its peoples. (It should be noted that the Ewe also live in Togo.)

Books

Aardema, Verna, reteller. *Anansi Does the Impossible: An Ashanti Tale*. Illustrated by Lisa Desimini. New York: Simon & Schuster Children's Publishing, 1997.

Aardema, Verna. *Anansi Finds a Fool: An Ashanti Tale*. Illustrated by Bryna Waldman. New York: Dial Books for Young Readers, 1992; 1992, paperback.

Aardema, Verna, reteller. *Oh, Kojo! How Could You!: An Ashanti Tale*. Illustrated by Marc Brown. New York: Pied Piper Books, 1984; 1988, paperback; N A L Dutton, 1993, paperback.

Berry, James, reteller. *Don't Leave an Elephant to Go and Chase a Bird*. Illustrated by Ann Grifalconi. New York: Simon & Schuster Children's Publishing, 1996.

Chocolate, Deborah M. Newton. *Kente Colors*. Illustrated by John Ward. New York: Walker Publishing Company, 1997; 1997, paperback.

Chocolate, Deborah M. Newton, reteller. *Spider and the Sky God: An Akan Legend.* (Legends of the World) Illustrated by Dave Albers. Mahwah, NJ: Troll Communications, 1997; 1997, paperback.

Dee, Ruby, reteller. *Tower to Heaven.* Illustrated by Jennifer Bent. New York: Henry Holt Books for Young Readers, 1995.

Haley, Gail E., reteller. *A Story, A Story: An African Tale.* Illustrated by reteller. New York: Atheneum Books for Young Readers, 1970; Aladdin Paperbacks, 1988.

Kimmel, Eric A., reteller. *Anansi and the Moss-Covered Rock.* Illustrated by Janet Stevens. New York: Holiday House, 1988; 1990, paperback.

Kimmel, Eric A., reteller. *Anansi and the Talking Melon.* Illustrated by Janet Stevens. New York: Holiday House, 1994; 1994, paperback.

Kimmel, Eric A., reteller. *Anansi Goes Fishing.* Illustrated by Janet Stevens. New York: Holiday House, 1992; 1992, paperback.

Lake, Mary Dixon, reteller. *The Royal Drum: An Ashanti Tale.* Illustrated by Carol O'Malia. Greenvale, NY: Mondo Publishing, 1996.

McDermott, Gerald, adapter. *Anansi the Spider: A Tale from the Ashanti.* Illustrated by adapter. New York: Henry Holt and Company, 1992, paperback; Henry Holt Books for Young Readers, 1995; 1995, paperback.

Medearis, Angela Shelf. *Too Much Talk.* Illustrated by Stefano Vitale. Cambridge, MA: Candlewick Press, 1995; 1997, paperback.

Mollel, Tololwa M., reteller. *Ananse's Feast: An Ashanti Tale*. Illustrated by Andrew Glass. New York: Clarion Books, 1997.

Souhami, Jessica. *The Leopard's Drum: An Asante Tale from West Africa*. Illustrated by author. New York: Little, Brown and Company, 1996.

"On the way, we stopped the car to watch two giraffes nibbling leaves from the tops of trees."
—Wilson-Max. *Furaha Means Happy.*

Kenya (Kenia, formerly East Africa Protectorate)

Three of the books set in Kenya present the country as seen by children.

I Am Eyes/Ni Macho, by Leila Ward, can be enjoyed by the youngest children. Each left-hand page contains a black-and-white drawing of a little girl with a one-line text noting items that she sees. The opposing page presents a color illustration of at least one of the objects, placed in a Kenyan setting. (It should be noted that Mount Kilimanjaro is in neighboring Tanzania.)

In *Furaha Means Happy*, by Ken Wilson-Max, a girl describes an outing to a lake for a family picnic. Interspersed with the double pages of text and accompanying illustrations are double pages depicting the objects mentioned, labeled in both English and Swahili. This word book includes a guide to pronunciation of the Swahili words, which range from gari (car) to kiboko (hippo).

Joan Barton Barsotti's *Christopher and Grandma on Safari* tells of the last day of Christopher's visit to the Masai Mara Game Reserve. He watches many wild animals from the safari van, but it is the spotting of the little brown giraffe that makes his safari complete.

In *Bringing the Rain to Kapiti Plain*, Verna Aardema

retells a folktale which comes from the Nandi people. The story is presented as an illustrated cumulative poem that shows a herdsman with a bow and arrow ending the drought on the Kapiti Plain.

Books

Aardema, Verna, reteller. *Bringing the Rain to Kapiti Plain: A Nandi Tale*. Illustrated by Beatriz Vidal. New York: Dial Books for Young Readers, 1981; 1981, paperback; 1983, paperback; Puffin Books, 1992, paperback; N A L Dutton, 1993, paperback.

Barsotti, Joan Barton. *Christopher and Grandma on Safari*. Illustrated by Carol Mathis. Camino, CA: Barsotti Books, 1996, paperback.

Ward, Leila. *I Am Eyes/Ni Macho*. Illustrated by Nonny Hogrogian. New York: Blue Ribbons Books, 1987, paperback; 1991, paperback.

Wilson-Max, Ken. *Furaha Means Happy: A Book of Swahili Words*. (Jump at the Sun) Illustrated by author. New York: Hyperion Books for Children, 2000.

"Inside, Mama sings a tula-tula hush-hush song to the baby."
—Mennen. *One Round Moon and a Star for Me.*

Lesotho
(formerly Basutoland)

Ingrid Mennen's *One Round Moon and a Star for Me* tells of the day a new baby comes to a little boy's home and of how his father reassures him that he is still his parents' child and that he, like the new baby, has a falling star.

Book

Mennen, Ingrid. *One Round Moon and a Star for Me.* Illustrated by Niki Daly. New York: Orchard Books, an imprint of Scholastic Inc., 1994.

"His royal drums carried the news of the feast far and wide throughout the jungle."
—Dee. *Two Ways to Count to Ten.*

Liberia

In *Two Ways to Count to Ten,* which is retold by Ruby Dee, it is the clever antelope, not the mighty beasts of the jungle, who counts to ten before the spear he has thrown falls to the ground.

Koi, the youngest son, receives only a kola tree for his inheritance in Verna Aardema's *Koi and the Kola Nuts.* However, his kindness in giving the tree's nuts to a snake, an ant, and a crocodile is more than repaid when they help him win the hand of a chief's daughter and half of his chiefdom.

Books

Aardema, Verna. *Koi and the Kola Nuts: A Tale from Liberia.* Illustrated by Joe Cepeda. New York: Atheneum Books for Young Readers, 1999.

Dee, Ruby, reteller. *Two Ways to Count to Ten: A Liberian Folktale.* Illustrated by Susan Meddaugh. New York: Henry Holt Books for Young Readers, 1995; Owlet Paperbacks for Young Readers, 1995, paperback.

"In the purple shade of the jacaranda they chewed the stiff, stringy pieces of cane and sweet juice ran down their chins."
—Williams. *When Africa Was Home.*

Malawi (formerly Nyasaland)

When Africa Was Home, by Karen Lynn Williams, tells of a small American boy who thoroughly enjoys being raised in Malawi. Homesick for Africa after his family returns to the United States, he rejoices when his father's work enables him to return to his African "mother" and his friend Yekha.

Seven-year-old Kondi displays perseverance and ingenuity in gathering the wire necessary to build a toy pickup truck in *Galimoto*, a book which is also written by Williams.

In *The Mean Hyena*, retold by Judy Sierra, the hyena gets his comeuppance after he places a tortoise in a tree. The tortoise paints stripes on the zebra and spots on the leopard, but the hyena ends up with a ragged coat and a defensive laugh.

Books

Sierra, Judy, reteller. *The Mean Hyena: A Folktale from Malawi.* Illustrated by Michael Bryant. New York: Lodestar Books, 1997, paperback.

Williams, Karen Lynn. *Galimoto*. Illustrated by Catherine Stock. New York: Lothrop, Lee & Shepard Books, 1990; Mulberry Books, 1991, paperback.

Williams, Karen Lynn. *When Africa Was Home*. Illustrated by Floyd Cooper. New York: Orchard Books, an imprint of Scholastic Inc., 1991; 1994, paperback.

"Listen to me, children of the Bright Country, and hear the great deeds of ages past."
—Wisniewski. *Sundiata.*

<u>Mali</u> (formerly Sudanese Republic, French Sudan)

Based on history, David Wisniewski's *Sundiata* is a book for the oldest children, who can follow Sundiata's thirteenth-century journey on the map at the front of the book. Unable to walk or to talk as a young child, Sundiata is not chosen as king when his father dies, and he goes into exile. When the land is invaded, Sundiata, now a man, returns with an army, is victorious in battle, and becomes Mali's ruler.

In Baba Wagué Diakité's *The Hatseller and the Monkeys*, it is only after BaMusa has eaten that he figures out how to trick the monkeys who have stolen his hats.

Books

Diakité, Baba Wagué, reteller. *The Hatseller and the Monkeys: A West African Folktale.* Illustrated by reteller. New York: Scholastic, 1999.

Wisniewski, David. *Sundiata: Lion King of Mali.* Illustrated by author. New York: Clarion Books, 1999.

"Up, up it flies until it is almost out of sight, then swoops back down to Abdul's head, bringing with it a story from the sky."
—Lewin. *The Storytellers.*

Morocco

Contemporary Fez is the setting of Ted Lewin's *The Storytellers*. As Abdul and his grandfather walk through the different marketplaces (the weavers' street, the copper and brass workers' street, ...), Abdul realizes that the two of them have the best job of all: storytelling.

Jonathan London's *Ali, Child of the Desert* takes place on the Sahara Desert as Ali goes with his father to sell camels at faraway Rissani. Separated from his father in a sandstorm, Ali bravely decides to stay with his camel at an oasis rather than go with the Berber goatherds he has met.

Books

Lewin, Ted. *The Storytellers*. Illustrated by author. New York: Lothrop, Lee & Shepard Books, 1998.

London, Jonathan. *Ali, Child of the Desert*. Illustrated by Ted Lewin. New York: Lothrop, Lee & Shepard Books, 1997.

"Tashira lived in a dry and dusty land."
—Claire. *The Sun, the Wind, and Tashira.*

Namibia
(formerly South-West Africa)

In *The Sun, the Wind, and Tashira*, Elizabeth Claire retells the Hottentot story of the color-loving Tashira, who decides to live with the sun that has made the sky blue and painted ever-changing sunsets. However, when the wind interferes with Tashira's sunward journey, the sun turns her into a rainbow.

It is a blue crane who comes to the rescue of two baby doves in *Jackal's Flying Lesson*, which is retold by Verna Aardema. The crane outwits the jackal who had earlier tricked a dove and swallowed her two children.

Books

Aardema, Verna, reteller. *Jackal's Flying Lesson: A Khoikhoi Tale*. Illustrated by Dale Gottlieb. New York: Alfred A. Knopf Books for Young Readers, 1995.

Claire, Elizabeth, reteller. *The Sun, the Wind, and Tashira: A Hottentot Tale from Africa*. (Mondo Folktales Series) Illustrated by Elise Mills. Greenvale, NY: Mondo Publishing, 1994; 1994, paperback.

"Sholo taught Banzar how to play the omele drum and compose the praise songs that honored the ancestors of the village chiefs."
—Medearis. *The Singing Man.*

Nigeria
Federal Republic of Nigeria

The books set in Nigeria include a book of poetry and seven folktales.

The Distant Talking Drum presents fifteen poems by the poet Isaac Olaleye, each accompanied by a full-page painting. Written from the perspective of a small boy, the book presents life in a Nigerian rain forest village: the farms, the school, the market, the storytelling,…and the rain.

Ashley Bryan's *The Story of Lightning & Thunder* is based on a folktale from southern Nigeria and tells how, because of Lightning's behavior, Thunder, who is a sheep, and Lightning, her son who is a ram, must leave the earth and go to live in the sky.

Based on an Ibibio myth, *Why the Sun & Moon Live in the Sky*, by Niki Daly, shows how, when Sun invites Sea and her children (fish, whales, etc.) to visit Sun and Moon's house, Sea completely floods the house, forcing the two of them to climb up to the sky. Considering that fiasco, it is not surprising that Moon chooses not to live with Sun again.

A Yoruba folktale is the basis for Angela Shelf Medearis's *The Singing Man*. Expelled from his village by the village elders because he wants to be a musician, Banzar travels from village to village learning to be and then becoming a praise singer. Chosen as the king of Lagos's personal musician, Banzar proudly returns to the village of his family.

The Flying Tortoise, retold by Tololwa M. Mollel, is a tale of the Igbo people. The crafty tortoise gets wings and flies with the birds to Skyland where he consumes all of the feast which has been prepared for them. But when it is time to return to earth, it is the birds who trick him, and to this day the embarrassed tortoise hides in his patched-up shell so that no one can tell that it is he and not a rock.

The fifth folktale comes from the Bini people. Retold by Mary-Joan Gerson, *Why the Sky Is Far Away* tells how in the beginning the sky was close to the earth and the people, when hungry, ate pieces of it. Unhappy because the people were wasteful with the amounts of sky they took, the sky moves upward too far for them to grasp and they must raise their own crops.

T. Obinkaram Echewa's *The Magic Tree*, the sixth folktale, is the story of an orphan boy who is cruelly treated by the villagers until he plants a magical udara tree.

The author of the seventh folktale is Ian Thomson, a native of Scotland who received the name Papa Oyibo because of his participation in the storytelling circle of the Yoruba. *Big Brother, Little Sister*, one of his original stories, tells of the mouse who pulls a thorn out of the foot of a young elephant. Becoming friends, the mouse becomes the big brother and the elephant the little sister.

Books

Bryan, Ashley. *The Story of Lightning & Thunder*. New York: Atheneum Books for Young Readers, 1993; Simon & Schuster Children's Publishing, 1999, paperback.

Daly, Niki. *Why the Sun & Moon Live in the Sky*. Illustrated by author. New York: Lothrop, Lee & Shepard Books, 1995.

Echewa, T. Obinkaram. *The Magic Tree: A Folktale from Nigeria*. Illustrated by E. B. Lewis. New York: Morrow Junior Books, 1999.

Gerson, Mary-Joan, reteller. *Why the Sky Is Far Away: A Nigerian Folktale*. Illustrated by Carla Golembe. New York: Little, Brown and Company, 1995, paperback.

Medearis, Angela Shelf. *The Singing Man: Adapted from a West African Folktale*. Illustrated by Terea Shaffer. New York: Holiday House, 1994; 1994, paperback.

Mollel, Tololwa M., reteller. *The Flying Tortoise: An Igbo Tale*. Illustrated by Barbara Spurll. New York: Houghton Mifflin Company, 1994.

Olaleye, Isaac. *The Distant Talking Drum: Poems from Nigeria*. Illustrated by Frané Lessac. Honesdale, PA: Wordsong, 1995.

Oyibo, Papa [aka Ian Thomson]. *Big Brother, Little Sister*. Illustrated by John Clementson. New York: Barefoot Books, 2000.

"Sebgugugu and his household lived near that cattle kraal for several years."
—Aardema. *Sebgugugu the Glutton.*

Rwanda
(formerly Ruanda)

Striking collages illustrate Verna Aardema's retelling for older children of a Bantu folktale, *Sebgugugu the Glutton.* Time and again the Lord of Rwanda comes to the rescue of the greedy and foolish Sebgugugu, but finally enough is enough and Sebgugugu's family and cows are taken from him.

Book

Aardema, Verna, reteller. *Sebgugugu the Glutton: A Bantu Tale from Rwanda, Africa.* Illustrated by Nancy L. Clouse. Lawrenceville, NJ: Africa World Press, 1993.

"When Mr. Nelson Mandela became president of the country, people danced and sang in the streets all day and all night."
—Sisulu. *The Day Gogo Went to Vote.*

South Africa
(formerly Union of South Africa)
Republic of South Africa

Specific Locations

Four of the provinces of South Africa are represented in the picture books described below.

Eastern Cape

Fly, Eagle, Fly!, which is retold by Christopher Gregorowski, is set in the Transkei Region. A farmer who has raised an eaglet as a chicken insists that it is a chicken. He is proven wrong by his friend—and by the bird, who shows that it is not a chicken of the land, but an eagle of the sky.

Over the Green Hills, by Rachel Isadora, describes the day that the young boy Zolani, a goat, and Zolani's mother, with a baby on her back and food and a chicken on her head, walk across the Transkei from their town of Mpame to his grandmother's house.

Gauteng

In Elinor Batezat Sisulu's *The Day Gogo Went to Vote* six-year-old Thembi tells how her one-hundred-year-old great-grandmother left their Soweto home for the first time in years to vote in South Africa's April 1994 elections.

KwaZulu-Natal

A book for the oldest children, *Marriage of the Rain Goddess*, by Margaret Olivia Wolfson, is based on a Zulu myth. Seeking a mate, the rain goddess decides upon a cattle herder. When he selects her instead of a beautiful young woman, she knows she has made the right choice.

Western Cape

Rosemary Kahn's *Grandma's Hat* is set in the Karoo Region. A grandmother tells her children how, when she was a child in the town of De Aar, the dreadful hat which her mother bought her ended up on a scarecrow's head instead of on hers.

In *Somewhere in Africa*, by Ingrid Mennen and Niki Daly, Ashraf enjoys living in the busy city of Cape Town—and enjoys reading the library book that describes the unfamiliar Africa of plains, lions, and crocodiles.

Charlie also lives in Cape Town in *Charlie's House*, by Reviva Schermbrucker. Charlie watches men build his family's iron sheet, leaky-roof shelter. Then with mud, clay, items he finds, and great creativity, he builds his own tiny house, complete with a milk carton refrigerator and a plastic bottle bathtub.

General

Alphabet, counting, and word books

Halala Means Welcome!, by Ken Wilson-Max, is a word book which alternates pages telling of the visit by a young boy to his Zulu friend's home with pages of individual pictures of some of the objects shown in the previous pages, this time labeled with their Zulu and English names. A pronunciation guide for each of the Zulu words is included at the end of the book.

Fables, fairy tales, folktales, legends, myths, and proverbs (including original works)

Nabulela, a North Nguni folktale retold by Fiona Moodie, tells of Nandi's dog who helps rescue her from the pit into which she has been pushed by her jealous playmates and of the young girl playmates who, as punishment, bravely lure the monster Nabulela from his lake to their kraal.

Historical figures

Mandela, Floyd Cooper's picture biography for the oldest children, presents the life of the South African leader from his birth in the Thembu village of Mvezo in 1918 to his election as president in 1994.

Nonfiction

The illustrations and brief text in Isadora's *A South African Night* show how at nighttime the people in Johannesburg go to bed, but the animals in Kruger National Park wake up and spend their nighttime hunting, eating, and drinking at the water hole.

Stories

Seven of the stories set in South Africa have been written by Hugh Lewin and tell about Jafta, his family, and his experiences.

A book for even the youngest children, *Jafta* shows how the small boy's actions resemble those of a hyena, an impala, a cheetah, and other South African animals.

Jafta's Mother introduces a mother who is like the sun, the sky, the hoopoe bird, and other parts of the environment.

Jafta's Father tells how Jafta misses his father, who has gone to the city to work and who has made him a hideout and a raft.

In *Jafta and the Wedding* Jafta relates what he and the other children did during the weeklong celebration of his older sister Nomsa's wedding.

Jafta and his mother travel by foot, cart, bus, and flatboat to reach the town where his father works in *Jafta—The Journey*.

In town with his parents, who are attending a funeral, Jafta plays with some children, sees his father's factory, and goes to a soccer game in *Jafta—The Town*.

In *Jafta—The Homecoming* Jafta remembers the many things that have happened at home since his father left, experiences that Jafta would have liked to have shared with him. But, things have also happened in South Africa, and Jafta's father finally returns.

Children wait for their fathers to return from the mines in *At the Crossroads*, by Isadora. Six children spend the entire night at the crossroads waiting for their fathers to return from a ten month absence.

Lindiwe gets her own flute in *The Song of Six Birds*, by Rene Deetlefs. Shocked by its piercing nonmusical sound, Lindiwe spends the day finding birds who give their songs to the flute and then, returning, shares its enchanting music with the village.

In Niki Daly's *Not So Fast, Songololo* young Malusi and his grandmother go on a shopping trip to the city. They both like to move slowly—until Malusi's grandmother unexpectedly buys him a pair of shoes and he proudly increases his pace.

Jamela thoughtlessly ruins the fabric for the dress her mother will wear to a wedding in *Jamela's Dress*, by Daly. Fortunately, the prize won by the photographer who has taken her picture pays for new material—enough for dresses for both her mother and Jamela.

Dianne Stewart's *Gift of the Sun* is the story of lazy Thulani, who after making a series of foolish trades ends up with sunflower seeds instead of a cow. However, thanks to the amazing properties of the sunflower seeds, Thulani is able to make a series of successful trades and, even more amazingly, stops sitting in the sun all day.

Books

Cooper, Floyd. *Mandela: From the Life of the South African Statesman*. Illustrated by author. New York: Philomel Books, 1996; Putnam Publishing Group, 1999, paperback.

Daly, Niki. *Jamela's Dress*. Illustrated by author. New York: Farrar, Straus & Giroux, 1999.

Daly, Niki. *Not So Fast, Songololo*. Illustrated by author. New York: Margaret K. McElderry Books, 1986; Aladdin Paperbacks, 1996.

Deetlefs, Rene. *The Song of Six Birds*. Illustrated by Lyn Gilbert. New York: Dutton Children's Books, 2000.

Gregorowski, Christopher, reteller. *Fly, Eagle, Fly!: An African Tale*. Illustrated by Niki Daly. New York: Margaret K. McElderry Books, 2000.

Isadora, Rachel. *At the Crossroads*. Illustrated by author. New York: Greenwillow Books, 1991; Mulberry Books, 1994, paperback.

Isadora, Rachel. *Over the Green Hills*. Illustrated by author. New York: Greenwillow Books, 1992.

Isadora, Rachel. *A South African Night*. Illustrated by author. New York: Greenwillow Books, 1998.

Kahn, Rosemary. *Grandma's Hat*. Illustrated by Terry Milne. New York: N A L Dutton, 1999, paperback.

Lewin, Hugh. *Jafta*. Illustrated by Lisa Kopper. Minneapolis: Carolrhoda Books, 1983, paperback.

Lewin, Hugh. *Jafta—The Homecoming*. Illustrated by Lisa Kopper. New York: Alfred A. Knopf Books for Young Readers, 1994.

Lewin, Hugh. *Jafta—The Journey.* Illustrated by Lisa Kopper. Minneapolis: Carolrhoda Books, 1994; 1994, paperback.

Lewin, Hugh. *Jafta—The Town.* Illustrated by Lisa Kopper. Minneapolis: Carolrhoda Books, 1994; 1994, paperback.

Lewin, Hugh. *Jafta and the Wedding.* Illustrated by Lisa Kopper. Minneapolis: Carolrhoda Books, 1983, paperback.

Lewin, Hugh. *Jafta's Father.* Illustrated by Lisa Kopper. Minneapolis: Carolrhoda Books, 1983; 1989, paperback.

Lewin, Hugh. *Jafta's Mother.* Illustrated by Lisa Kopper. Minneapolis: Carolrhoda Books, 1983; 1989, paperback.

Mennen, Ingrid, and Niki Daly. *Somewhere in Africa.* Illustrated by Nicolaas Maritz. New York: Dutton Children's Books, 1992, paperback.

Moodie, Fiona, reteller. *Nabulela: A South African Folk Tale.* Illustrated by reteller. New York: Farrar, Straus & Giroux, 1997.

Schermbrucker, Reviva. *Charlie's House.* Illustrated by Niki Daly. New York: N A L Dutton, 1999, paperback.

Sisulu, Elinor Batezat. *The Day Gogo Went to Vote: South Africa, April 1994.* Illustrated by Sharon Wilson. New York: Little, Brown, and Company, 1996; 1999, paperback.

Stewart, Dianne. *Gift of the Sun: A Tale from South Africa.* Illustrated by Jude Daly. New York: Farrar, Straus & Giroux, 1996.

Wilson-Max, Ken. *Halala Means Welcome!: A Book of Zulu Words.* Illustrated by author. New York: Hyperion, 1998.

Wolfson, Margaret Olivia. *Marriage of the Rain Goddess: A South African Myth.* Illustrated by Clifford Alexander Parms. New York: Barefoot Books, 1999.

"The next moment he stared in panic as a herd of elephants stampeded out of the grove."
—Mollel. *Big Boy.*

Tanzania (formerly Tanganyika)
United Republic of Tanzania

General

Fables, fairy tales, folktales, legends, myths, and proverbs (including original works)

Bimwili & the Zimwi, by Verna Aardema, is a tale from the island of Zanzibar. Kidnapped by the magical Zimwi, Bimwili is forced to sing from inside a drum at village meeting places. She sings a different song when she realizes she is in her own village, thereby enabling her family to rescue her.

Francesca Martin's *Clever Tortoise* is set by Lake Nyasa (Lake Malawi). When Elephant and Hippopotamus disturb the other animals by boasting of their superiority, Clever Tortoise tricks them into a tug-of-war in which, unbeknownst to each of them, they are tugging against each other instead of against the tortoise.

Three Tanzanian tales are placed in modern settings.

Shadow Dance, by Tololwa M. Mollel, tells how the kind Salome is captured by the tricky crocodile she has helped. She is finally saved, thanks to her clever thinking.

Tatu is responsible for tending her little brother in Mollel's *Subira Subira*. Faced with his constantly fighting her, Tatu goes to a spirit woman for help. Following her advice by securing three whiskers from a lion, Tatu discovers that it is not the whiskers that solve the problem, but the patience which she has learned. The words and music of the song Tatu sings are appended.

Big Boy, by Mollel, is about the little boy, Oli. Longing to be big, Oli gets up from his nap and sneaks out to the woods where the wish granted by the magic Tunukia-zawadi bird convinces him that there are advantages to being little.

Poetry and songs

In *Is It Far to Zanzibar?* Niki Grimes presents thirteen poems about Tanzania, with one specifically about Zanzibar.

Stories

Mollel's *Kele's Secret* tells of small Yoanes, who has the job of searching his coffee farm for hens' eggs. It is the hen Kele who chooses the most unusual place of all—and the brave Yoanes who, mastering his fear of a dreaded monster, enters a scary rain shelter and discovers a treasure trove of eggs.

Also set on a coffee farm is Mollel's *My Rows and Piles of Coins*. Saruni saves the money he earns helping his mother so that he can buy a bicycle to carry her goods to market. When he unexpectedly receives a bicycle, he continues to save his coins, this time for a cart.

In *Elizabeti's Doll*, by Stephanie Stuve-Bodeen, when young Elizabeti becomes a big sister, she decides to have a baby doll of her own. Choosing a rock, she names it Eva and cares for it until it disappears. This story, which has a happy ending, should appeal especially to young children who have a new sibling.

In the sequel, *Mama Elizabeti*, Elizabeti finds that taking care of her now-older baby brother is much different than tending to Eva. Obedi causes problems when she tries to do her chores, and she finds it impossible to carry both him and the water jug. Then Obedi solves the problem by taking his first steps—and Elizabeti discovers that there are advantages to having a real baby.

Books

Aardema, Verna. *Bimwili & the Zimwi: A Tale from Zanzibar*. Illustrated by Susan Meddaugh. New York: N A L Dutton, 1992, paperback.

Grimes, Nikki. *Is It Far to Zanzibar?: Poems about Tanzania*. Illustrated by Betsy Lewin. New York: Lothrop, Lee & Shepard Books, 2000.

Martin, Francesca. *Clever Tortoise: A Traditional African Tale*. Cambridge, MA: Candlewick Press, 2000.

Mollel, Tololwa M. *Big Boy*. Illustrated by E. B. Lewis. New York: Clarion Books, 1994; 1997, paperback.

Mollel, Tololwa M. *Kele's Secret*. Illustrated by Catherine Stock. New York: Dutton, 1997, paperback.

Mollel, Tololwa M. *My Rows and Piles of Coins*. Illustrated by E. B. Lewis. New York: Clarion Books, 1999.

Mollel, Tololwa M. *Shadow Dance*. Illustrated by Donna Perrone. Boston: Houghton Mifflin Company, 1998.

Mollel, Tololwa M. *Subira Subira*. Illustrated by Linda
    Saport. New York: Clarion Books, 2000.
Stuve-Bodeen, Stephanie. *Elizabeti's Doll*. Illustrated by
    Christy Hale. New York: Lee & Low Books, 1998.
Stuve-Bodeen, Stephanie. *Mama Elizabeti*. Illustrated by
    Christy Hale. New York: Lee & Low Books, 2000.

"The sky is fire-red, but a cool breeze rustles the leaves of the great gray baobab tree as Manyoni sets off down the path."
—Stock. *Where Are You Going, Manyoni?*

Zimbabwe (formerly Rhodesia, Southern Rhodesia)

In John Steptoe's *Mufaro's Beautiful Daughters* it is not the beautiful, but scheming and thoughtless Manyara whom the King marries, but the equally beautiful, but kind Nyasha, who unknowingly had befriended the king when he took the form of a garden snake.

Children will enjoy searching the vast landscapes for the wildlife and for Manyoni in Catherine Stock's *Where Are You Going, Manyoni?* All by herself, Manyoni crosses the veld near the Tobwani Dam on the Limpopo River until, joined by her friend, she reaches the school.

Books

Steptoe, John. *Mufaro's Beautiful Daughters: An African Tale.* Illustrated by author. New York: Lothrop, Lee & Shepard Books, 1987; Mulberry Books, 1993, paperback.

Stock, Catherine. *Where Are You Going, Manyoni?* Illustrated by author. New York: Morrow Junior Books, 1993.

<u>Asia</u>

"We climb into the cold blue light, toward sheer fields of snow and ice."
—McKay. *Caravan.*

Afghanistan

In Lawrence McKay, Jr.'s *Caravan* a ten-year-old Kirghiz boy makes a 250 mile round-trip journey with his father's caravan. Traveling through the Pamirs, part of the Hindu Kush Mountains, the horse-riding Jura is responsible for three camels which carry furs and felts that his father trades for grain at the distant marketplace.

Book

McKay, Lawrence, Jr. *Caravan.* Illustrated by Darryl Ligasan. New York: Lee & Low Books, 1995.

"After a hard day's travel, the caravan stopped at a lonely khan, an inn, built into a mountainside."
—San Souci. *A Weave of Words.*

Armenia

Armenia was formerly a constituent republic of the Union of Soviet Socialist Republics (U.S.S.R.), which was dissolved in 1991. Picture books set in the area of the former U.S.S.R. for which no other specific location is given are described under Russia (Russian Federation). Books set in the ancient country of Armenia, which is now divided between Armenia, Iran, and Turkey, are included here.

In Robert D. San Souci's *A Weave of Words* it is fortunate that the educated Anait requires Prince Vachagan to learn to read, write, and learn a trade before she will marry him. When he is imprisoned with others in a cave, the message he weaves into a carpet enables Anait, now the queen, to lead an army to free him.

The Golden Bracelet, which is retold by David Kherdian, is a version of the same tale. Here King Haig goes out to search for his servant, who, with a number of other men, has been enslaved in a dungeon by a sorcerer. It is a golden cloth complete with a hidden message and a map that he weaves for the eyes of Queen Anahid.

The Contest, an Armenian folktale which is adapted by Nonny Hogrogian, tells of two robbers who, unbeknownst to each of them, are betrothed to the same woman. Discovering the deception, they enter into a contest in which the cleverest shall win the hand of the woman. They both perform clever tasks and then have the cleverest idea of all: neither one will marry the unworthy woman.

Inspired by an Armenian tale, Hogrogian's *One Fine Day*, a Caldecott Medal winner, relates a cumulative story that shows everything the fox must go through to get his tail reattached.

Books

Hogrogian, Nonny, adapter. *The Contest*. Illustrated by author. New York: Greenwillow Books, 1976.

Hogrogian, Nonny. *One Fine Day*. Illustrated by author. New York: Simon & Schuster Books for Young Readers, 1971; Aladdin Paperbacks, 1974, paperback.

Kherdian, David, reteller. *The Golden Bracelet*. Illustrated by Nonny Hogrogian. New York: Little, Brown and Company, 1996; Holiday House, 1998.

San Souci, Robert D., reteller. *A Weave of Words: An Armenian Tale*. Illustrated by Raúl Colón. New York: Orchard Books, an imprint of Scholastic, Inc., 1998.

"Brother Sun was just setting and the heart-shaped leaves of the banyan tree seemed to rattle uneasily."
—Mao Wall. *Judge Rabbit and the Tree Spirit.*

Cambodia (Kampuchea)

Angkat, a book for older children by Jewell Reinhart Coburn, presents a Cinderella story which varies in many respects from the familiar one. Angkat's father does not die, but joins her stepmother and her one stepsister in conspiring against her; through trickery her stepsister becomes daughter Number One; Angkat is aided by a magical fish; a bird takes one of her slippers to the prince; and after the prince and Angkat are wed, Angkat is killed by her family, but is later restored to life.

Jeanne M. Lee's *Silent Lotus* tells how a girl, who is deaf-mute, learns to express herself through dancing at the king's court.

Minfong Ho and Saphan Ros are the authors of *The Two Brothers*, a folktale for the oldest children about two brothers who fulfill the abbot's prophecy—the older one, who right away takes the abbot's advice, and the younger one, who only after many difficulties chooses to heed the abbot's words.

Written in both English and Khmer, *Judge Rabbit and the Tree Spirit*, which is told by Lina Mao Wall, reveals a wise rabbit, who is able to determine which of two look-alike men is a wife's real husband.

Books

Coburn, Jewell Reinhart. *Angkat: The Cambodian Cinderella.* Illustrated by Eddie Flotte. Auburn, CA: Shen's Books, 1998.

Ho, Minfong, and Saphan Ros. *The Two Brothers.* Illustrated by Jean Tseng and Mou-sien Tseng. New York: Lothrop, Lee & Shepard Books, 1995.

Lee, Jeanne M. *Silent Lotus.* Illustrated by author. New York: Farrar, Straus & Giroux, 1991; Sunburst Books, 1994, paperback.

Mao Wall, Lina, told by. *Judge Rabbit and the Tree Spirit: A Folktale from Cambodia.* Adapted by Cathy Spagnoli. Illustrated by Nancy Hom. San Francisco: Children's Book Press, 1991.

"Now China is an enormous country with the tallest mountains, the longest rivers, and the thickest jungles—and many, many animals live there."
—Whitfield. *The Animals of the Chinese Zodiac.*

China
<u>People's Republic of China</u>

Specific Locations

The picture books described are set in four provinces (Henan, Shandong, Sichuan, and Yunnan), one municipality (Beijing), one autonomous region (Tibet), and one special administrative region (Hong Kong).

Beijing (Peking, formerly Peiping)

A cricket performs an invaluable service for his master in *The Cricket's Cage*, which is retold by Stefan Czernecki. Kuai Xiang, a carpenter, is about to lose his head if he cannot design a magnificent tower for each corner of the wall surrounding the Forbidden City. The cricket comes up with a design for his new cricket cage, and after Kuai Xiang builds it, it is accepted as the model for the towers.

Amy Lowry Poole sets her retelling of an Aesop's fable at the Emperor's original summer palace, Yuanmingyuan. In *The Ant and the Grasshopper* the ants work hard each day reconstructing their house and gathering food, while the grasshopper, mocking the ants' industriousness, enjoys the carefree life of entertaining the Emperor. When winter comes, the court leaves the summer palace and the ants are snug in their home. It is then that the grasshopper finally realizes how foolish he has been.

Henan (Honan)

Emily Arnold McCully's book for older children, *Beautiful Warrior*, is set in the Shaolin Monastery west of Zhengzhou where Wu Mei is a Buddhist nun and a kung fu master. The story tells how she teaches kung fu, both its technique and the inner strength it requires, to a young woman who rebels at marrying a brigand.

Hong Kong (Hongkong)

In Riki Levinson's *Our Home Is the Sea*, a young boy enjoys the sights of modern-day Hong Kong as he travels from school to his houseboat home. However, despite the attractions of the city, he longs to be a fisherman like his father and grandfather.

Nei Monggol (Inner Mongolia)

The region, Mongolia, includes Mongolia (Outer Mongolia), the Nei Monggol (Inner Mongolia) Autonomous Region of China, and Tuva. Picture books set in the region of Mongolia are described under Mongolia (Outer Mongolia).

Shandong (Shantung)

The Beggar's Magic, which is retold by Margaret and Raymond Chang, is the story originating in Shandong Province of a beggar priest, who performs tricks of kindness. All the villagers learn of his magical powers when, in appreciation of their own kindnesses toward him, he transforms the pears and cart of a miserly farmer into a pear tree.

An old woman must learn to be kind in Laurence Yep's *Tiger Woman*, a book for older readers which has its origin in a Shandong folk song. After refusing to share her bean curd with a beggar, the woman's comments turn her successively into a tiger, an ox, a sparrow, an elephant, and a pig before she once again becomes an old woman—this time a kind one.

Sichuan (Szechuan, Szechwan)

A book for older children, *The Dragon's Pearl*, retold by Julie Lawson, tells of the boy Xiao Sheng, who brings good fortune to himself and his mother when he finds a magic pearl. Then, when he inadvertently swallows the pearl, he becomes a dragon and, living in the Min River, brings rain every year to the countryside.

Tibet (Xizang, Hsi-tsang)

Mordicai Gerstein's *The Mountains of Tibet* tells the story of the Tibetan man who longed to see the world and the galaxies. When he died as an old man, he was given the option of returning to life anywhere he wished and, after looking at the universe, chose Tibet.

In Alan Schroeder's *The Stone Lion* the brother who is honest, kind, and caring of the environment is given gold and silver coins by a stone lion, but the dishonest, greedy brother's hand is trapped in the lion's mouth until the brother repents.

Demi's *The Donkey and the Rock* retells the folktale of a poor and honest man's donkey which accidentally breaks the jar of oil owned by an equally poor and honest man. When the wise king arrests and tries both the donkey and the rock upon which the jar had been placed, the money charged the curious spectators is given to the man whose oil was spilled.

The renowned ducktective, Miss Mallard, travels to Tibet to find her lost nephew in Robert Quackenbush's *Danger in Tibet*, part of a series for older readers. She not only finds her nephew, but also is helped by the Abominable Snowduck, solves a bank robbery, meets the High Lama, and saves his hidden city from being developed into a resort.

Yunnan (Yün-nan)

Jennifer Armstrong's *Chin Yu Min and the Ginger Cat* is set near Kunming. It tells the story of a haughty woman who learns the meaning of friendship from a ginger cat.

The folktale, *White Tiger, Blue Serpent*, which is retold by Grace Tseng, has its origin in Yunnan Province. Kai works hard for a thousand days so that his mother can weave him a most beautiful brocade. When it is blown across the river to the fertile land of the goddess Qin, Kai bests a white tiger and a blue serpent and then benefits from another wind created by Qin as this time the animals, birds, trees, and flowers depicted on the brocade are blown off and bring fertility to his side of the river.

General

Celebrations

An original tale for older children, David Bouchard's *The Dragon New Year* shows how the celebration of the Chinese New Year might have originated. Thanks to the bonfire lit by the Buddha and the noise made on a chopping block by the woman who had lost her son to the terrible dragon New Year, the dragon departs and New Year comes to be celebrated by the light and noise of fireworks and cymbals.

In Amy Tan's *The Moon Lady*, a book for older children, three sisters hear from their grandmother of her adventures as a little girl at the Moon Festival. On that eventful occasion she covers her clothes with the blood of an eel, falls off a floating teahouse, is rescued by a fisherman, and, lost, discovers her secret wish.

Fables, fairy tales, folktales, legends, myths, and proverbs (including original works)

Most of the picture books on China are folktales with no specific locations.

The folktales include two Cinderella stories, one Beauty and the Beast story, and a Red Riding Hood story.

Yeh-Shen, which is retold by Ai-Ling Louie, tells of an orphan girl who is mistreated by her father's other wife and their daughter. When the fish whom Yeh-Shen has befriended is killed by her stepmother, Yeh-Shen's needs are met by its magical bones, which provide her with a gown for the festival. She runs off from the festival when she fears her stepsister has recognized her, and her lost golden slipper eventually arrives in the hands of the king of an island kingdom. He discovers Yeh-Shen when she retrieves the lost slipper so that she may regain the favor of the fish bones. The preface in this book notes that the Cinderella story appeared in China centuries before the first known Cinderella story in Europe. It also includes a copy of an early Chinese version.

The Cinderella story, Wishbones, which is retold by Barbara Ker Wilson, resembles the Louie version, but differs in some of the details. For instance, Yeh Hsien's father does not die, the fishbones provide Yeh Hsien with fine goods before the time of the festival, the cave setting is emphasized, and the story reveals the fate of the fishbones.

Full- and double-page paintings illustrate Laurence Yep's The Dragon Prince. In this Beauty and the Beast tale, Seven, the youngest of seven sisters, weds a dragon to save her father's life and is transported by the dragon to a land under the sea where, touched by her beauty and kindness, he turns into a prince. All goes well with the couple until the homesick Seven returns to visit her family and is tricked by her jealous sister, Three, who assumes her identity. Not deceived, the prince finds his lost love and takes her and the old woman who has cared for her back to his palace in the sea.

In Lon Po Po, a Caldecott Medal winner translated

and illustrated by Ed Young, instead of Red Riding Hood going to her grandmother's house, the wolf, pretending to be their grandmother, is let into the house of three little girls. When the eldest one realizes that he is a wolf, she devises a clever plan whereby she and her sisters escape to the top of a gingko nut tree and then kill the wolf while he is attempting to taste one of the nuts.

Animals are featured in a number of the folktales. In addition to his story of the wolf, Young has written four of them.

His *Night Visitors* tells of a young man who does not want to destroy the ants which are eating his family's rice. Thanks to a dream (?), he finds the means whereby he can protect the rice, while preserving the ants' lives.

Young's *Mouse Match* is a book which opens out accordion-fashion. Papa mouse wants the most powerful husband for his daughter. After seeking first the sun and then the cloud, the wind, and the mountain, he discovers that the most powerful of all is the mouse.

The Lost Horse, by Young, relates how the wise man Sai recognizes that what would appear to be misfortunes and good fortune regarding his horse will prove to be otherwise. The book includes the original story in Chinese and a pocket at the end which contains articulated plastic puppets of the horse, Sai, and his son. There is a warning on the cover that because of choking danger with the puppets, the book should not be used with children under three.

The fourth book by Young, *Cat and Rat*, is one of four books explaining how the animals of the Chinese zodiac were selected and describing the supposed characteristics of persons born in each animal's year. According to the Young story, when the emperor holds a race with years to be named for the twelve winners, Rat pushes his best friend Cat out of contention and finishes first, thereby creating lasting enmity between Cat and Rat.

Why Rat Comes First, retold by Clara Yen, is based on her father's original folktale. In this story the curious Jade King wishes to see all the animals of China and is disappointed when only twelve respond to his invitation. When the animals cannot agree whether the rat or the ox deserves to be the name of the first year, the Jade King lets some children on the earth decide, and the clever rat wins the contest.

Based on a legend of about A.D. 600, Susan Whitfield's *The Animals of the Chinese Zodiac* tells how, at the invitation of the sick and lonely Buddha, twelve animals journey to visit him. As he sees them coming, he decides to name the years after them, starting with the first to arrive, the rat. Both the text and the watercolor illustrations present each animal as a very distinct individual.

In *The Rooster's Antlers*, which is retold by Eric A. Kimmel, the Jade King selects the animals on the basis of their characteristics. The rooster is upset that the dragon is chosen for an earlier year than his, which he attributes to his loaning, at the behest of the centipede, of his antlers to the dragon. Thus, today roosters like to eat centipedes and crow at the dragon in the sky who has never returned the rooster's antlers. There is a distinctive blue background throughout this book.

In *How the Ox Star Fell from Heaven*, retold by Lily Toy Hong, the ox who is sent as a messenger to earth misstates the message. As a result, he is banished from heaven and, falling to earth, makes it possible for people to fulfill his mixed-up message, that they shall be able to eat three meals a day.

Darcy Pattison's *The River Dragon* is an original folktale in which a goldsmith plots to have a river dragon prevent a blacksmith from wedding his daughter. Twice the blacksmith is saved from the dragon through the help of fortune cookies, but the third time he must rely on his own ingenuity.

Dragonsong, by Russell Young, is an original fable for the oldest children about another dragon, the young Chiang-An. When it is announced that a dragon will be chosen for the year 2000 to become keeper of a village's mountain, Chiang-An visits the dragons of Stonehenge, an African river, Niagara Falls, and Teotihuacan. Drawing upon the songs of their wisdom, he composes the song which wins him the position.

Da Wei's Treasure, which is retold by Margaret and Raymond Chang, relates the experiences of Da Wei, who, thanks to his father's prized possession, is led to an undersea mansion where he is befriended by a kitten. Taking the kitten back to his house, Da Wei is surprised to learn both its origin and that it is in reality a mortal woman, a woman whom he happily marries.

Numerous animals are featured in *A Chinese Zoo*, which is adapted by Demi. Each of the book's double-page spreads includes a fable, an illustrated Chinese fan which depicts the fable, and the proverb it expresses.

Demi's retelling, *The Dragon's Tale and Other Animal Fables of the Chinese Zodiac*, also presents fables, in this instance, brightly illustrated tales of the twelve animals of the Chinese zodiac.

Demi uses Chinese paints and brushes for the detailed

full-page paintings that illustrate the Hans Christian Andersen tale, *The Nightingale*. The emperor, who secures the most marvelous thing in China, a gray nightingale, banishes it from his kingdom and then discovers that it cannot be replaced by a bejeweled artificial bird.

It is not a nightingale, but cranes, that are featured in *Lord of the Cranes*, which is retold by Kerstin Chen. When Tian, the Lord of the Cranes, goes disguised as a beggar into the city, he meets Wang, a kind innkeeper, who feeds him gratis every evening. In return Tian paints three cranes on the inn wall. Many come to see the cranes who descend from the wall to dance for the inn's patrons, thereby bringing business and wealth to Wang.

Children are the main characters in eleven folktales.

Diane Wolkstein's *The Magic Wings* shows how all the women and girls of the town, including the princess and the queen, follow the example of the goose girl and try to fly. However, only the flower-loving goose girl is granted the power to do so.

Demi's *The Empty Pot* tells of a China of long ago in which everyone loves flowers. Yet surprisingly, it is the boy Ping, the one child who cannot grow a flower to show the emperor, who is rewarded for his honesty and courage.

A child who loves to paint is the title character in two versions of an old Chinese folktale.

In Demi's *Liang and the Magic Paintbrush* the boy Liang uses his magic brush to help others, but, unfortunately, it draws the attention of the greedy emperor who wishes to use it to get what he wants. A watercolor illustration accompanies text on each page.

In *Tye May and the Magic Brush*, adapted by Molly Garrett Bang, it is a girl, Tye May, who loves to paint and whose paintings, as in the Demi version, come to life. This book differs from the Demi book in some of the story's details and also in that it is a chapter book with an illustration appearing on each page or with a full-page picture facing a page of text.

Tikki Tikki Tembo, which is retold by Arlene Mosel, is the tale of a little boy who has an incredibly long name. Children should enjoy the repetitive use of his name in this story which contrasts his rescue from a well with that of his short-named younger brother.

Whether or not he is sad, the boy in Yep's *The City of Dragons* has such a sad face that no one wants to be depressed by his presence. Leaving his village, he goes to the underwater city of the dragons where his sad face causes dragons to weep tears of pearls. He then returns with pearls and dragon-woven silk to his home where the villagers have already regretted their previous behavior.

Jane Yolen's *The Emperor and the Kite* features Djeow Seow, the emperor's eighth child, who is so small that she is completely overlooked. However, when the emperor is imprisoned in a tower, it is Djeow Seow who manages to get food to him and then come to his rescue.

In Leong Vá's *A Letter to the King*, which is written in Chinese and English, Ti Ying's actions enable her father to be freed from prison, thereby proving to him as well as to the villagers that daughters can help their parents.

Elizabeth Hillman's *Min-Yo and the Moon Dragon* is an original tale explaining how stars came to be in the sky. Min-Yo, like Djeow Seow, is very small, and it is because of her lightness that she is chosen by the emperor to climb the frail cobweb ladder to the moon to see if the moon dragon can prevent the moon from falling into the earth.

Min-Yo climbs the ladder, discovers a very likable moon dragon, and, together, they discover that it is the diamonds placed in a moon cave that are causing the moon to fall.

The Cricket Warrior, retold by Margaret and Raymond Ching, tells of Wei nian who loses the large fighting cricket which is to save his family's land and his father from jail. Wei nian bravely takes the place of the cricket, and, although he is but a small cricket, he becomes the champion fighting cricket of the emperor's court. His deeds bring relief from debt and an orchard to his parents and then the greatest gift of all, the return to them of their son, the boy Wei nian.

A fighting cricket also appears in *The Jade Horse, the Cricket and the Peach Stone*, a folktale-like original story by Ann Tompert. However, it is not a cricket, salt, or a jade horse which the boy Pan Su presents to the emperor. It is a peach—and it is a gift of lasting joy.

Two of the folktales tell of grown siblings.

Claire Huchet Bishop's *The Five Chinese Brothers* is the 1938 retelling of a Chinese folktale about five identical brothers, each with an amazing attribute, who cooperate to prevent the executioner from killing the first brother (or one of the others). Although this book is among the best-known picture books set in China, its stereotypical depiction of the brothers, the drowning of a small boy, and the emphasis on different ways of killing may cause some to find it inappropriate for young children.

The Seven Chinese Brothers, by Margaret Mahy, is similar to the Bishop book. However, in this version, there are seven brothers possessing different capabilities, the offending brother gets in trouble for helping tired workers repair the Great Wall (not for a child's drowning), and the watercolors and text give a more humane approach to the story. The emperor in this folktale is Ch'in Shih Huang, who ruled China from 259 to 210 B.C.

Weaving is a common thread of six of the picture books.

In *The Seventh Sister*, which is retold by Cindy Chang, Mei and her sisters weave the tapestry of the sky which must lie over the earth every night. When she falls in love with Chang, a cowherd, Mei is too distracted to do her work. As a solution, Chang joins her as a star, but, separated by the Milky Way, the two can be together just once a year.

Legend of the Milky Way, which is retold by Jeanne M. Lee, tells a somewhat different story. In this version the heavenly king's seventh daughter, who is a weaver, is attracted to the flute music of a peasant, marries him, and, when his buffalo companion dies, weaves him a cloak from the buffalo's hide. When the queen discovers her missing daughter, she takes her back to the heavens. Thanks to the buffalo cloak, the peasant ascends into the sky, but is foiled again by the queen who draws a river, the Milky Way, to separate the couple whom she turns into stars. As in the Chang version, the two reunite once a year.

A tapestry reflecting an old widow's dream is the focal point of both *The Enchanted Tapestry*, retold by Robert D. San Souci, and *The Weaving of a Dream*, retold by Marilee Heyer. When the tapestry is taken by fairies, only the youngest of the widow's three sons will brave danger to recover it. Upon his return the scene depicted in the tapestry becomes real, and the widow, the youngest son, and one of the fairies live together in the setting which she has woven. The books differ somewhat in the details of the folktale. Both include full- and double-page paintings.

Demi's *The Magic Tapestry* tells an almost identical story. However, the tapestry is a heavenly tapestry, the mother weaves tears and blood from her weary eyes into her work, and the recovered tapestry heals her blindness. This book also includes large colorful illustrations.

Hong's *The Empress and the Silkworm* is based on the legend of the Empress Si Ling-Chi's discovery of silk in about 2640 B.C. When a cocoon falls into her tea, she unwinds it and has the thread woven into a magnificent robe for the emperor, Huang-Ti.

Two very different folktales feature shells.

In *The Shell Woman & the King*, retold by Yep, Shell, a girl from the sea who can turn herself into a seashell, marries a man, Uncle Wu. The jealous king captures the couple and demands that Shell become his queen or bring him three wonders. She cleverly completes the three tasks, thereby saving herself and her husband.

In *White Wave*, retold by Wolkstein, a farmer each day brings leaves to feed the snail he has found. He discovers that it is in reality a moon goddess, and all goes well until he seeks to touch her hair. She disappears into the air, but leaves him the gift of her shell.

Drought and a thunder lord/thunder god are the subjects of the retellings of two Chinese tales.

In Yep's retelling, *The Junior Thunder Lord*, Yue, who as a boy learned the importance of aiding those who are less fortunate, helps and befriends the ugly giant, Bear Face. When Bear Face realizes the plight of Yue's village, he reveals himself as a junior thunder lord and lets Yue help him to bring rain to the village.

Ah-mei risks her life to bring water to her village in *The Long-Haired Girl*, which is retold by Doreen Rappaport.

However, her life is spared thanks to the ingenuity of an old man who tricks the thunder god.

Ten Suns, retold by Eric A. Kimmel, reveals why the earth needs one sun, not ten and not none. In the crisis caused when the ten brother suns cross the sky at the same time, the Archer of Heaven shoots down nine of the suns who turn into crows. Now each morning the crows greet the rising sun, their brother.

In *How the Rooster Got His Crown*, which is retold by Poole, the world began with six, not ten suns. An archer, at the behest of the emperor and the elders, shoots the reflections of five of them. A rooster's "cockle doodle do" entices the frightened sixth sun to come out from the cave in which he has been hiding and to shine upon the earth.

In *The Treasure Chest*, which is retold by Rosalind C. Wang, the kindness which Laifu shows a fish enables him to perform three seemingly impossible tasks and thereby not only marry his intended, but also save both of them and the villagers from a villainous ruler.

It would be hard to match the foolishness of the Emperor, his high chancellor, his imperial minister, and his people in Demi's *The Emperor's New Clothes*. In this retelling of the Andersen tale, which is set in a Chinese province, it is only the forthrightness of one small child that saves the Emperor from continuing folly.

In Arnold Lobel's original folktale, *Ming Lo Moves the Mountain*, Ming Lo's foolishness saves him and his wife from their uncomfortable life at the foot of a mountain. However, unbeknownst to them, the couple has moved, not the mountain.

On the other hand, it is Sung's cleverness that saves

him from the ghost who is going to take his life in Yep's *The Man Who Tricked a Ghost*.

Cleverness also plays a vital role in *The Greatest Treasure*, by Demi. The rich miserly Pang uses his cleverness to get his poor neighbor to stop playing his distracting flute music. However, it is the flute player and his wife who, even more clever, bring the gift of music and of happiness to Pang and his family.

Cleverness and perseverance enable the peasant Pong Lo to win the hand of a princess in Helena Clare Pittman's *A Grain of Rice*, an original story for older children which is set in the fifteenth century. Pong Lo works his way up in the imperial staff, heals the princess's illness, and then, in a manner similar to that found in three of the picture book folktales from India, places the emperor in the uncomfortable situation where he has promised Pong Lo more grains of rice than exist in the world.

In Marguerite W. Davol's *The Paper Dragon*, it is wisdom that enables the artist Mi Fei to persuade a destructive dragon to go back to sleep. He fulfills the dragon's three tasks by bringing it a paper lantern, a paper fan, and a paper scroll embodying love in its depiction of his neighbors' faces. Each page of text in this book opens out into a three-page-wide painting by Robert Sabuda. It should be noted that younger children may need help in handling the pages.

Paper craft is also featured in Margaret Bateson-Hill's *Lao Lao of Dragon Mountain*, which is written in English and Chinese. The old woman who delights the villagers with her exquisite paper cuts is called upon by the emperor to perform the impossible task of transforming paper into jewels while imprisoned and freezing in a mountain tower.

She is rescued by the Ice Dragon and now rides on his back, cutting out and spreading upon the earth blossoms, flowers, apples, nuts, and snowflakes.

Demi's *The Stonecutter* is a variant of *Mouse Match*, described earlier in this category. However, instead of a mouse who is dissatisfied with a mouse husband for his daughter, it is a stonecutter who repeatedly is granted his wishes to be greater than he was before and then at last chooses to be what he was originally, a stonecutter.

In the amusing *Two of Everything*, retold by Hong, a farmer finds a magic pot, which doubles everything that is placed inside it, including the farmer and his wife.

Three picture books tell the story of Mu Lan, who, disguised as a soldier, takes her father's place in the Emperor's army and achieves distinction before returning to her family. Available in several bilingual versions, Wei Jiang and Cheng An Jiang's *The Legend of Mu Lan* is written in prose in contrast to *China's Bravest Girl* and *The Song of Mu Lan*, which are described in the poetry category. In the Jiangs' book Mu Lan lies that she is her father's daughter and uses lantern-carrying goats to trick the enemy in a battle at what is now the city of Chengde in Hebei Province.

Nonfiction

Children may want to follow the kite-making directions at the end of Demi's *Kites*, which is for older children. This book explains how the Chinese fly kites that represent specific wishes, cut the strings of kites representing misfortune, and hold an annual kite festival.

Poetry and songs

Two bilingual (English/Chinese) books, *China's Bravest Girl*, by Charlie Chin, and *The Song of Mu Lan*, by Lee, present the legend of Mu Lan in poetry as opposed to *The Legend of Mu Lan*, which is described at the end of the Fables... category. The Chin tale concludes with Mu Lan marrying her soldier companion. The Lee version is distinguished by double-page watercolor illustrations and a succinct verse.

A book for older children, *Ling Cho and His Three Friends*, by V. J. Pacilio, relates through a long narrative poem how a kind farmer tries to help three poorer friends, how each deceives him, and how he wisely deals with their deceit.

Maples in the Mist, translated by Mingfong Ho, contains sixteen illustrated short poems which were written for children by fourteen poets of the Tang Dynasty (A.D. 618-907).

Even the youngest children should enjoy listening to the nursery rhymes and searching the illustrations for the objects mentioned in *Dragon Kites and Dragonflies*, which is adapted by Demi.

Stories

Marjorie Flack's *The Story about Ping* tells of a young duck who searches the Yangtze River for the boat that is home to him and his extended family.

The *Chinese Siamese Cat*, by Amy Tan, explains why, thanks to a kitten and an ink pot, Chinese cats have the same features as Siamese cats.

In Ting-xing Ye's *Weighing the Elephant*, a talented baby elephant fails to perform for the emperor who has seized him. Threatened with banishment unless someone can determine his weight, he is rescued by his young keeper, who cleverly employs the Archimedean principle.

Children may enjoy duplicating the tangrams illustrating Ann Tompert's *Grandfather Tang's Story*. The story tells how two fox fairies, changing into different animals, discover the importance of their friendship.

In *The Willow Pattern Story*, which is for older children, Allan Drummond uses the design on willow pattern china as the basis for the tale of a mandarin's daughter and servant who, falling in love, experience both joy and suffering until, dying, they became doves.

Xiaolong, the title character in Lensey Namioka's *The Laziest Boy in the World*, is so lazy that he barely moves. This changes on the night that a thief comes into the house, and Xiaolong expends enough energy to tip rice soup onto the floor, thereby causing the thief to fall and be caught.

The Squiggle, by Carole Lexa Schaefer, shows how a little girl's imagination transforms a string she finds into such objects as a dragon and a great wall. This book can provide an introduction to China for even very young children who have developed a sense of imagination.

In Margaret Holloway Tsubakiyama's *Mei-Mei Loves the Morning* a little girl in a modern Chinese city spends the morning with her grandfather. Together they ride on his bicycle to the park where they enjoy the company of their friends.

Books

Andersen, Hans Christian. *The Nightingale*. Illustrated by Demi. San Diego: Voyager Books, 1988, paperback.

Armstrong, Jennifer. *Chin Yu Min and the Ginger Cat*. Illustrated by Mary GrandPré. New York: Crown Publishing Group, 1996, paperback.

Bang, Molly Garrett, adapter. *Tye May and the Magic Brush*. Illustrated by adapter. New York: Mulberry Books, 1992, paperback.

Bateson-Hill, Margaret. *Lao Lao of Dragon Mountain*. Illustrated by Francesca Pelizzoli. Chinese text by Manyee Wan. Paper cuts by Sha-liu Qu. New York: Zero to Ten, 1998.

Bishop, Claire Huchet. *The Five Chinese Brothers*. Illustrated by Kurt Wiese. New York: G.P. Putnam's Sons, 1938; Putnam Publishing Group, 1988.

Bouchard, David. *The Dragon New Year: A Chinese Legend*. Illustrated by Zhong-Yang Huang. Atlanta: Peachtree Publishers, 1999.

Chang, Cindy, reteller. *The Seventh Sister: A Chinese Legend*. (Legends of the World) Illustrated by Charles Reasoner. Mahwah, NJ: Troll Communications, 1996, paperback; 1997.

Chang, Margaret, and Raymond Chang, retellers. *The Beggar's Magic: A Chinese Tale*. Illustrated by David Johnson. New York: Margaret K. McElderry Books, 1997.

Chang, Margaret, and Raymond Chang, retellers. *The Cricket Warrior: A Chinese Tale*. Illustrated by Warwick Hutton. New York: Atheneum Books for Young Readers, 1994.

Chang, Margaret, and Raymond Chang, retellers. *Da Wei's Treasure: A Chinese Tale*. Illustrated by Lori McElrath-Eslick. New York: Simon & Schuster Children's Publishing, 1999.

Chen, Kerstin, reteller. *Lord of the Cranes: A Chinese Tale*. (A Michael Neugebauer Book) Illustrated by Jian Jiang Chen. Translated by J. Alison James. New York: North-South Books, 2000.

Chin, Charlie. *China's Bravest Girl: The Legend of Hua-Mu Lan*. Illustrated by Tomie Arai. Chinese translation by Wang Xing Chu. San Francisco: Children's Book Press, 1993; 1997, paperback.

Czernecki, Stefan, reteller. *The Cricket's Cage: A Chinese Folktale*. Illustrated by reteller. New York: Hyperion Books for Children, 1997.

Davol, Marguerite W. *The Paper Dragon*. Illustrated by Robert Sabuda. New York: Atheneum Books for Young Readers, 1997.

Demi, adapter. *A Chinese Zoo: Fables and Proverbs*. Illustrated by adapter. San Diego: Harcourt, 1987.

Demi. *The Donkey and the Rock*. Illustrated by author. New York: Henry Holt and Company, 1999.

Demi, adapter. *Dragon Kites and Dragonflies: A Collection of Chinese Nursery Rhymes*. Illustrated by adapter. San Diego: Harcourt, 1986.

Demi, reteller. *The Dragon's Tale and Other Animal Fables of the Chinese Zodiac*. Illustrated by reteller. New York: Bill Martin Books for Young Readers, 1995.

Demi. *The Emperor's New Clothes: A Tale Set in China*. New York: Margaret K. McElderry Books, 2000.

Demi. *The Empty Pot*. Illustrated by author. New York: Henry Holt Books for Young Readers, 1995; Bill Martin Books for Young Readers, 1996, paperback.

Demi. *The Greatest Treasure*. Illustrated by author. New York: Scholastic, 1998.

Demi. *Kites: Magic Wishes That Fly Up to the Sky*. Illustrated by author. New York: Crown Publishers, 1999.

Demi. *Liang and the Magic Paintbrush*. Illustrated by author. New York: Henry Holt Books for Young Readers, 1995, paperback.

Demi, reteller. *The Magic Tapestry: A Chinese Folktale*. Illustrated by reteller. New York: Henry Holt and Company, 1995.

Demi. *The Stonecutter*. Illustrated by author. New York: Crown Books for Young Readers, 1995.

Drummond, Allan. *The Willow Pattern Story*. Illustrated by author. New York: North-South Books, 1992; 1995, paperback.

Flack, Marjorie. *The Story about Ping*. Illustrated by Kurt Wiese. New York: Viking Children's Books, 1933; Puffin, 1977, paperback; 1989.

Gerstein, Mordicai. *The Mountains of Tibet*. Illustrated by author. New York: Harper Trophy, 1989, paperback.

Heyer, Marilee. *The Weaving of a Dream: A Chinese Folktale*. Illustrated by author. New York: Puffin, 1989, paperback.

Hillman, Elizabeth. *Min-Yo and the Moon Dragon*. Illustrated by John Wallner. San Diego: Harcourt, 1992; Voyager Books, 1996, paperback.

Ho, Minfong, translator. *Maples in the Mist: Children's Poems from the Tang Dynasty*. Illustrated by Jean Tseng and Mou-sien Tseng. New York: Lothrop, Lee & Shepard Books, 1996.

Hong, Lily Toy. *The Empress and the Silk Worm*. Illustrated by author. Morton Grove, IL: Albert Whitman & Company, 1995.

Hong, Lily Toy, reteller. *How the Ox Star Fell from Heaven*. Illustrated by reteller. Morton Grove, IL: Albert Whitman & Company, 1995, paperback.

Hong, Lily Toy, reteller. *Two of Everything: A Chinese Folktale*. Illustrated by reteller. Morton Grove, IL: Albert Whitman & Company, 1993.

Jiang, Wei, and Cheng An Jiang. *The Legend of Mu Lan: A Heroine of Ancient China/Truyen Thuyet Moc Lan: Anh Thu cua Co Dai Trung Quoc*. Illustrated by authors. Monterey, CA: Victory Press, 1997.

Kimmel, Eric A., reteller. *The Rooster's Antlers: A Story of the Chinese Zodiac*. Illustrated by YongSheng Xuan. New York: Holiday House, 1999.

Kimmel, Eric A., reteller. *Ten Suns: A Chinese Legend*. Illustrated by Yongsheng Xuan. New York: Holiday House, 1998.

Lawson, Julie, reteller. *The Dragon's Pearl*. Illustrated by Paul Morin. New York: Oxford University Press, 1992; Clarion Books, 1993.

Lee, Jeanne M., reteller. *Legend of the Milky Way*. New York: Owlet Paperbacks for Young Readers, 1995, paperback.

Lee, Jeanne M. *The Song of Mu Lan*. Illustrated by author. Asheville, NC: Front Street, 1995.

Levinson, Riki. *Our Home Is the Sea*. Illustrated by Dennis Luzak. New York: Puffin Unicorn, 1992, paperback.

Lobel, Arnold. *Ming Lo Moves the Mountain*. Illustrated by author. New York: Mulberry Books, 1993; 1993, paperback.

Louie, Ai-Ling, reteller. *Yeh-Shen: A Cinderella Story from China*. Illustrated by Ed Young. New York: Philomel Books, 1982; Paperstar, 1996, paperback.

McCully, Emily Arnold. *Beautiful Warrior: The Legend of the Nun's Kung Fu*. Illustrated by author. New York: Scholastic, 1998.

Mahy, Margaret. *The Seven Chinese Brothers*. Illustrated by Jean Tseng and Mou-sien Tseng. New York: Scholastic, 1992, paperback.

Mosel, Arlene, reteller. *Tikki Tikki Tembo*. Illustrated by Blair Lent. New York: Henry Holt Books for Young Readers, 1989, paperback; 1995; 1995, paperback; Lectorum Publishing, 1994.

Namioka, Lensey. *The Laziest Boy in the World*. Illustrated by YongSheng Xuan. New York: Holiday House, 1998.

Pacilio, V. J. *Ling Cho and His Three Friends*. Illustrated by Scott Cook. New York: Farrar, Straus & Giroux, 2000.

Pattison, Darcy. *The River Dragon*. Illustrated by Jean Tseng and Mou-sien Tseng. New York: Lothrop, Lee & Shepard Books, 1991.

Pittman, Helena Clare. *A Grain of Rice*. Illustrated by author. New York: Bantam Doubleday Dell Books for Young Readers, 1992, paperback; 1995, paperback.

Poole, Amy Lowry, reteller. *The Ant and the Grasshopper*. Illustrated by reteller. New York: Holiday House, 2000.

Poole, Amy Lowry, reteller. *How the Rooster Got His Crown*. Illustrated by reteller. New York: Holiday House, 1999.

Quackenbush, Robert. *Danger in Tibet: A Miss Mallard Mystery*. Illustrated by author. New York: Pippin Press, 1989.

Rappaport, Doreen. *The Long-Haired Girl: A Chinese Legend*. Illustrated by Yang Ming-Yi. New York: Dial Books for Young Readers, 1995, paperback.

San Souci, Robert D., reteller. *The Enchanted Tapestry: A Chinese Folktale*. Illustrated by László Gál. New York: Dial Books for Young Readers, 1990, paperback.

Schaefer, Carole Lexa. *The Squiggle*. Illustrated by Pierr Morgan. New York: Crown, 1996; Crown Publishing Group, 1999, paperback.

Schroeder, Alan. *The Stone Lion*. Illustrated by Todd L. W. Doney. New York: Charles Scribner's Sons Books for Young Readers, 1994.

Tan, Amy. *The Chinese Siamese Cat*. Illustrated by Gretchen Schields. New York: Macmillan Books for Young Readers, 1994.

Tan, Amy. *The Moon Lady*. Illustrated by Gretchen Schields. New York: Macmillan Books for Young Readers, 1992; Aladdin Paperbacks, 1995.

Tompert, Ann. *Grandfather Tang's Story*. Illustrated by Robert Andrew Parker. New York: Crown Books for Young Readers, 1990; 1997, paperback.

Tompert, Ann. *The Jade Horse, the Cricket, and the Peach Stone*. Illustrated by Winson Trang. Honesdale, PA: Boyds Mills Press, 1996.

Tseng, Grace. *White Tiger, Blue Serpent*. Illustrated by Jean Tseng and Mou-sien Tseng. New York: Lothrop, Lee & Shepard Books, 1999.

Tsubakiyama, Margaret Holloway. *Mei-Mei Loves the Morning*. Illustrated by Cornelius Van Wright and Ying-Hwa Hu. Morton Grove, IL: Albert Whitman & Company, 1999.

Vá, Leong. *A Letter to the King*. Illustrated by author. Translated from Norwegian by James Anderson. New York: HarperCollins Children's Books, 1991.

Wang, Rosalind C., reteller. *The Treasure Chest: A Chinese Tale*. Illustrated by Will Hillenbrand. New York: Holiday House, 1995.

Whitfield, Susan. *The Animals of the Chinese Zodiac*. Illustrated by Philippa-Alys Browne. Northampton, MA: Crocodile Books, An imprint of Interlink Publishing Group, Inc., 1998.

Wilson, Barbara Ker, reteller. *Wishbones: A Folk Tale from China*. Illustrated by Meilo So. New York: Bradbury Press, 1993.

Wolkstein, Diane. *The Magic Wings: A Tale from China*. Illustrated by Robert Andrew Parker. New York: Dutton Children's Books, 1983, paperback.

Wolkstein, Diane, reteller. *White Wave: A Chinese Tale*. Illustrated by Ed Young. New York: T Y Crowell Junior Books, 1979; Harcourt, 1996.

Ye, Ting-xing. *Weighing the Elephant*. Illustrated by Suzane Langlois. Toronto: Annick (Distributed by Firefly Books), 1998; 1998, paperback.

Yen, Clara, reteller. *Why Rat Comes First: A Story of the Chinese Zodiac*. Illustrated by Hideo C. Yoshida. San Francisco: Children's Book Press, 1991.

Yep, Laurence. *The City of Dragons*. Illustrated by Jean Tseng and Mou-sien Tseng. New York: Scholastic Hardcover, 1995; Scholastic, 1997, paperback.

Yep, Laurence. *The Dragon Prince: A Chinese Beauty & the Beast Tale*. Illustrated by Kam Mak. New York: HarperCollins Publishers, 1997; Harper Trophy, 1999, paperback.

Yep, Laurence. *The Junior Thunder Lord*. Illustrated by Robert Van Nutt. Mahwah, NJ: BridgeWater Books, 1996; Troll Communications, 1996, paperback.

Yep, Laurence. *The Man Who Tricked a Ghost*. Illustrated by Isadore Seltzer. Mahwah, NJ: Troll Medallion, 1995, paperback; BridgeWater Books, 1997.

Yep, Laurence, reteller. *The Shell Woman & the King: A Chinese Folktale*. Illustrated by Yang Ming-Yi. New York: Dial Books for Young Readers, 1993, paperback.

Yep, Laurence. *Tiger Woman*. Illustrated by Robert Roth. Mahwah, NJ: BridgeWater Books, 1995, paperback; Troll Communications, 1996, paperback.

Yolen, Jane. *The Emperor and the Kite*. Illustrated by Ed Young. New York: Philomel Books, 1983; Paperstar, 1998, paperback.

Young, Ed. *Cat and Rat: The Legend of the Chinese Zodiac*. Illustrated by author. New York: Henry Holt and Company, 1995; 1998, paperback.

Young, Ed, translator. *Lon Po Po: A Red-Riding Hood Story from China*. Illustrated by translator. New York: Philomel Books, 1989; Paperstar, 1996, paperback.

Young, Ed. *The Lost Horse: A Chinese Folktale*. Illustrated by author. San Diego: Harcourt, 1998.

Young, Ed. *Mouse Match: A Chinese Folktale*. Illustrated by author. San Diego: Harcourt, 1997.

Young, Ed. *Night Visitors*. Illustrated by author. New York: Philomel Books, 1995.

Young, Russell. *Dragonsong: A Fable for the New Millennium*. Illustrated by Civi Cheng. Auburn, CA: Shen's Books, 2000.

"He stood on the center island stand that morning, in the middle of the busy intersection in the center of the town, eyeing the honking taxis and beeping three-wheeled open autorickshaws and rumbling paint-decorated lorries and bicycles with their bells clanging and the oxcarts from the country all around him."
—Shank. *The Sanyasin's First Day.*

India
Republic of India

Specific Locations

The picture books described below are set in the states of Kerala, Rajasthan, and Uttar Pradesh.

Kerala

The ten brief stories in Eknath Easwaran's *The Monkey and the Mango* reveal the special relationship that the author had with his grandmother when he was a boy. He learns many spiritual values through the wisdom she brings to his experiences with such creatures as fireflies, red ants, a mongoose, a pigeon, and a monkey.

Rajasthan

Jami Parkison's *Amazing Mallika* takes place in Ranthambhore Park, a wildlife sanctuary. A tiger cub's hot temper gets her into trouble until, remaining calm, she is able to climb out of the underground chamber into which she has fallen.

Uttar Pradesh

Two books are set in the ancient city of Benares, which is also known as Varanasi, Banaras, and Kasi.

The Monkey Bridge, by Rafe Martin, retells a tale from the Jataka collection of fables. In it the king of Benares learns a valuable lesson from the monkey king and, as a result, there are two trees of delicious fruit, one the home of monkeys in the Himalaya and the other in Benares.

In *Sacred River*, a book for older children, Ted Lewin uses text and watercolor illustrations to present the experiences of the many Hindus who make pilgrimages to Benares to be purified in the sacred waters of the Ganges River and to scatter on the river the ashes of those who have died.

Cherry Tree, by Ruskin Bond, takes place in Mussoorie, which is in the Himalayan foothills where there are few fruit trees. Six year old Rakhi plants the seed from a Kashmirian cherry in the soil of her grandfather's garden. Carefully tended, the seed grows into a tall tree with cherries and beautiful blossoms.

General

Alphabet, counting, and word books

A banyan tree and wild animals are among the objects counted in Jim Haskins's *Count Your Way through India,* a book for older children. The numbers are presented in English and Hindi.

Fables, fairy tales, folktales, legends, myths, and proverbs (including original works)

Martin's *The Brave Little Parrot* retells a Jataka tale. The parrot, who is trying to put out a forest fire all by herself by repeatedly carrying tiny amounts of water from the river to the fire, attracts the attention of a god, whose tears put out the fire, restore the forest, and give the parrot colored feathers.

Another Jataka tale is related in Paul Galdone's *The Monkey and the Crocodile*. The crocodile's two plans to catch and eat the monkey are foiled by the even more clever monkey.

Aaron Shepard's *Savitri* is the retelling for older children of a tale from the poem The Mahabharata. The princess Savitri outsmarts the god of death, thereby saving the life of her beloved husband, Satyavan.

Rama and the Demon King, which is retold by Jessica Souhami, tells how Rama, his brother, and an army of monkeys rescue Rama's wife from the ten-headed demon king who has kidnapped her.

Another book by Souhami, *No Dinner!*, relates the tale of a woman and her granddaughter who foil the wolf, the bear, and the tiger who threaten the grandmother as she travels between their two homes.

The god Brahma, disguised as a fish, repays Manu for his kindness in Roberta Arenson's *Manu and the Talking Fish*. Heeding the fish's advice, Manu builds a large boat and, filling it with seeds, animals, and wise men, rides out a flood and then creates a new home.

In Melissa Kajpust's retelling, *The Peacock's Pride*, the beautiful and vain peacock is humbled by the koel, a bird whose dull appearance belies its exquisite voice.

The Very Hungry Lion, which is adapted by Gita Wolf, tells how a lazy, hungry lion is outwitted by a sparrow, a lamb, and a deer.

Each of six blind men feels a different part of an elephant in an easy reader, *The Blind Men and the Elephant*, which is retold by Karen Backstein. A prince resolves their conflicting impressions of the elephant by informing them that the whole of an elephant is a combination of its parts.

The oldest children who are learning the concept of multiplication should be interested in three versions of a folktale which focuses on the continuing doubling of what is initially the number "1", a single grain of rice. Two of the picture books relate the quantity of rice to the sixty-four squares of a chessboard.

In *The King's Chessboard*, by David Birch, a wise man seeks no reward for his service to the king, but the proud king foolishly promises him that for each square of his chessboard, the number of grains of rice will be doubled. Later, after the king sees the wagons of rice being conveyed to the wise man, he realizes that the total quantity by the sixty-fourth day will be more than all the rice in India. Summoning the wise man, the king discovers that it was only his own vanity that insisted upon a reward. This book is set in the ancient area of Deccan, which now comprises the state of Maharashtra and parts of the states of Andhra Pradesh, Karnataka, Madhya Pradesh, and Orissa.

The other versions of the folktale are not given a specific location.

In *The Token Gift,* by Hugh William McKibbon, it is the inventor of chess who is given the reward of rice by the king, whose generals have used the game to develop their military strategies. When soon afterward the king realizes his mistake, he appoints as king the inventor, who has always longed to do something for the world. Then realizing that he has already performed a service to the world, the wise inventor abdicates and reinstates the original king.

The rajah in Demi's *One Grain of Rice* reneges on his promise to return the rice he has collected from the villagers when there is a famine. Clever Rani brings to the rajah some rice which has fallen from one of his baskets. As a reward she requests and receives the doubling of a grain of rice for thirty (not sixty-four) days so that the villagers may eat and extracts a pledge from the rajah that in the future he will collect rice only for his own needs.

Stories

In *Maya, Tiger Cub,* by Theresa Radcliffe, tiger cubs Maya and Sameer are left alone when their mother leaves to locate water. A nearby hyena eats some deer remnants and then threatens Maya, who bravely displays her ferocity. Illustrations by John Butler add to this portrayal of life in the forest.

The Naming Day for a litter of kittens is the subject of Marsha Diane Arnold's *Heart of a Tiger.* Incredibly, the runt of the litter would like to be named after a Bengal tiger.

After trailing the tiger for days and saving the tiger's life, he proves himself worthy of the name, Heart of a Tiger.

Tigers are also featured in Helen Bannerman's *The Story of Little Babaji*, which is a revised edition of her *The Story of Little Black Sambo*. The offensive pictures have been removed and are replaced by illustrations by Fred Marcellino which place the story in its originally intended setting of India. Further, the offensive names have been replaced by Indian names. This book tells the story of how tigers trick Little Babaji into giving them his clothes and his umbrella. Then, because of their vanity, they turn into butter which is used to make his family's pancakes.

Aleph Kamal's *The Bird Who Was an Elephant* presents a day in the life of an Indian village as it is experienced by a bird.

Older children may enjoy two versions of Rudyard Kipling's *Rikki-Tikki-Tavi*, the exciting story of the brave mongoose who destroys the two cobras, their eggs, and the brown snake which threaten the English family that has befriended him.

In one version, Lambert Davis's full-page acrylic paintings illustrate Kipling's text.

In the other book, Jerry Pinkney both retells the story and dramatizes it through large watercolor paintings.

A banyan tree is the village center in Barbara Bash's *In the Heart of the Village*. The sacred tree, which spreads as its branches become trunks, is the site of activities from early morning when a woman brings offerings through daytime when a market and a school are held under its shade to evening when the villagers watch dancing. The tree also serves as home to many birds and monkeys.

Life in a busy modern town is reflected in Ned Shank's *The Sanyasin's First Day*. The plumber, the policeman, and the farmer, as well as the sanyasin, successfully complete the first day at their new jobs.

Books

Arenson, Roberta. *Manu and the Talking Fish*. Illustrated by author. New York: Barefoot Books, 2000.

Arnold, Marsha Diane. *Heart of a Tiger*. Illustrated by Jamichael Henterly. New York: Dial Books for Young Readers, 1995, paperback.

Backstein, Karen, reteller. *The Blind Men and the Elephant*. (Hello Reader! Series) Illustrated by Annie Mitra. New York: Scholastic, 1992, paperback.

Bannerman, Helen. *The Story of Little Babaji*. (Michael Di Capua Books) Illustrated by Fred Marcellino. New York: HarperCollins Children's Books, 1996.

Bash, Barbara. *In the Heart of the Village: The World of the Indian Banyan Tree*. (Tree Tales Series) Illustrated by author. San Francisco: Sierra Club Books for Children, 1996.

Birch, David. *The King's Chessboard*. Illustrated by Devis Grebu. New York: Dial Books for Young Readers, 1988; Puffin Pied Piper, 1993, paperback.

Bond, Ruskin. *Cherry Tree*. Illustrated by Allan Eitzen. Honesdale, PA: Boyds Mills Press, 1996, paperback.

Demi. *One Grain of Rice: A Mathematical Folktale*. New York: Scholastic, 1997; 1997, paperback.

Easwaran, Eknath. *The Monkey and the Mango: Stories of My Granny*. Illustrated by Ilka Jerabek. Tomales, CA: Nilgiri Press, 1996.

Galdone, Paul. *The Monkey and the Crocodile: A Jataka Tale from India*. Illustrated by author. New York: Clarion Books, 1987, paperback.

Haskins, Jim. *Count Your Way through India*. (Count Your Way Books) Illustrated by Liz Brenner Dodson. Minneapolis: Carolrhoda Books, 1990; 1992, paperback.

Kajpust, Melissa. *The Peacock's Pride*. Illustrated by Jo'Anne Kelly. New York: Hyperion Books for Children, 1997.

Kamal, Aleph. *The Bird Who Was an Elephant*. Illustrated by Frané Lessac. New York: Lippincott Children's Books, 1990.

Kipling, Rudyard. *Rikki-Tikki-Tavi*. Adapted by Jerry Pinkney. Illustrated by adapter. New York: Morrow Junior Books, 1997.

Kipling, Rudyard. *Rikki-Tikki-Tavi*. Illustrated by Lambert Davis. San Diego: Harcourt, 1992.

Lewin, Ted. *Sacred River*. Illustrated by author. New York: Clarion Books, 1995.

McKibbon, Hugh William. *The Token Gift*. Illustrated by Scott Cameron. Toronto: Annick (Distributed by Firefly Books), 1996, paperback.

Martin, Rafe. *The Brave Little Parrot*. Illustrated by Susan Gaber. New York: G. P. Putnam's Sons, 1998.

Martin, Rafe. *The Monkey Bridge*. Illustrated by Fahimeh Amiri. New York: Random House, 1997.

Parkison, Jami. *Amazing Mallika*. Illustrated by Itoko Maeno. Kansas City, MO: MarshMedia, 1996.

Radcliffe, Theresa. *Maya, Tiger Cub*. Illustrated by John Butler. New York: Viking, 1999.

Shank, Ned. *The Sanyasin's First Day*. Illustrated by Catherine Stock. Tarrytown, NY: Marshall Cavendish, 1999.

Shepard, Aaron. *Savitri: A Tale of Ancient India*. Illustrated by Vera Rosenberry. Morton Grove, IL: Albert Whitman & Company, 1992.

Souhami, Jessica. *No Dinner!: The Story of the Old Woman and the Pumpkin*. Illustrated by author. Tarrytown, NY: Marshall Cavendish, 2000.

Souhami, Jessica, reteller. *Rama and the Demon King: An Ancient Tale from India*. Illustrated by reteller. New York: DK Publishing, 1997.

Wolf, Gita, adapter. *The Very Hungry Lion: A Folktale*. Illustrated by Indrapramit Roy. Toronto: Annick (Distributed by Firefly Books), 1996.

"A traditional Balinese family eats rice for breakfast, lunch, and dinner."
—Gelman. *Rice Is Life*.

Indonesia (formerly Netherlands Indies) <u>Republic of Indonesia</u>

In Judy Sierra's *The Dancing Pig*, twin Balinese girls are kidnapped by an ogress, who has tricked them into believing she is their mother. Before the ogress can eat them, they are rescued by the animals they have befriended: frogs whose music entices the ogress from her house, a sarong-clad pig who dances the Legong with the ogress, and a mouse whose gnawing frees the twins.

Rice Is Life, by Rita Golden Gelman, is also set on the island of Bali. While the text traces the process of growing rice from its planting to its harvesting, an accompanying narrative poem describes the creatures of the sawah, the rice field.

Komodo!, by Peter Sis, tells of a dragon-loving boy who goes with his parents to the island of Komodo to see the Komodo dragon. The dragon show is overrun with tourists, but, when the boy goes off on his own, he sees one—and, perhaps, many komodo dragons.

In Doug Cushman's *The Mystery of the Monkey's Maze* the detective Seymour Sleuth goes to the island of Borneo to discover who is trying to prevent Dr. Tann from locating the Black Flower of Sumatra. Children can analyze the clues to find the culprit—and then discover what happens when the flower is finally found.

Books

Cushman, Doug. *The Mystery of the Monkey's Maze.* Illustrated by author. New York: HarperCollins Children's Books, 1999.

Gelman, Rita Golden. *Rice Is Life.* Illustrated by Yangsook Choi. New York: Henry Holt and Company, 2000.

Sierra, Judy. *The Dancing Pig.* Illustrated by Jesse Sweetwater. San Diego: Harcourt, 1999.

Sis, Peter. *Komodo!* Illustrated by author. New York: Greenwillow Books, 1993.

*"Once, in the royal city of Isfahan, there lived a young man
named Ahmed, who had a wife named Jamell."*
—Shepard. *Forty Fortunes.*

Iran (formerly Persia)

Books set in the ancient country of Armenia, which is
now divided between Armenia, Iran, and Turkey, are
described under Armenia.

A book for older children, *The Stone*, by Dianne
Hofmeyr, is based on a tale told to Marco Polo by the
residents of the Persian town of Saveh where he noticed the
tombs of Balthasar, Melchior, and Jasper. According to the
story, the three astronomers follow a strange bright star and
give the young boy they find the gifts of gold (in case he is
a king), myrrh (if a healer), and incense (if a holy man). On
the way back they open the box the child has given them
and finding a stone that bursts into fire, realize that the
child is all three of the men and that the stone, representing
the strength and ardor of belief, is to be shared by all.

The Cinderella story which Shirley Climo retells in
The Persian Cinderella is set in fifteenth century Persia. In
this version Settareh is given her gown by the fairy in a
small cracked jug which Settareh has bought; she loses an
anklet, not a slipper; and the hairpins which her stepsisters
push into her hair on the day of her wedding turn her into a
turtledove until they are removed by the prince.

Aaron Shepard's *Forty Fortunes* is set in Isfahan (Esfahan) when it was the capital of Persia (mainly in the seventeenth century). To please his wife, Ahmed becomes a diviner and, by luck, recovers forty stolen chests of royal treasures. He then wisely retires from his divining career.

In *The Legend of the Persian Carpet*, retold by Tomie dePaola, the king's prized diamond is stolen and dropped by the thief upon rocks where the sunlight reflected by the now many pieces forms a brilliant multicolored land cover. Not wanting to leave this beautiful spot, the king agrees to return to his palace if the Persian weavers and dyers can create an equally splendid carpet to fill the room where the diamond once shone.

Books

Climo, Shirley. *The Persian Cinderella*. Illustrated by Robert Florczak. New York: HarperCollins Publishers, 1999.

dePaola, Tomie, reteller. *The Legend of the Persian Carpet*. Illustrated by Claire Ewart. New York: G. P. Putnam's Sons, 1993.

Hofmeyr, Dianne. *The Stone: A Persian Legend of The Magi*. Illustrated by Jude Daly. New York: Farrar, Straus & Giroux, 1998.

Shepard, Aaron. *Forty Fortunes: A Tale of Iran*. Illustrated by Alisher Dianov. New York: Clarion Books, 1999.

*"Over many lands came caravans of camels, six thousand
strong, swaying and rocking as they padded single file
across the sands and plains on their way to Baghdad."*
—Heide and Gilliland. *The House of Wisdom.*

Iraq (Irak)

The House of Wisdom, by Florence Parry Heide and
Judith Heide Gilliland, is a book for the oldest children
which is set in the ninth century when Baghdad was a
world trade and intellectual center. Ishaq admires the
passion of his father who translates manuscripts in the
House of Wisdom, a magnificent library. Ishaq also wishes
to be a scholar, but it is not until he collects books in many
distant places, including Athens, and then reads a book
which Aristotle may have authored, that he too becomes
inspired. An end note identifies Ishaq as the world's
leading translator of Aristotle's writings.

There are many twists from the traditional Cinderella
story in Rebecca Hickox's *The Golden Sandal*. The fairy
godmother is a red fish, the formal ball is a women's henna
for a bride, the bride's brother's horse finds the sandal
in a river, the brother's mother is the one who searches
for the sandal's owner, and the stepmother tries to prevent
the wedding.

Books

Heide, Florence Parry, and Judith Heide Gilliland. *The House of Wisdom*. Illustrated by Mary Grandpré. New York: DK Publishing, 1998.

Hickox, Rebecca. *The Golden Sandal: A Middle Eastern Cinderella Story*. Illustrated by Will Hillenbrand. New York: Holiday House, 1998; 1998, paperback.

"Because of its location, the area now called Israel has long been a crossroads of the Middle East, important for trade and conquest."
—Haskins. *Count Your Way through Israel.*

Israel
State of Israel

Books set in Palestine, not a separate country, but a region coextensive with Israel and part of Jordan, are described in the section, Palestine.

The numbers one through ten are written in both Hebrew and English in Jim Haskins's *Count Your Way through Israel*, a book for older children, which touches upon the country's diversity, produce, exports, animals, and the Jewish people and religion.

Book

Haskins, Jim. *Count Your Way through Israel*. (Count Your Way Books) Illustrated by Rick Hanson. Minneapolis: Carolrhoda Books, 1990; 1992, paperback.

"On the banks of the river Nagara, where the long-necked cormorants fish at night, there once lived a poor widow and her son."
—Snyder. *The Boy of the Three-Year Nap.*

Japan

Specific Locations

Some of the picture books are set in specific regions.

Chubu

Marcia Vaughan's *Dorobo the Dangerous* is set near Mount Fuji, which is on the border of the Shizuoka and Yamanashi prefectures. It relates the story of a crane who receives the help needed to stop a fox's thievery. The book features the repetitive use of the crane's catchy song.

The Dragon Kite, by Nancy Luenn, tells of another thief, Ishikawa, who spends four years learning to build a dragon kite so that he can help feed the poor by stealing the golden dolphins from atop the Nagoya castle in Aichi prefecture. Riding the kite, Ishikawa steals the dolphins' fins and then sets the kite free. Later, when he, his family, and his kitemaker mentor are arrested, they are all rescued by the kite's dragon, who is grateful for his freedom.

The Drums of Noto Hanto, by J. Alison James, tells of a true event that has been celebrated since 1576 by the peoples of the Noto Peninsula in Ishikawa prefecture. When ships of samurai try to conquer their village, the villagers outwit them by setting fires, donning masks, and playing the drums that usually herald the advent of each season. The text is punctuated by the distinctive sounds of the different drums.

Set in the prefecture of Gifu, *The Boy of the Three-Year Nap*, by Dianne Snyder, tells of the lazy boy who devises a clever plan to wed a rich merchant's daughter and of his hard-working mother who also comes up with a clever plan.

Chugoku

In *The Samurai's Daughter*, a book for older children which is retold by Robert D. San Souci, Tokoyo is as brave as a samurai. She travels by herself across Japan to the Oki Islands in Shimane prefecture and dives into the sea to destroy a serpent.

Shimane prefecture is also the source of the folktale, *Tasty Baby Belly Buttons*, by Judy Sierra. A five-year-old girl, who as a baby was found in a melon, utilizes her skills of dumpling cooking and sword fighting to rescue the babies of her village who have been kidnapped by oni (monsters) who want to feast on their belly buttons.

Hokkaido

In *The Bears' Autumn*, by Keizaburo Tejima, a baby bear dives for and catches his first salmon, but he can't catch the moonlight sparkling on the water.

Another young animal, a wild Dosanko colt, survives a harsh winter in *Wild Horse Winter*, by Tetsuya Honda. With his mother and the other hungry horses he leaves the prairie, is buried in snow drifts in the forest, and then journeys to the sea where there is food: kelp.

Kanto

Yoshi's Feast, by Kimiko Kajikawa, is set in Yedo in the days before it became known as Tokyo. The stingy Yoshi refuses to buy any of his neighbor Sabu's broiled eels, but savors their delicious smells. When he says he will pay for the smell of the eels only with the sound of his money box, Sabu retaliates by cooking ill-smelling samma. Fortunately, the two neighbors resolve their differences when Yoshi, dancing around with his jingling money box, attracts customers for Sabu's eels.

Chibi, by Barbara Brenner and Julia Takaya, is a two chapter true story set in Tokyo. The first chapter tells how a wild duck nests in an office park and, with the help of a caring photographer, leads her ten ducklings across eight lanes of traffic to a new home in a moat in the Imperial Gardens. The second chapter tells how the smallest duckling, together with his mother and all but one of his siblings, survives a typhoon.

In Mimi Otey Little's *Yoshiko and the Foreigner*, Yoshiko overcomes her reluctance to speak to a foreigner, an American Air Force officer who is lost in Tokyo. She secretly continues to see him and then, thanks to his honoring of the Japanese culture, receives her parents' blessing to go to America to marry him.

Sayonara, Mrs. Kackleman, by Maira Kalman, is the amusing story of a sister and brother who fly to Tokyo where they tour the city environs. They visit a school, enjoy

Japanese restaurants, encounter a haiku-reciting frog, and go to a Noh play.

Kinki

Jean Merrill's folktale adaptation, *The Girl Who Loved Caterpillars*, is set in Kyoto. Izumi is not concerned with fashion, attracting noblemen, or the gossiping about her, but loves the caterpillars which boys collect for her.

In *The Bee and the Dream*, adapted by Jan Freeman Long, Shin buys his friend's dream and travels to Naniwa (now Osaka) to dig up a jar of gold. Tricked by a wealthy man, he returns empty-handed, only to discover that bees have transported the treasure to his home.

The farmer never does rescue the girl who is imprisoned in a swamp in Yoshiko Uchida's retelling, *The Magic Purse*. However, he bravely carries a letter to her parents who live in a different swamp near Osaka, travels to the shrine at Iseh (probably Ise in Mie prefecture), lives comfortably the rest of his life, and never forgets the girl.

Jack, the title character of *Jack the Dog*, by John A. Rowe, falls asleep on a ship docked in London and unexpectedly travels to Osaka. As a prerequisite for a cup of tea, he must dress up in a Japanese costume, which he procures from some trash cans outside a Kabuki theater. However, before getting his first sip of tea, he discovers that his fantastic experience is only a dream.

Kyushu

A first grader's school sports day turns out to be an unforgettable one in Allen Say's *The Bicycle Man*. Shortly after World War II, two American soldiers, one with red hair and the other an African-American, unexpectedly become participants, the one serving as ringmaster and the other performing incredible tricks on a bicycle.

Tohoku

Michael P. Waite's *Jojofu* is based on a folktale set in Aomori prefecture. The hunting dog Jojofu saves Takumi's life three times and then saves the lives of his other dogs.

General

Alphabet, counting, and word books

Jim Haskins's *Count Your Way through Japan* introduces the country to older children through such topics as Mount Fuji and chopsticks.

Celebrations

In David Kudler's *The Seven Gods of Luck* Kenji, Sachiko, and their mother are too poor to buy food for a New Year's feast. Much to their surprise, they are provided with a feast by the statues of the Seven Gods of Luck who appreciate the children's kindness to them.

Fables, fairy tales, folktales, legends, myths, and proverbs (including original works)

Six picture books feature animals.

In *The Loyal Cat*, which is retold by Lensey Namioka, the cat Huku uses his magical powers to bring the priest Tetsuzan enough money to maintain his temple.

Retold by Arthur A. Levine, *The Boy Who Drew Cats* tells of young Kenji's cat paintings which cause him to be banished from one temple, but rescue a second temple from the Goblin Rat who has usurped it.

Tony Johnston's adaptation, *The Badger and the Magic Fan*, relates the humorous story of the magic fan which lengthens and shortens noses and of the badger who gets his comeuppance for misusing it.

In Sheila Hamanaka's retelling, *Screen of Frogs*, an encounter with an enormous frog changes the values and lifestyle of the lazy, spendthrift Koji.

A pair of mandarin ducks saves the lives of a chief steward and a kitchen maid in Katherine Paterson's *The Tale of the Mandarin Ducks*. Appearing as imperial messengers, the ducks provide a feast and a home for the couple who have shown the drake kindness.

In *The Greatest of All*, which is retold by Eric A. Kimmel, a mouse who lives in the emperor's palace finds his daughter's choice of a field mouse spouse completely beneath his standards. After failing to convince the emperor, the sun, a cloud, the wind, and a wall to marry her, he discovers that the field mouse is the best choice.

A baby boy found in a peach, an origami doll which comes to life, a girl who climbs a silk strand into the sky, a woman who is really a crane, and a woman who is really a snow woman people seven of the Japanese tales.

Momotaro, the title character of *Peach Boy*, which is retold by Gail Sakurai, grows up to be strong and brave. With help from a dog, a monkey, and a pheasant he defeats some thieving, destructive ogres, and thenceforth the four of them and his elderly parents live together happily.

Williams H. Hooks retells the same story in his book, *Peach Boy*, which is a reader. Here it is a hawk rather than a pheasant who comes to the aid of Momotaro.

In *Little Oh*, an original folktale by Laura Krauss Melmed, an origami doll becomes an alive paper girl and then, after being chased by a dog, riding a river on part of a teacup, and flying on the neck of a crane, she returns to her home and her mother where she becomes a real girl with not only a mother, but also a father and a brother.

The Long Silk Strand, by Laura E. Williams, is a book for older children that deals with Yasuyo's coping with her grandmother's death. Thanks to her grandmother's silk strand of memories, Yasuyo comes to appreciate her own life, secure in the assurance of her grandmother's continuing presence.

The Crane Wife, which is retold by Ena Keo, tells how Sachi, who has become vain and greedy, breaks his promise to his wife, thereby discovering that she is the crane he had tended and that she has left him forever.

In Odds Bodkin's retelling, *The Crane Wife*, the sail maker's wife weaves her feathers into magic sails. Breaking his promise, the sail maker goes behind the screen to look at her and she flies away, never to return.

A man also breaks his promise in San Souci's *The Snow Wife*, and his wife, who is in reality a snow woman, disappears. However, in this instance, the man, Minokichi, makes a perilous journey to the Wind God and his wife is returned to him.

Women are the main characters in four of the books.

Alan Schroeder's *Lily and the Wooden Bowl* is about a girl who, at her grandmother's request, wears a bowl on her head to hide her beauty. When she marries her beloved Kumaso, the bowl splits apart.

The Funny Little Woman, which is retold by Arlene Mosel, details the subterranean adventure of the woman who is forced to cook rice for some oni, but then escapes with their magic paddle.

In Irene Hedlund's *Mighty Mountain and the Three Strong Women*, Mighty Mountain becomes the best sumo wrestler in Japan, thanks to three generations of women, each of whom is stronger than he is.

In a folktale retold by Uchida, *The Wise Old Woman*, the title character completes three seemingly impossible challenges, thereby saving her village and convincing its lord that old people are useful.

Four folktales feature men: two farmers, a gardener, and a stonecutter.

The farmer in *The Farmer and the Poor God*, which is retold by Ruth Wells, learns much from the Poor God: how to weave sandals, how to apply himself to work, and how there are things more important than riches.

The wise old farmer in *The Wave*, adapted by Margaret Hodges, burns his own rice fields to save four hundred villagers from a tidal wave.

The gardener in Laura Langston's *The Magic Ear* receives a magic shell in return for saving a baby sea bream. With it he finds a lump of gold and heals the nobleman's daughter, whom he subsequently marries.

The power-hungry stonecutter in Gerald McDermott's *The Stonecutter* resembles the father mouse in *The Greatest of All*. He becomes a prince, the sun, a cloud, and finally a mountain before realizing that he has no power over a stonecutter.

Historical figures

Grass Sandals, by Dawnine Spivak, tells of the travels of the Japanese poet Basho Matsuo, who in the seventeenth century walked about Japan observing and writing poems in his diary. His journey is presented through text, pictures, a map, Japanese characters, and his haiku.

In Tim Myers's *Basho and the Fox* a fox and Basho both want to eat some delicious wild cherries. The fox proposes that if Basho writes a good haiku, he can enjoy the cherries. After rejecting the great poet's first two haikus, the fox accepts the third one—because it mentions a fox.

Three books written and illustrated by Say are included here because together they present the lives of his grandfather and his mother—and also tell of the author who moved from his native Japan to California when he neared adulthood. All three stories focus on the theme of homesickness and finding one's own place.

Grandfather's Journey, a Caldecott medal winner, relates how Say's grandfather went on a journey to the United States where he fell in love with California. He returned to Japan to get married, and he and his bride moved to San Francisco. Homesick for Japan, the family moved back with their daughter when she was a teenager. World War II prevented him from taking a trip he'd planned to California.

Tea with Milk tells the story from the standpoint of Say's mother, giving more details of her life. She enjoyed growing up in San Francisco and hated to leave it. Homesick for San Francisco and unhappy with having to repeat high school and learning how to be a Japanese "lady", she went to work in a department store in Osaka where she met her future husband. They married and went to live in Yokohama.

Tree of Cranes tells of an incident that occurred in Say's life as a little boy. Homesick for California at Christmas time, his mother dug up a tree in the yard, decorated it with paper cranes and candles, and gave her son his first Christmas present.

Sadako, Eleanor Coerr's book for the oldest children, tells the story of Sadako Sasaki, a girl who died from leukemia caused by exposure to the Hiroshima bomb explosion. An active, aspiring runner prior to experiencing the disease, Sadako tries to fold one thousand paper cranes so that she can live a long life. Although she completes only 644, the remaining 356 are folded by her friends and classmates for burial with her. Her statue and cranes folded by children on Peace Day are now part of the Hiroshima Peace Park in Hiroshima prefecture.

Nonfiction

Holly Littlefield's *Colors of Japan* is a book for the oldest children that presents Japan through its many colors, such as the pink of its cherry blossoms, the red of the sun on its flag, and the tan of its tatami mats.

Stories

The sea is the setting of four stories.

In *The Sea and I*, by Harutaka Nakawatari, the young son of a fisherman watches for his father's boat to come in from a storm.

It is whales whom Takumi watches in Arnica Esterl's *Okino and The Whales*. His mother tells him the story of his great-grandmother who lived for a time in the palace of the whales.

The fisherwomen in Lili Bell's *The Sea Maidens of Japan* are ama, who dive to the ocean floor where they gather seafood. With the help of a sea turtle, Kiyomi overcomes her fear of the water and becomes one of the sea maidens.

A boy who likes to build things finds a magic fan in the sea in Keith Baker's *The Magic Fan*. He relies on the fan to show him what to build until the fan is lost in a tidal wave and the boy learns to follow his own vision. Unique fan-like semicircular paintings enhance the story.

Fumiko Takeshita's *The Park Bench*, which is written in Japanese and English, records through text and illustrations a day in the life of a town park bench. Children should enjoy searching the pictures for the animals and people mentioned in the text and especially for the park worker, who appears in almost every painting.

Takaaki Nomura's *Grandpa's Town* also is written in both Japanese and English. When a young boy accompanies his grandfather to the public bath, he discovers the reason that his grandfather does not want to leave his town.

The grandfather in Brenda Lena Fazio's *Grandfather's Story* has a dream and discovers that there is still much to do in his life.

No one will listen to young Yukio's scary dream in *The Dream Eater*, by Christian Garrison. Indeed, all the villagers are having nightmares until Yukio rescues the creature who eats bad dreams.

Children are also featured in six of the other stories.

In Melmed's *The First Song Ever Sung* a little boy asks each family member as well as the dog, some fish, and some birds what was the first song—and each gives a different answer, based on his own experiences.

Mi-chan makes snow bunnies in Masako Hidaka's *Girl from the Snow Country*.

In Virginia Kroll's *A Carp for Kimiko* another little girl, Kimiko, cannot have a carp kite to fly on Children's Day because she is not a boy. However, the next morning she receives her own live carp.

The youngest children should enjoy hearing about Mariko's early morning routine in *Rise and Shine, Mariko-chan!*, by Chiyoko Tomioka. Mariko gets dressed, eats her breakfast, watches her two older sisters set off for school, carries her father's briefcase to the car as her parents leave for work, and then boards the yellow bus that takes her to her school.

It takes six school years for his classmates to appreciate Chibi in Taro Yashima's *Crow Boy*.

With his older brother, an American boy goes to Japan to meet Kenji and his family in *Moshi Moshi*, by Jonathan London. The three boys spend time in Tokyo, Kyoto, and on the family's orange farm in Kagoshima prefecture in the Kyushu region. By the end of the visit the American boy decides he would like to become Kenji's pen pal.

In David Wisniewski's *The Warrior and the Wise Man* grown twins race to complete five tasks, with the winner to succeed their emperor father. Although Tozaemon the warrior wins the challenge, in so doing he provokes such hostility that his life is saved only by the wisdom of his brother, who is then chosen as the next emperor.

Sato and the Elephants, by Juanita Havill, tells of a boy who grew up longing to be an ivory carver like his father, but, discovering a bullet within some ivory, realizes that he cannot promote the killing of elephants—and decides to switch to stone carving.

Books

Baker, Keith. *The Magic Fan*. Illustrated by author. San Diego: Harcourt, 1989; Voyager Books, 1997, paperback.

Bell, Lili. *The Sea Maidens of Japan*. Illustrated by Erin McGonigle Brammer. Nashville, TN: Ideals Children's Books, 1997.

Bodkin, Odds, reteller. *The Crane Wife*. Illustrated by Gennady Spirin. San Diego: Harcourt, 1998.

Brenner, Barbara, and Julia Takaya. *Chibi: A True Story from Japan*. Illustrated by June Otani. New York: Clarion Books, 1999.

Coerr, Eleanor. *Sadako*. Illustrated by Ed Young. New York: G.P. Putnam's Sons, 1993; Paperstar, 1997, paperback.

Esterl, Arnica. *Okino and the Whales*. Illustrated by Marek Zawadzki. San Diego: Harcourt, 1995.

Fazio, Brenda Lena. *Grandfather's Story*. Illustrated by author. Seattle: Sasquatch Books, 1996.

Garrison, Christian. *The Dream Eater*. Illustrated by Diane Goode. New York: Aladdin Paperbacks, 1986.

Hamanaka, Sheila, reteller. *Screen of Frogs: An Old Tale.* Illustrated by reteller. New York: Orchard Books, 1993.

Haskins, Jim. *Count Your Way through Japan.* (Count Your Way Books) Illustrated by Martin Skoro. Minneapolis: Carolrhoda Books, 1987; 1987, paperback.

Havill, Juanita. *Sato and the Elephants.* Illustrated by Jean Tseng and Mou-sien Tseng. New York: Lothrop, Lee & Shepard Books, 1993.

Hedlund, Irene. *Mighty Mountain and the Three Strong Women.* Illustrated by author. English version by Judith Elkin. Volcano, CA: Volcano Press, 1990.

Hidaka, Masako. *Girl from the Snow Country.* Illustrated by author. Translated by Amanda Mayer Stinchecum. Brooklyn, NY: Kane/Miller Book Publishers, 1986; 1999, paperback.

Hodges, Margaret, adapter. *The Wave: Adapted from Lafcadio Hearn's Gleanings in Buddha Fields.* Illustrated by Blair Lent. Boston: Houghton Mifflin Company, 1964.

Honda, Tetsuya. *Wild Horse Winter.* Illustrated by author. Based on English translation by Susan Matsui. San Francisco: Chronicle Books, 1995, paperback.

Hooks, William H. *Peach Boy.* Illustrated by June Otani. New York: Bantam Doubleday Dell Books for Young Readers, 1992.

James, J. Alison. *The Drums of Noto Hanto.* Illustrated by Tsukushi. New York: DK Ink, 1999.

Johnston, Tony, adapter. *The Badger and the Magic Fan: A Japanese Folktale.* (Whitebird Books). Illustrated by Tomie dePaola. New York: G. P. Putnam's Sons, 1990.

Kajikawa, Kimiko. *Yoshi's Feast.* Illustrated by Yumi Heo. New York: DK Ink, 2000.

Kalman, Maira. *Sayonara, Mrs. Kackleman*. Illustrated by author. New York: Viking Children's Books, 1989, paperback; Puffin, 1991, paperback.

Keo, Ena, reteller. *The Crane Wife*. Illustrated by Cheryl Kirk Noll. Austin, TX: Raintree Steck-Vaughn Publishers, 1998.

Kimmel, Eric A., reteller. *The Greatest of All: A Japanese Folktale*. Illustrated by Giora Carmi. New York: Holiday House, 1991; 1991, paperback.

Kroll, Virginia. *A Carp for Kimiko*. Illustrated by Katherine Roundtree. Watertown, MA: Charlesbridge Publishing, 1993; 1996, paperback.

Kudler, David. *The Seven Gods of Luck*. Illustrated by Linda Finch. Boston: Houghton Mifflin Company, 1997.

Langston, Laura. *The Magic Ear*. Illustrated by Victor Bossou. Custer, WA: Orca Book Publishers, 1995.

Levine, Arthur A, reteller. *The Boy Who Drew Cats: A Japanese Folktale*. Illustrated by Frédéric Clément. New York: Dial Books for Young Readers, 1994, paperback.

Little, Mimi Otey. *Yoshiko and the Foreigner*. Illustrated by author. New York: Farrar, Straus & Giroux, 1996.

Littlefield, Holly. *Colors of Japan*. (Colors of the World) Illustrated by Helen Byers. Minneapolis: Carolrhoda Books, 1997; 1997, paperback.

London, Jonathan. *Moshi Moshi*. Illustrated by Yoshi Miyake. Brookfield, CT: Milbrook Press, 1998.

Long, Jan Freeman, adapter. *The Bee and the Dream: A Japanese Tale*. Illustrated by Kaoru Ono. New York: Dutton Children's Books, 1996, paperback.

Luenn, Nancy. *The Dragon Kite*. Illustrated by Michael Hague. New York: Voyager Books, 1983, paperback.

McDermott, Gerald, adapter. *The Stonecutter: A Japanese Folk Tale*. Illustrated by adapter. San Diego: Harcourt, 1995, paperback.

Melmed, Laura Krauss. *The First Song Ever Sung*. Illustrated by Ed Young. New York: Lothrop, Lee & Shepard Books, 1993.

Melmed, Laura Krauss. *Little Oh*. Illustrated by Jim LaMarche. New York: Lothrop, Lee & Shepard Books, 1997.

Merrill, Jean, adapter. *The Girl Who Loved Caterpillars: A Twelfth Century Tale from Japan*. Illustrated by Floyd Cooper. New York: Philomel Books, 1992; Paperstar, 1997, paperback.

Mosel, Arlene, reteller. *The Funny Little Woman*. Illustrated by Blair Lent. New York: Dutton Children's Books, 1972, paperback; Puffin, 1993, paperback.

Myers, Tim. *Basho and the Fox*. Illustrated by Oki S. Han. Tarrytown, NY: Marshall Cavendish, 2000.

Nakawatari, Harutaka. *The Sea and I*. Illustrated by author. Translated by Susan Matsui. New York: Sunburst Books, 1994, paperback.

Namioka, Lensey, reteller. *The Loyal Cat*. Illustrated by Aki Sogabe. San Diego: Browndeer Press, 1995.

Nomura, Takaaki. *Grandpa's Town*. Illustrated by author. Translated by Amanda Mayer Stinchecum. Brooklyn: Kane/Miller Book Publishers, 1991; 1995, paperback.

Paterson, Katherine. *The Tale of the Mandarin Ducks*. Illustrated by Leo Dillon and Diane Dillon. New York: Lodestar Books, 1990, paperback; Puffin Unicorn, 1995, paperback.

Rowe, John A. *Jack the Dog*. Illustrated by author. New York: Picture Book Studio, 1993.

Sakurai, Gail, reteller. *Peach Boy: A Japanese Legend.* (Legends of the World) Illustrated by Makiko Nagano. Mahwah, NJ: Troll Communications, 1997; 1997, paperback.

San Souci, Robert D. *The Samurai's Daughter: A Japanese Legend.* Illustrated by Stephen T. Johnson. New York: Puffin, 1997, paperback.

San Souci, Robert D., reteller. *The Snow Wife.* Illustrated by Stephen T. Johnson. New York: Dial Books for Young Readers, 1993, paperback.

Say, Allen. *The Bicycle Man.* Illustrated by author. Boston: Houghton Mifflin Company, 1982; Sandpiper Paperbacks, 1989, paperback.

Say, Allen. *Grandfather's Journey.* Illustrated by author. Boston: Houghton Mifflin Company, 1993.

Say, Allen. *Tea with Milk.* Illustrated by author. Boston: Houghton Mifflin Company, 1999.

Say, Allen. *Tree of Cranes.* Illustrated by author. Boston: Sandpiper Paperbacks, 1991.

Schroeder, Alan. *Lily and the Wooden Bowl.* Illustrated by Yoriko Ito. New York: Picture Yearling, 1997, paperback.

Sierra, Judy. *Tasty Baby Belly Buttons.* Illustrated by Meilo So. New York: Alfred A. Knopf, 1999; 1999, paperback.

Snyder, Dianne. *The Boy of the Three-Year Nap.* Illustrated by Allen Say. Boston: Houghton Mifflin Company, 1988; 1993, paperback.

Spivak, Dawnine. *Grass Sandals: The Travels of Basho.* Illustrated by Demi. New York: Simon & Schuster Books for Young Readers, 1997.

Takeshita, Fumiko. *The Park Bench.* Illustrated by Mamoru Suzuki. Translated by Ruth A. Kanagy. Brooklyn, NY: Kane/Miller Book Publishers, 1988; 1989, paperback.

Tejima, Keizaburo. *The Bears' Autumn*. Illustrated by author. Translated from the Japanese by Susan Matsui. New York: Green Tiger Press, 1991.

Tomioka, Chiyoko. *Rise and Shine, Mariko-chan!* Illustrated by Yoshiharu Tsuchida. New York: Scholastic, 1992, paperback.

Uchida, Yoshiko, reteller. *The Magic Purse*. Illustrated by Keiko Narahashi. New York: Margaret K. McElderry Books, 1993.

Uchida, Yoshiko, reteller. *The Wise Old Woman*. Illustrated by Martin Springett. New York: Margaret K. McElderry Books, 1994.

Vaughan, Marcia. *Dorobo the Dangerous*. Illustrated by Kazuko Stone. Parsippany, NJ: Silver Burdett Press, 1994; 1994, paperback.

Waite, Michael P. *Jojofu*. Illustrated by Yoriko Ito. New York: Lothrop, Lee & Shepard Books, 1996.

Wells, Ruth, reteller. *The Farmer and the Poor God: A Folktale from Japan*. Illustrated by Yoshi. New York: Simon & Schuster Books for Young Readers, 1996.

Williams, Laura E. *The Long Silk Strand*. Illustrated by Grayce Bochak. Honesdale, PA: Boyds Mills Press, 1995.

Wisniewski, David. *The Warrior and the Wise Man*. Illustrated by author. New York: Lothrop, Lee & Shepard Books, 1989.

Yashima, Taro. *Crow Boy*. Illustrated by author. New York: Viking Children's Books, 1955, paperback; Puffin, 1976, paperback.

Jordan (formerly Transjordan)
Hashemite Kingdom of Jordan

Books set in Palestine, not a separate country, but a region coextensive with Israel and part of Jordan, are described in the section, Palestine.

"In the valley below, they could see a river and, in the distance, a village."
—Rumford. *The Cloudmakers.*

Kazakhstan (Kazakstan, formerly Kazakh Soviet Socialist Republic)
Republic of Kazakhstan

Kazakhstan was formerly a constituent republic of the Union of Soviet Socialist Republics (U.S.S.R.), which was dissolved in 1991. Picture books set in the area of the former U.S.S.R. for which no other specific location is given are described under Russia (Russian Federation).

Based on a true event that took place in A.D. 751, James Rumford's *The Cloudmakers* tells of an old Chinese man and his grandson who save themselves from slavery by demonstrating to the great sultan of the victorious Arab army that they can make "clouds". Thus, the Chinese art of papermaking is introduced to the Arabs.

Book

Rumford, James. *The Cloudmakers*. Illustrated by author. Boston: Houghton Mifflin Company, 1996.

"She climbed through forests of striped bamboo and wild banana trees, past plants curved like rooster tail feathers, and over rocks shaped like sleeping dragons."
—Xiong. *Nine-in-One, Grr! Grr!*

Laos
Lao People's Democratic Republic

Thanks to the Eu bird in *Nine-in-One, Grr! Grr!*, which is told by Blia Xiong, the first tiger has only one cub every nine years instead of nine cubs every year, thereby keeping the world from being overpopulated by tigers.

Book

Xiong, Blia, told by. *Nine-in-One, Grr! Grr!: A Folktale from the Hmong People of Laos.* Adapted by Cathy Spagnoli. Illustrated by Nancy Hom. San Francisco: Children's Book Press, 1989; 1993, paperback.

"On foot, he crossed the vast, grassy plains that stretched like a great green sea."
—Yep. *The Khan's Daughter.*

Mongolia (Outer Mongolia, formerly Mongolian People's Republic)

The region, Mongolia, includes Mongolia (Outer Mongolia), the Nei Monggol (Inner Mongolia) Autonomous Region of China, and Tuva. Picture books set in the region of Mongolia are described here.

In Laurence Yep's *The Khan's Daughter* a sheepherder wins the hand of the Khan's daughter even though he completes only two of the tasks demanded of him.

Jay Williams's *Everyone Knows What a Dragon Looks Like* is set in a storybook city located between China and what would appear to be Mongolia with its plains and horsemen. No one believes the fat old man who arrives in the city claiming to be a dragon. However, because the boy who is the gate-sweeper is kind to him, the man saves the city from invading wild horsemen.

Books

Williams, Jay. *Everyone Knows What a Dragon Looks Like*. Illustrated by Mercer Mayer. New York: Aladdin Paperbacks, 1984, paperback.

Yep, Laurence. *The Khan's Daughter: A Mongolian Folktale*. Illustrated by Jean Tseng and Mou-sien Tseng. New York: Scholastic, 1997.

"The Governor's palace stood among mountains that touched the sky."
—Park and Park. *The Royal Bee.*

North Korea
Democratic People's Republic
of Korea

Korea was partitioned into North Korea and South Korea after World War II. Korean picture books for which no specific North Korean location is given are described under South Korea.

The Royal Bee, by Frances and Ginger Park, tells of the winning of a contest of knowledge attended by the governor. This story, which is based on the experience of the authors' grandfather, tells how Song-ho, who is so poor that he is not allowed to go to school, learns by listening outside the school door. After finally being permitted inside the classroom, he represents the school at the Royal Bee and wins the contest.

Book

Park, Frances, and Ginger Park. *The Royal Bee*. Illustrated by Christopher Zhong-Yuan Zhang. Honesdale, PA: Boyds Mills Press, 2000.

*"In the evenings we climbed the stairs to the roof of
Sitti's house to look at the sky, smell the air, and take
down the laundry."*
—Nye. *Sitti's Secrets.*

Palestine

Not a separate country, but a region, Palestine is
coextensive with Israel and part of Jordan.

In *Sitti's Secrets,* by Naomi Shihab Nye, an American
girl, visiting her grandmother on the West Bank, is able to
communicate with her even though they speak different
languages—and she manages to discover whether her
grandmother does indeed have striped hair.

Book

Nye, Naomi Shihab. *Sitti's Secrets.* Illustrated by Nancy
Carpenter. New York: Four Winds Press, 1994;
Aladdin Paperbacks, 1997.

"From where he lay, Miguel saw the eagle surging upward again, and he understood why it had plunged to earth—in its talons it carried the long body and hooded head of a king cobra."
—Allen. *Eagle*.

Philippines
Republic of the Philippines

In Francisco Arcellana's *The Mats*, which is for children who are older, Papa brings home sleeping mats made specifically for each family member, including three of the children who are deceased.

Four children and a teacher take a trek into the forest in Judy Allen's *Eagle*, which is also a book for older children. Despite his best efforts young Miguel remains terrified of a large eagle until, diving for food, the eagle saves Miguel from a cobra.

Books

Allen, Judy. *Eagle*. Illustrated by Tudor Humphries. Cambridge, MA: Candlewick Press, 1996, paperback.

Arcellana, Francisco. *The Mats*. Illustrated by Hermès Alègrè. Brooklyn, NY: Cranky Nell Books, 1999.

"A long time ago, in a simple farmhouse in Korea, there lived a kindly old rice farmer and his wife."
—Reasoner. *The Magic Amber.*

South Korea
Republic of Korea

Korea was partitioned into North Korea and South Korea after World War II. Korean picture books for which no specific North Korean location is given are described here.

Specific Locations

Seoul

In Sook Nyul Choi's *Yunmi and Halmoni's Trip*, New Yorker Yunmi accompanies her grandmother on a trip to Seoul. She enjoys her visit, but worries that her grandmother will remain in her native Korea.

Juno's grandmother lives outside Seoul in Soyung Pak's *Dear Juno*. Even though American Juno cannot read Korean, he and his grandmother are able to communicate by letter—through the items and pictures that they enclose.

General

Fables, fairy tales, folktales, legends, myths, and proverbs (including original works)

Two of the folktales are Cinderella stories. Instead of a fairy godmother, both Cinderellas, Pear Blossom and Kongi, are helped by a frog/toad, an ox, and some sparrows.

In Shirley Climo's *The Korean Cinderella* the stepmother and stepsister are especially mean, calling Pear Blossom "Pigling" and trying to get rid of her. Pear Blossom never gets a magnificent dress, but is spotted in her rags by the magistrate who finally weds her.

Kongi and Potgi, which is adapted by Oki S. Han and Stephanie Haboush Plunkett, includes angels who clothe Kongi in finery. Kongi is seen by the prince at his bride-choosing party, and her stepmother and stepsister eventually repent their behavior.

The generosity of a poor, older couple is rewarded by the gift of a magic amber in *The Magic Amber*, retold by Charles Reasoner. Indeed, because they are generous in wealth as well as in poverty, they are provided for even after the amber stone is stolen.

Magic Spring, retold by Nami Rhee, tells of another poor, older couple, who long for a child. The man is led by a bluebird to a magical spring where one taste of the water transforms him into a young man. When he tells his wife of the spring she too becomes young, but when he tells his selfish, rich old neighbor, the man turns into a baby, who becomes the couple's child.

Despite its title, *The Chinese Mirror*, adapted by Mirra Ginsburg, is set in a Korean village where the mirror one of the villagers has brought home confuses the family members and a neighbor, each of whom sees a different, but seemingly real person in the mirror.

In Daniel San Souci's retelling of the Korean tale, *In the Moonlight Mist*, first a deer and then the heavenly king reward a woodcutter for his kindness. Even though he errs in not following all the deer's instructions, he is reunited in heaven with his wife, daughter, and mother.

Retold by Yangsook Choi, *The Sun Girl and the Moon Boy* tells of a tiger who eats a mother and almost eats her two children. However, the girl becomes the sun, the boy the moon, and their mother the stars.

Julia Gukova's colorful illustrations in *The Mole's Daughter* enhance this adaptation of the tale of the foolish mole who decides that his beautiful daughter deserves better than a mole for a husband. After unsuccessfully requesting the hand of the sky, the sun, a cloud, and the wind, his wise daughter manages to convince him that it would be better for her to marry the mole who has bested her father's next candidate, a stone wall.

Suzanne Crowder Han tells two stories, written in English and Korean, of a clever rabbit.

In one, *The Rabbit's Judgment*, the rabbit is able to save a man from the tiger whom he has rescued.

In the other, *The Rabbit's Escape*, the rabbit saves himself from the Dragon King who wishes to eat his liver.

A third rabbit story by Han, *The Rabbit's Tail*, is written only in English. This folktale tells of a tiger who mistakenly becomes afraid of a dried persimmon, a thief who mistakenly steals the tiger instead of an ox, and a rabbit who, because of the mix-ups, loses his long tail.

The Green Frogs, which is retold by Yumi Heo, tells of two frogs who consistently disobey their mother until the one time that they should have done so.

The proverbs selected by Daniel D. Holt for *Tigers, Frogs, and Rice Cakes* are presented in English and Korean and illustrated with bright watercolor paintings. This book, which is for older children, includes an explanation of each of the proverbs.

Nonfiction

A book for older children, Jim Haskins's *Count Your Way through Korea* includes the numerals from one to ten in Korean as well as English. The items counted include the players needed for seesaw and types of seasonings.

Stories

An illustrated chapter book for older children, Haemi Balgassi's *Peacebound Trains* tells how Sumi likes to sit on a rock watching trains as she longs for her mother to return from the military. Her grandmother tells Sumi of the train she once took long ago, riding on the crowded roof with Sumi's young uncle and her mother, who was a baby, as they escaped from Seoul to Pusan during the Korean War.

Books

Balgassi, Haemi. *Peacebound Trains*. Illustrated by Chris K. Soentpiet. New York: Clarion Books, 1996.
Choi, Sook Nyul. *Yunmi and Halmoni's Trip*. Illustrated by Karen Dugan. Boston: Houghton Mifflin Company, 1997.

Choi, Yangsook, reteller. *The Sun Girl and the Moon Boy*. Illustrated by reteller. New York: Knopf Books for Young Readers, 1997.

Climo, Shirley. *The Korean Cinderella*. Illustrated by Ruth Heller. New York: HarperCollins Children's Books, 1993; Harper Trophy, 1996, paperback.

Ginsburg, Mirra, adapter. *The Chinese Mirror: Adapted from a Korean Folktale*. Illustrated by Margot Zemach. San Diego: Gulliver Books, 1988; Harcourt, 1991, paperback.

Han, Oki S., and Stephanie Haboush Plunkett, adapters. *Kongi and Potgi: A Cinderella Story from Korea*. Illustrated by Oki S. Han. New York: Dial Books for Young Readers, 1996, paperback.

Han, Suzanne Crowder. *The Rabbit's Escape*. Illustrated by Yumi Heo. New York: Henry Holt and Company, 1995.

Han, Suzanne Crowder. *The Rabbit's Judgment*. Illustrated by Yumi Heo. New York: Henry Holt and Company, 1995.

Han, Suzanne Crowder. *The Rabbit's Tail: A Story from Korea*. Illustrated by Richard Wehrman. New York: Henry Holt and Company, 1999.

Haskins, Jim. *Count Your Way through Korea*. (Count Your Way Books) Illustrated by Dennis Hockerman. Minneapolis: Carolrhoda Books, 1989; 1989, paperback.

Heo, Yumi, reteller. *The Green Frogs: A Korean Folktale*. Illustrated by reteller. Boston: Houghton Mifflin Company, 1996.

Holt, Daniel D., selector. *Tigers, Frogs, and Rice Cakes: A Book of Korean Proverbs*. Illustrated by Soma Han Stickler. Translated by selector. Auburn, CA: Shen's Books, 1999.

The Mole's Daughter: An Adaptation of a Korean Folktale. Illustrated by Julia Gukova. Toronto: Annick (Distributed by Firefly Books), 1998; 1998, paperback.

Pak, Soyung. *Dear Juno.* Illustrated by Susan Kathleen Hartung. New York: Viking Penguin, 1999.

Reasoner, Charles, reteller. *The Magic Amber: A Korean Legend.* (Legends of the World) Illustrated by reteller. Mahwah, NJ: Troll Communications, 1994, paperback; 1997.

Rhee, Nami. *Magic Spring: A Korean Folktale.* (A Whitebird Book) Illustrated by reteller. New York: G. P. Putnam's Sons, 1993.

San Souci, Daniel, reteller. *In the Moonlight Mist: A Korean Tale.* Illustrated by Eujin Kim Neilan. Honesdale, PA: Boyds Mills Press, 1999.

"Whenever it rained they used banana or yam leaves for umbrellas, or covered their heads with... ... sacks, cloths or baskets."
—Wettasinghe. *The Umbrella Thief.*

Sri Lanka
(formerly Ceylon)

Sybil Wettasinghe's *The Umbrella Thief* reveals how the unusual thief who steals Kiri Mama's umbrellas unwittingly does him a favor.

Book

Wettasinghe, Sybil. *The Umbrella Thief.* Illustrated by author. Brooklyn: Kane/Miller Book Publishers, 1987.

"Mai grabbed her pa´ndau and ran through the muddy lanes of brown huts all the way to the camp border."
—Shea. *The Whispering Cloth.*

Thailand (formerly Siam)

Minfong Ho's *Hush!* is a rhythmic lullaby which should appeal to even the youngest children. Putting the baby down to sleep, the mother quiets all the animals, including a mosquito and a water buffalo; joins them in sleep; and then, when everything is quiet, the baby awakes.

The title character in *The Man Who Caught Fish*, by Walter Lyon Krudop, always catches a fish when he dips the string at the end of his pole into water. He then gives a fish apiece to those around him. When the king tries trickery, inducement, and imprisonment to make the man give him more than one fish, he not only fails, but is sentenced to become the new fish-catching man.

In Pegi Deitz Shea's *The Whispering Cloth*, a book for the oldest children, Mai, a Hmong refugee from Laos, has grown up in Thailand's Ban Vinai refugee camp. Her grandmother teaches her to stitch. After practice and stitching borders, Mai stitches her own pa´ndau, a cloth that tells the story of her life from her escape across the Mekong River with her grandmother to her hoped-for move to America.

Books

Ho, Minfong. *Hush!: A Thai Lullaby*. Illustrated by Holly Meade. New York: Orchard Books, 1996.

Krudop, Walter Lyon. *The Man Who Caught Fish*. Illustrated by author. New York: Farrar, Straus & Giroux, 2000.

Shea, Pegi Deitz. *The Whispering Cloth: A Refugee's Story*. Illustrated by Anita Riggio. Stitched by You Yang. Honesdale, PA: Boyds Mills Press, 1996, paperback.

"Mounting his little donkey, he rode to the marketplace and, after a whole morning's thought and bargaining, he selected a cow and led her home."
—Walker. *Watermelons, Walnuts and the Wisdom of Allah and Other Tales of the Hoca.*

Turkey

Books set in the ancient country of Armenia, which is now divided between Armenia, Iran, and Turkey, are described under Armenia.

In *Watermelons, Walnuts and the Wisdom of Allah and Other Tales of the Hoca* a picture on each page illustrates Barbara Walker's telling of eighteen tales about the wise—and foolish—Nasreddin Hoca, who has become a Turkish folk hero.

Jane Yolen's *Little Mouse & Elephant* is the retelling of a Turkish tale of the vain mouse who is so foolish that he misinterprets the animals' reactions to his foolishness.

The setting of the Greek legend, *The Trojan Horse*, a book for older children which is retold by Warwick Hutton, is the ancient city of Troy, located at what is now Hissarlik in Turkey. After unsuccessfully besieging Troy for ten years, the Greeks build a gigantic wooden horse which the unsuspecting Trojans take into their city. During the night the horse is opened, revealing its contents of soldiers, who, together with the Greek army waiting offshore, destroy the now gateless Trojan stronghold.

Two books, *The Midas Touch,* by Jan Mark, and *King Midas*, by John Warren Stewig, place another Greek tale in a Turkish setting.

In the Mark version the god Dionysus gives King Midas the touch of gold, which he asks for on the spur of the moment as he had not previously wanted it. Then, when the frantic king fears starvation because all his food turns to gold, Dionysus comes to his rescue by telling him to jump into the Pactolus River. King Midas loses his terrible power—and the sands of the river turn golden.

King Midas had been consumed by the desire for gold in the Stewig version. He is given the golden touch by a stranger and in this version also has it removed by jumping into the Pactolus River. In this book King Midas has a beloved daughter, Marygold. After the king's golden touch is removed, not only does the Pactolus River sand turn gold, but also there appears a golden tint in Marygold's hair and later in the hair of her children.

Books

Hutton, Warwick, reteller. *The Trojan Horse.* Illustrated by reteller. New York: Margaret K. McElderry Books, 1992.

Mark, Jan. *The Midas Touch.* Illustrated by Juan Wijngaard. Cambridge, MA: Candlewick Press, 1999.

Stewig, John Warren. *King Midas: A Golden Tale.* Illustrated by Omar Rayyan. New York: Holiday House, 1999.

Walker, Barbara. *Watermelons, Walnuts and the Wisdom of Allah and Other Tales of the Hoca.* Illustrated by Harold Berson. Lubbock, TX: Texas Tech University Press, 1991.

Yolen, Jane, reteller. *Little Mouse & Elephant: A Tale from Turkey*. Illustrated by John Segal. New York: Simon & Schuster Books for Young Readers, 1995.

Tuva (formerly Tuva Autonomous Soviet Socialist Republic)

The region, Mongolia, includes Mongolia (Outer Mongolia), the Nei Monggol (Inner Mongolia) Autonomous Region of China, and Tuva. Picture books set in the region of Mongolia are described under Mongolia (Outer Mongolia).

"That afternoon Duc and I were up in our favorite guava tree when I spotted someone on the village road."
—Breckler. *Sweet Dried Apples.*

Vietnam (Viet Nam, formerly Democratic Republic of Vietnam and Republic of Vietnam) <u>Socialist Republic of Vietnam</u>

Jeanne M. Lee's *Toad Is the Uncle of Heaven* relates the folktale of toad's trip to the King of Heaven to get rain for the parched earth. Thanks to the toad and his friends (some bees, a rooster, and a tiger), the king not only brings rain to the world, but also addresses the toad by the respectful title, "uncle", and tells him that the next time he needs rain he should just croak.

The Golden Slipper, retold by Darrell Lum, is the Cinderella-like tale of a young girl, Tam, who is kind to a catfish, a rooster, and a horse. It is these three animals plus an unusual woman who dress Tam in fine clothes and enable her to go to the Autumn Festival. There the prince, searching for the owner of the slipper he has found, discovers her and seeks her hand in marriage.

It is the Vietnam War which is the setting of Rosemary Breckler's *Sweet Dried Apples*, a book for older children. When the father of a little girl and her brother goes off to war, their grandfather, an herb doctor, comes to help care for them. He becomes ill during the fighting, but, using the herbs the children have prepared for him, manages to treat all those needing his medicines before he dies—and the family escapes Vietnam.

Set after the Vietnam War that caused the Sarus cranes to leave the Mekong Delta, *Grandfather's Dream,* by Holly Keller, shows how Nam's grandfather's dream for the return of the cranes is fulfilled and, as a result, the wetland is not turned into rice fields.

The Lotus Seed, by Sherry Garland, spans the period from 1945 to the near present. When a Vietnamese girl sees the last emperor Bao Dai cry when he is forced to abdicate, she takes a lotus seed from his garden to preserve his memory. She keeps this prized possession when she becomes a wife and a mother and as she escapes by boat from the fighting and comes to live in the United States. When her grandson takes the seed and plants it in the mud, a lotus flower blooms. The woman gives one of its seeds to each of her grandchildren so that they can remember her.

Maxine Trottier's *The Walking Stick* also begins in the pre-Vietnam War period, when Van as a boy finds a stick beneath a tree near a Buddhist temple. It ends many years later when his American granddaughter returns to the temple the walking stick that Van had held as he led her grandmother and her mother out of war-torn Vietnam.

More than twenty years after he escaped the fighting in Vietnam, the Vietnamese-American father in *My Father's Boat*, by Garland, teaches his young son the shrimp trade on his shrimp boat in the Gulf of Mexico. They think of another fisherman, their father and grandfather, who stayed in Vietnam and who now fishes from his boat in the South China Sea.

In Eva Boholm-Olsson's *Tuan*, Tuan is a five-year-old boy who goes to day care and likes to ride a water buffalo. When he is bitten by a rabid dog, his mother and the doctor worry that there will not be enough rabies vaccine.

Books

Boholm-Olsson, Eva. *Tuan*. Illustrated by Pham van Dôn. Translated by Dianne Jonasson. Stockholm: R & S Books (Distributed by Farrar, Straus & Giroux), 1988.

Breckler, Rosemary. *Sweet Dried Apples: A Vietnamese Wartime Childhood*. Illustrated by Deborah Kogan Ray. Boston: Houghton Mifflin Company, 1996.

Garland, Sherry. *The Lotus Seed*. Illustrated by Tatsuro Kiuchi. San Diego: Harcourt, 1993; 1997, paperback.

Garland, Sherry. *My Father's Boat*. Illustrated by Ted Rand. New York: Scholastic, 1998.

Keller, Holly. *Grandfather's Dream*. Illustrated by author. New York: Greenwillow Books, 1994.

Lee, Jeanne M., reteller. *Toad Is the Uncle of Heaven: A Vietnamese Folktale*. Illustrated by reteller. New York: Owlet Paperbacks for Young Readers, 1995, paperback.

Lum, Darrell, reteller. *The Golden Slipper: A Vietnamese Legend*. (Legends of the World) Illustrated by Makiko Nagano. Mahwah, NJ: Troll Communications, 1997.

Trottier, Maxine. *The Walking Stick*. Illustrated by Annouchka Gravel Galouchko. New York: Stoddart Kids, 1999.

Australia and Oceania

"It was baking hot now, and Wombat shuffled into the shade of a giant eucalyptus tree."
—Morpurgo. *Wombat Goes Walkabout.*

Australia
Commonwealth of Australia

Specific Locations

Seven of the picture books described below are set in a specific state or territory.

New South Wales

My Place, by Nadia Wheatley, is a book for the oldest children. It traces the history of a specific piece of land in Sydney going backwards by decade from 1988 when it was occupied by a little girl named Laura and her family to 1788 when Barangaroo spent the summer there in an Aboriginal camp. A double-page illustration, a map of the immediate neighborhood drawn by the child who lived there, and the accompanying text provide a look at both the property and the family who occupied the land in each decade. This is a book which children can examine for hours: seeing how the property has changed both in the illustrations and the maps; looking at the different generations of some of the families who lived there; noting how the land was occupied at times by convict servants and settlers from Germany, Greece, Ireland, and the United

States; and discovering that, despite all the changes, the large fig tree has remained.

Northern Territory

Robyn Eversole's *Flood Fish* shows how, when it rains, large fish suddenly appear in the typically dry bed of the Finke River. In this story a boy, his siblings, and his grandfather speculate as to the source of these fish, a mystery that still baffles scientists.

Queensland

In the collage-illustrated *Where the Forest Meets the Sea*, by Jeannie Baker, a small boy explores the remote Daintree Rainforest.

Toad Overload, by Patricia Seibert, provides a true account of the 101 large toads brought into Queensland in 1935 to destroy beetles that were eating the sugarcane crop. Unfortunately, toads were not suited to the climate of Australia's sugarcane fields. The rapidly multiplying toads generally did not eat the beetles and migrated to towns where they populated the gardens and lawns. Now numbering in the millions, these toads create a nuisance for many residents in a large area of Queensland.

South Australia

The contrast between the opal-mining town of Coober Pedy and the city of Adelaide is revealed in Robyn Eversole's *The Gift Stone*. The colors in the opals bring joy to a miner's young daughter, but she would prefer living with her grandparents in Adelaide where there are the colors of trees and flowers. Discovering a large opal, she gives it to her grandmother, thereby providing enough money that she can stay with them.

In Colin Thiele's *Farmer Schulz's Ducks*, Farmer Schulz is determined that his ducks be able to cross the road each day as they go and return from their swim in the Onkaparinga River. When the traffic to and from Adelaide makes the ducks' crossing unsafe, Farmer Schulz, on the advice of young Anna, tries first a duck crossing sign and then building a duck bridge. These failing, Anna comes up with her best idea: a duck pipe.

Tasmania

In Baker's *The Hidden Forest* a diver introduces Ben to the wonders of an underwater kelp forest.

General

Alphabet, counting, and word books

Even the youngest children should enjoy the amusing poem and illustrations in the counting book, *One Woolly Wombat*, by Rod Trinca and Kerry Argent. The Australian animals depicting the numbers one through fourteen include riddle-writing kookaburras and yo-yo-spinning dingoes.

Fables, fairy tales, folktales, legends, myths, and proverbs (including original works)

The four picture books in this category reflect the Aboriginal influence in their art, their inspiration, and/or the stories themselves.

Arone Raymond Meeks's *Enora and the Black Crane*, a book for older children, relates an Aboriginal story that explains how all the birds except the black crane came to have colorful feathers.

It is not a black crane which gets its distinctive features in Rudyard Kipling's *The Sing-Song of Old Man Kangaroo*. Rather, it is the kangaroo who attains his distinctive shape and his hopping gait after being chased around Australia by a dingo.

Pheasant and Kingfisher, by Catherine Berndt, tells how the men Bookbook and Bered-bered escape those who are throwing spears at them by turning, respectively, into a pheasant and a kingfisher—and how each continues to call out his name.

The title character in Susan L. Roth's collage-illustrated *The Biggest Frog in Australia* is so thirsty that he swallows all the water on the island as well as in the clouds above. It is not until two eels make him laugh that the water is released and returned to its rightful locations.

Nonfiction

Like *Toad Overload*, described under Queensland, *The Story of Rosy Dock*, by Baker, reveals the change that occurs when a non-native element, in this instance the rosy dock plant, is introduced into the environment. Baker's brief text and collages show the Finke River (which is located in South Australia as well as the Northern Territory) as it looks in the cycles of rain and drought and as its landscape has been altered by the rosy dock which one woman planted in her garden years ago.

The text and illustrations in Alison Lester's *My Farm* depict a year in her childhood, a year busy with chores and fun. Among the times remembered are riding down the road at night in her pajamas to bring back panicked cattle, waterskiing on wet grass behind a farm truck, painting a horse like a zebra, and finally getting a pony.

Poetry and songs

Graeme Base's *My Grandma Lived in Gooligulch* presents through a humorous poem and many double-page illustrations the story of kangaroo-riding Grandma, the animals who live with her, and the journey which she and a wombat take in a pelican's beak. The inside covers contain a picture of twenty-two Australian animals and birds, which children can identify by using the book's picture key.

Stories

Not surprisingly, Australia's unusual animals are featured in many of the picture books.

Young Kangaroo, by Margaret Wise Brown, describes the growing up of a joey, who shortly after birth crawls into his mother's pouch, smells the world before he can see it, grabs from the pouch for food to eat, leaves the pouch for brief intervals, and, after being dumped from the pouch by his mother who is escaping from dingoes, is reunited with her.

Marcia Vaughan's *Snap!* is the story of a joey who wants to play after a long day in his mother's pouch. His new acquaintances—a bush mouse, a green tree snake, a platypus, and an echidna—introduce him to some new games—but the group gets an unpleasant surprise when they get involved in the crocodile's game.

In Mem Fox's *Koala Lou*, young Koala Lou feels she needs to regain her mother's love after the birth of siblings. She fails to win the Bush Olympics tree climbing competition, but discovers that her mother still loves her.

Patty Sheehan's *Kylie's Song* tells of another young koala who is unhappy first because she is teased for her singing and then because, when she decides to conform, she gives up the singing she loves. Gaining the courage to sing again, she brings happiness to the other animals.

In Michael Morpurgo's *Wombat Goes Walkabout*, Wombat encounters a kookaburra, a wallaby, a possum, an emu, a boy, and a koala as he searches for his mother. Each of them can do wonderful things, while he can only dig and think. However, when a fire comes, it is Wombat's strengths that save him and his new friends, who join him after the fire in finding his mother.

A different wombat is placed in a stew pot by Dingo in *Wombat Stew*, a second book by Vaughan. However, Platypus, Emu, Lizard, Echidna, and Koala add their own "delicious" ingredients to the stew, thereby saving Wombat.

Food is also the focal point of Fox's *Possum Magic*. Grandma Poss and the invisible Hush travel about Australia, trying out food in Adelaide, Melbourne, Sidney,

Brisbane, Darwin, Perth, and Hobart until Hush finally becomes visible again.

Animals play an important role in both John Winch's *The Old Man Who Loved to Sing* and his *The Old Woman Who Loved to Read*.

When the old man forgets to sing, it is the animals who have loved his singing who awaken the valley with their music—and also awaken the old man who once again sings.

The old woman leaves the busy city to find time to read, but discovers that farm life, including taking care of an orphan lamb in the spring, pumping water for the animals in the summer, and rescuing them via bathtub from fall floods leaves no time for reading. Finally, when she has a spare moment, she sits in her chair with a book and, surrounded by a bevy of Australian animals, falls asleep.

Fred and Grace are anthropomorphic mice in Susanna Rodell's *Dear Fred*. Grace writes to her half-brother Fred from the urban apartment she and her mother have moved to in the United States, describing her new life and remembering her times with Fred at her old house with a backyard in Australia.

The setting is the emphasis of two other picture books.

Baker's *Window* is a wordless, collage-illustrated picture book, which features double-page illustrations of the view from a house window. As a boy grows from an infant to a man so the landscape changes in each picture from the wooded area surrounding the house to an increasingly residential neighborhood to a city complete with McDonald's. Only the cat remains the same, and children may enjoy searching for it in each of the pictures.

Henry Wilson shows that he knows precisely where he lives in *My Place in Space*, by Robin and Sally Hirst. Henry places the location of his house not only as a street address, but also in a town in Australia in the Southern Hemisphere and in a particular place in the universe.

The 1983 victory of an older Australian farmer in a 542 mile race is the inspiration of Marsha Diane Arnold's amusing story, *The Pumpkin Runner*. An older sheep rancher, who gets his energy from eating pumpkins, beats his much younger, more traditional competitors in a Melbourne-Sydney race—and in the process discovers that he does not need to rely on pumpkins.

Santa and Samantha strike up a monthly correspondence in Margaret Wild's *Thank You, Santa*. As a result, Santa's littlest reindeer is able to pull the sleigh on Christmas eve and an Australian polar bear receives the Christmas gift he most wants.

In Jeanie Adams's *Going for Oysters* an Aborigine girl and her family go to the river where she chops off mangrove roots covered with oysters, enjoys opening the shells and eating the oysters, goes swimming, catches a salmon, and is scared when she hears the noise of Yaatamay, the Carpet Snake.

Books

Adams, Jeanie. *Going for Oysters*. Illustrated by author. Morton Grove, IL: Albert Whitman & Company, 1993.
Arnold, Marsha Diane. *The Pumpkin Runner*. Illustrated by Brad Sneed. New York: Dial Books for Young Readers, 1998.
Baker, Jeannie. *The Hidden Forest*. Illustrated by author. New York: Greenwillow Books, 2000.

Baker, Jeannie. *The Story of Rosy Dock*. Illustrated by author. New York: Greenwillow Books, 1995.

Baker, Jeannie. *Where The Forest Meets the Sea*. Illustrated by author. New York: Greenwillow Books, 1988.

Baker, Jeannie. *Window*. Illustrated by author. New York: Greenwillow Books, 1991.

Base, Graeme. *My Grandma Lived in Gooligulch*. Illustrated by author. New York: Harry N. Abrams, 1995.

Berndt, Catherine. *Pheasant and Kingfisher: Originally told by Nganalgindja in the Gunwinggu Language*. Illustrated by Arone Raymond Meeks. Greenvale, NY: Mondo Publishing, 1994, paperback.

Brown, Margaret Wise. *Young Kangaroo*. Illustrated by Jennifer Dewey. New York: Hyperion Books for Children, 1993.

Eversole, Robyn. *Flood Fish*. Illustrated by Sheldon Greenberg. New York: Crown Books for Young Readers, 1995.

Eversole, Robyn. *The Gift Stone*. Illustrated by Allen Garns. New York: Alfred A. Knopf, 1998.

Fox, Mem. *Koala Lou*. Illustrated by Pamela Lofts. San Diego: Harcourt, 1989; Gulliver Books, 1994, paperback.

Fox, Mem. *Possum Magic*. Illustrated by Julie Vivas. San Diego: Gulliver Books, 1990; 1991, paperback.

Hirst, Robin, and Sally Hirst. *My Place in Space*. Illustrated by Roland Harvey with Joe Levine. New York: Orchard Books, 1992, paperback.

Kipling, Rudyard. *The Sing-Song of Old Man Kangaroo*. Illustrated by John Alfred Rowe. New York: Picture Book Studio, 1991.

Lester, Alison. *My Farm*. Illustrated by author. Boston: Houghton Mifflin Company, 1994; 1999, paperback.

Meeks, Arone Raymond. *Enora and the Black Crane.* Illustrated by author. New York: Scholastic, 1993.

Morpurgo, Michael. *Wombat Goes Walkabout.* Illustrated by Christian Birmingham. Cambridge, MA: Candlewick Press, 2000.

Rodell, Susanna. *Dear Fred.* Illustrated by Kim Gamble. New York: Ticknor & Fields Books for Young Readers, 1995.

Roth, Susan L. *The Biggest Frog in Australia.* Illustrated by author. New York: Simon & Schuster Books for Young Readers, 1996; Simon & Schuster Children's Publishing, 2000.

Seibert, Patricia. *Toad Overload: A True Tale of Nature Knocked Off Balance in Australia.* Illustrated by Jan Davey Ellis. Brookfield, CT: Millbrook Press, 1996.

Sheehan, Patty. *Kylie's Song.* Illustrated by Itoko Maeno. Santa Barbara, CA: Advocacy Press, 1988.

Thiele, Colin. *Farmer Schulz's Ducks.* Illustrated by Mary Milton. New York: HarperCollins Children's Books, 1988.

Trinca, Rod, and Kerry Argent. *One Woolly Wombat.* (A Cranky Nell Book) Illustrated by Kerry Argent. Brooklyn NY: Kane/Miller Book Publishers, 1985; 1987, paperback.

Vaughan, Marcia. *Snap!* Illustrated by Sascha Hutchinson. New York: Scholastic, 1996.

Vaughan, Marcia. *Wombat Stew.* Illustrated by Pamela Lofts. Parsippany, NJ: Silver Burdett Press, 1985; 1985, paperback.

Wheatley, Nadia. *My Place.* Illustrated by Donna Rawlins. Brooklyn: Kane/Miller Book Publishers, 1994, paperback.

Wild, Margaret. *Thank You, Santa*. Illustrated by Kerry
    Argent. New York: Scholastic Hardcover, 1992;
    Scholastic, 1994, paperback.
Winch, John. *The Old Man Who Loved to Sing*. Illustrated
    by author. New York: Scholastic, 1996; 1998, paperback.
Winch, John. *The Old Woman Who Loved to Read*.
    Illustrated by author. New York: Holiday House, 1997;
    1997, paperback.

"Afterward, they sat side by side on the beach and watched the glittering waves tumble, one after another, to shore."
—Wolfson. *Turtle Songs.*

Fiji
(Fiji Islands)

Margaret Olivia Wolfson's *Turtle Songs* is set on the island of Kandavu (Kadavu). When the princess and her small daughter, who dream of giant sea turtles, are kidnapped, they sing to the sea god, who rescues them by turning them into turtles. They still come back to Kandavu whenever the women and girls of their village, Namuana, sing the songs the princess taught them.

Book

Wolfson, Margaret Olivia. *Turtle Songs: A Tale for Mothers and Daughters.* Illustrated by Karla Sachi. Hillsboro, OR: Beyond Words Publishing, 1999.

<u>Europe</u>

"When Mr. Beethoven first lived in Vienna, he would sit down with orchestras to play his music, without a single note written out."
—Nichol. *Beethoven Lives Upstairs.*

Austria

Two picture books tell of the life of Wolfgang Amadeus Mozart.

Young Mozart, by Rachel Isadora, focuses on Mozart's life as a child prodigy, touring Europe with his parents and his sister, Nannerl. It also surveys Mozart's adult life, presenting his wife and sons; his friendship with Franz Joseph Haydn; his composition of The Marriage of Figaro, Don Giovanni, and The Magic Flute; and his death at the age of thirty-five.

Julie Downing's *Mozart Tonight*, a book for older children, focuses on the performance of Don Giovanni in Prague and the financial need for it to be successful. It looks back at Mozart's growing up in Salzburg, his concert performances about Europe, his encounter with the new Archbishop of Salzburg, and his love of Vienna.

Another famous composer, Ludwig van Beethoven, rents a room in Christoph's house in *Beethoven Lives Upstairs*, a book for the oldest children by Barbara Nichol. The story is told through correspondence between the boy and his uncle from September 7, 1822 to March 31, 1825. At first, Christoph cannot stand the noisy and eccentric Beethoven and wishes he would move out. However, he gradually comes to appreciate the musician and is amazed when he attends the first performance of Beethoven's Ninth Symphony.

Ruth Sawyer's *The Remarkable Christmas of the Cobbler's Sons* tells how the king of the goblins comes to a cobbler's hut in the Tirolean mountains. After being disagreeable to the cobbler's three cold and hungry sons, he magically fills their pockets with oranges, candy, baked goods, and coins.

Books

Downing, Julie. *Mozart Tonight*. Illustrated by author. New York: Bradbury Press, 1991; Aladdin Paperbacks, 1994, paperback.

Isadora, Rachel. *Young Mozart*. Illustrated by author. New York: Viking Penguin, 1997; Puffin Books, 1999.

Nichol, Barbara. *Beethoven Lives Upstairs*. Illustrated by Scott Cameron. New York: Orchard Books, an imprint of Scholastic Inc., 1999, paperback.

Sawyer, Ruth. *The Remarkable Christmas of the Cobbler's Sons*. Illustrated by Barbara Cooney. New York: Viking Children's Books, 1994, paperback; Viking Penguin, 1997, paperback.

"On the morning we left for America, however, everything rested quietly in the trunk which Grandfather and Avrom-Leyb had loaded onto the wagon."
—Bresnick-Perry. *Leaving for America.*

Belarus (Byelarus, formerly Belorussian Soviet Socialist Republic)

Belarus was formerly a constituent republic of the Union of Soviet Socialist Republics (U.S.S.R.), which was dissolved in 1991. Picture books set in the area of the former U.S.S.R. for which no other specific location is given are described under Russia (Russian Federation).

Three of the books tell of Jewish children who emigrate to the United States.

A book for older children, *Streets of Gold*, by Rosemary Wells, is based on the memoir of Mary Antin, "The Promised Land", which tells of her 1894 journey as a twelve year old from Polatsk to Boston. Portions of her diary are printed in borders next to the text. In what was then Russia, Mary was not permitted to go to school, her father's grocery store was closed by the czar's police, and her house and belongings taken away. Mary's father goes to the United States and sends money until the family has enough to take the train to Hamburg and thence a boat to Boston. When she had been in Boston for only half a year,

Mary Antin wrote a poem in her new language, English, that was published in the Boston Herald.

In *Leaving for America*, Roslyn Bresnick-Perry tells of how in 1929, when she was a little girl, she and her mother leave the Jewish town of Wysokie-Litewskie to join her father in the United States. It is a time of packing and of saying good-bye to her best friend and her relatives.

All the Lights in the Night, by Arthur A. Levine, which is for older children, tells of Moses and his younger brother Benjamin who travel in a potato cart from their home to Minsk where they take a train to Warsaw to get their papers and by train again and by ship to Palestine. Throughout their land journey, Benjamin is comforted by the story of Hanukkah and by their celebration of it with the tiny brass lamp which had been their grandmother's. The lamp then enables both of them to have enough money for their ship passage.

Maxine Rose Schur's *The Peddler's Gift* tells of Schnook, the supposedly foolish peddler from Pinsk, who travels to Leibush's village, which is on the road from Moscow to Minsk. When Leibush runs through the rainy night to return the dreidel he has taken from Schnook, he discovers just how different the wise and compassionate Schnook is from the other peddlers and thenceforth calls him by his real name, Shimon.

Books

Bresnick-Perry, Roslyn. *Leaving for America*. Illustrated by Mira Reisberg. San Francisco: Children's Book Press, 1992.

Levine, Arthur A. *All the Lights in the Night.* Illustrated by James E. Ransome. New York: Tambourine Books, 1991; Mulberry Books, 1997, paperback.

Schur, Maxine Rose. *The Peddler's Gift.* Illustrated by Kimberly Bulcken Root. New York: Dial Books for Young Readers, 1999.

Wells, Rosemary. *Streets of Gold.* Illustrated by Dan Andreasen. New York: Dial Books for Young Readers, 1999; 1999, paperback.

"Every morning, their king rode alone and unarmed along the streets of Denmark's capital, Copenhagen."
—Deedy. *The Yellow Star.*

Denmark

The picture book set in Greenland, a self-governing entity of Denmark, is described under Greenland.

A book for older children, by Carmen Agra Deedy, *The Yellow Star* relates a legend arising during the German occupation of Copenhagen. Thanks to King Christian, the Nazi flag does not fly atop the palace and many non-Jewish Danes join with Jewish residents in wearing the dreaded yellow star, thereby making it impossible to pick out those who are Jewish.

Book

Deedy, Carmen Agra. *The Yellow Star: The Legend of King Christian X of Denmark.* Illustrated by Henri Sørensen. Atlanta: Peachtree Publishers, 2000.

"Birdie was a cheerful old woman who lived with her marmalade cat in a bitty cottage just outside the village."
—Riggio. *Beware the Brindlebeast.*

England

Picture books whose setting embraces England and one or more other parts of the United Kingdom are described under United Kingdom.

Specific Locations

A number of England's counties are represented in picture books.

Cornwall and Isles of Scilly

In *Duffy and the Devil*, a Cornish folktale retold by Harve Zemach, Duffy makes a bargain with the devil that he will do all of her spinning and knitting. In return, she must go off with him at the end of three years if she cannot guess his name. Fortunately, the squire whom Duffy marries discovers the devil's name. As the devil vanishes, all his spinning turns into ashes and the squire finds himself unclad.

Sarah Garland's *Seeing Red* tells how Trewenna hates the scratchy red petticoat that her grandmother wants her to wear—that is, until the day that Napoleon's soldiers make a surprise landing at her village. Then, thanks to Trewenna, the village women and girls use their red petticoats to drive the French fleet away from Cornwall.

Mowser, a Cornish cat, lives a life of contentment with his fisherman pet, Tom, in *The Mousehole Cat*, by Antonia Barber. However, when severe weather, the Great Storm-Cat, keeps the fishermen home, their village has no food. Right before Christmas Mowser and Tom sail out into the storm and manage to catch a boatload of fish. Then, thanks to Mowser's purring in anticipation of the coming fish dinners, the Great Storm-Cat also purrs and, in the quieting waters, Tom and Mowser safely bring their fish to the welcoming villagers.

Cumbria

In the seventeen picture books described below, Beatrix Potter created a much-beloved cast of animals who are all interrelated, whether by family, shared experiences, or even by frequenting the same shops. A great number of these books are set in or near Sawrey or near Derwent Water in the Lake District of Cumbria, although the scenes in some were drawn from other locations (Taylor et al., 1987, pp. 95-161). Since the text of the stories makes it impossible for Peter Rabbit, for instance, to be separated in locale from his cousin, Benjamin Bunny, or for Benjamin and Flossie to be separated from their baby rabbits, the books are all included here under Cumbria. Two picture books about Beatrix Potter are, however, described under Historical figures.

In *The Tale of Peter Rabbit* three of Mrs. Rabbit's children—Flopsy, Mopsy, and Cottontail—are good little bunnies, but the fourth, the disobedient Peter, goes to Mr.

McGregor's garden. Unfortunately, he gets sick from eating the farmer's vegetables and is chased by Mr. McGregor. When, minus his clothes, he finally gets home, Mrs. Rabbit gives him camomile tea, while his sisters get to eat supper.

The Tale of Benjamin Bunny takes place immediately after *The Tale of Peter Rabbit*. Knowing that Mr. and Mrs. McGregor have gone out for the day, Benjamin and his ailing cousin Peter go back to Mr. McGregor's garden to retrieve Peter's clothes, which have been placed on a scarecrow. They get the clothes as well as some onions, but do not anticipate the presence of Mr. McGregor's cat.

When Benjamin Bunny grows up, he marries Peter's sister, Flopsy. In *The Tale of Mr. Tod*, their children, who are tiny rabbit babies, are kidnapped by Tommy Brock, a badger. Benjamin and Peter track him to one of the houses of the fox, Mr. Tod, but are unable to get in. However, when Mr. Tod returns to the house, he and Tommy Brock get into a dreadful fight which provides the opportunity for Peter and Benjamin to rescue the babies. This is a book for older children.

Benjamin and Flopsy's children are known as the Flopsy Bunnies. In *The Tale of the Flopsy Bunnies* the little bunnies are captured by Mr. McGregor when they fall asleep after eating a great amount of lettuce from his rubbish heap. Thanks to the helpful Thomasina Tittlemouse, the bunnies are freed from the sack in which he has placed them. Then their parents use the sack to play a trick on the McGregors.

Mrs. Tittlemouse is revealed as a fastidious housekeeper in *The Tale of Mrs. Tittlemouse*. However, she has trouble keeping her home tidy because of the intruders, who include Babbity Bumble, a bee, and Mr. Jackson, a toad.

Another of Peter's sisters, grown-up Cottontail, is one of the animals featured in *Appley Dapply's Nursery Rhymes*. Appley Dapply is a pie-loving mouse.

Also living in Sawrey is a family of cats, Tabitha Twitchit and her children, Mittens, Moppet, and Tom Kitten.

In *The Tale of Samuel Whiskers*, a book for older children, Mittens hides in a jar, Moppet hides in a flour barrel, and Tom Kitten hides in the chimney. However, Tom Kitten encounters a rat, Samuel Whiskers, in a room off the chimney. Samuel and his wife roll Tom up in dough and plan to eat him. Fortunately, Tabitha and her cousin Ribby discover where he is and engage a dog to remove a plank in the attic floor. Tom is safely reunited with his family, and Samuel Whiskers and his wife depart the premises.

Tabitha Twitchit dresses the three kittens in finery to attend her tea in *The Tale of Tom Kitten*. However, they not only mess up their clothes, but lose them altogether to the three Puddle-ducks, one of whom is Jemima Puddle-duck.

The Tale of Jemima Puddle-duck tells of the most foolish Jemima who lays her eggs amidst the feathers of a fox's woodshed. Fortunately, on the occasion on which she is to have dinner with the fox, the fox is chased off by the dog Kep and two puppies, and Jemima is saved from being the main course.

The *Tale of the Pie and the Patty Pan*, a book for older children, tells of the tea which the cat Ribby holds for Duchess, a dog. Because Duchess does not want to eat mouse pie, she tries to substitute her own veal and ham pie, which leads to most unexpected consequences. The patty pans as well as some of the food for the tea come from Tabitha Twitchit's store.

Another shop in the community is Ginger and Pickles, which is run by Ginger, a cat, and Pickles, a dog, and is featured in *The Tale of Ginger and Pickles*. Ginger and Pickles get much more business than Tabitha Twitchit because they give credit. Unfortunately, they also receive no money, with Samuel Whiskers running up an especially large bill. When the dog license and taxes come due, Ginger and Pickles close the shop. It is finally reopened by Sally Henny Penny, who offers penny bargains.

Among the customers at Ginger and Pickles are the dolls, Lucinda and Jane. In *The Tale of Two Bad Mice* the mice Tom Thumb and his wife Hunca Munca enter the dollhouse when Lucinda and Jane are away. Upset because the appetizing food in the house is not real, they destroy it, make a mess in the house, and take some of the dolls' belongings. However, they later amend for their behavior as Tom Thumb gives the dolls a sixpence and Hunca Munca sweeps their dollhouse daily.

The Tale of Mr. Jeremy Fisher tells of another of Ginger and Pickles' customers, the frog, Mr. Jeremy Fisher. Fishing for minnow on a lily-leaf boat, Mr. Jeremy is snatched by a trout, but, fortunately, the trout does not like the taste of his raincoat. Mr. Jeremy is released and even hosts a dinner for his friends, but it is of grasshopper, not of minnow.

A small girl, Lucie, discovers what has happened to her lost handkerchiefs in *The Tale of Mrs. Tiggy-winkle*. Mrs. Tiggy-winkle, a hedgehog, has been washing and ironing them as well as doing the laundry for such animals as Cock Robin, Sally Henny Penny, and Squirrel Nutkin.

The Tale of Squirrel Nutkin tells a story of the impertinent squirrel, who annoys the owl that lets the squirrels take nuts from his island. On the sixth day the seemingly impervious owl snatches up Squirrel Nutkin, but he is able to escape.

When Timmy Willie, a country mouse, crawls into a hamper, he makes an unexpected visit to town in *The Tale of Johnny Town-mouse*. Although Johnny Town-mouse tries to make Timmy Willie comfortable, the country mouse longs for his own home, his garden, and his friend Cock Robin. Later after Timmy Willie has gone back to the country, Johnny Town-mouse returns the visit, but decides that he prefers town life.

Aunt Pettitoes cannot take care of all her piglets in *The Tale of Pigling Bland*, a book for older children. One piglet, Pigling Bland, is sent to be hired out at the Lancashire market. Becoming lost and taken to a farmer's house, he discovers a girl piglet whom the farmer has stolen. They escape across the bridge to Westmorland.

Devon

The Tale of Little Pig Robinson, which is also by Potter, is a book for the oldest children. Little Pig Robinson, who has a silver ring in his nose, is sent off by his aunts to do the marketing. After a trek to town and time spent selling his aunts' goods and buying the items on their list, the young pig is kidnapped by a ship's cook. Robinson comes to enjoy the ship, especially the food, until he discovers that he is being fattened for the captain's birthday dinner. Thanks to the ship's pussy cat, he escapes to the island where the Bong tree grows. The pig prefers the tropical life to that in Devon—and is later visited by the honeymooning Pussy Cat and his bride, who is, of course, the Owl.

When Leon moves to Plymouth, he acquires an imaginary friend, Bob, in *Leon and Bob* by Simon James. Bob accompanies Leon everywhere until Leon meets a new neighbor, a real boy named Bob.

Dorset

Four picture books telling of the life of Mary Anning of Lyme Regis are described under Historical figures.

Gloucestershire

Potter's *The Tailor of Gloucester* relates for older children the story of the poor, old tailor in Gloucester who becomes so ill that it is unlikely he will finish the wedding coat and waistcoat which he is making for the mayor. However, thanks to the mice who live in his kitchen and belatedly to his cat, the wedding clothes are made in time—and the tailor becomes rich.

Greater London

Initially the main character in Michael Bond's children's novels, Paddington Bear is now featured in a number of picture books, also written by Bond.

In *Paddington Bear* the small bear, just arrived from Peru, meets Mr. and Mrs. Brown in London's Paddington Station. Naming him Paddington, they take him home with them. After creating havoc in the bathroom, a harbinger of his future adventures, Paddington falls asleep in an armchair in his new home near Hyde Park.

Paddington Bear: My Scrapbook is illustrated with maps, photographs, newspaper clippings, and pictures. It chronicles Paddington's life in Peru: his separation from his parents in an earthquake, his time with his Aunt Lucy, and her sending him abroad on an ocean liner. The book covers his meeting with the Browns, described in *Paddington Bear*, and introduces Mr. Curry and Mr. Gruber.

In *Paddington Bear and the Christmas Surprise*, Paddington and his family go to a department store so that they can see Santa Claus and ride through a Christmas display. After a disastrous experience capped by Paddington's knocking out the store lights, the family hastily leaves. However, the newspaper account of the mysterious bear at the store creates a boom in its business, and the family returns for a rewarding outing, capped this time by a jar of marmalade for Paddington.

Paddington goes with his friend, Mr. Gruber, to the Little Venice part of London in *Paddington Bear and the Busy Bee Carnival*. Paddington wins one of the contests when he finds forty-two things which start with the letter B.

Paddington Rides On! uses a comic strip format to tell how Paddington, who longs to be a cowboy, ends up lassoing a television cowboy's horse and performing in a wild west show.

A comic strip format is also used in *Paddington Meets the Queen*. As a result of his efforts to taste Windsor marmalade, Paddington rides with Queen Elizabeth II in her coach, is briefly imprisoned in the Tower of London, and takes marmalade sandwiches from Buckingham Palace.

Two picture books, written for the youngest children, present poems about the appealing bear.

Paddington Bear All Day Long tells of Paddington getting up; eating breakfast, lunch, and tea; and going to bed.

Paddington tears past just-opening stores as he goes to get a bun in *Paddington Bear Goes to Market*.

Five other Paddington books introduce letters, opposites, colors, numbers, and words to even the youngest children.

Paddington's ABC shows one object for each letter of the alphabet, each pictured with Paddington in a full-page illustration.

Paddington demonstrates such opposites as neat/messy and full/empty in *Paddington's Opposites*.

Paddington's not altogether successful experiences with the laundry and room decorating serve to present different colors and color mixing in *Paddington's Colors*.

Paddington's 123 is a counting book that extends from one Paddington Bear to twenty marmalade sandwiches.

A great number of objects are presented in *Paddington's First Word Book* as it traces Paddington's experiences starting with his arrival in London.

Another well-known book character, Madeline, travels from Paris to London with eleven other little girls and Miss Clavel in *Madeline in London*, by Ludwig Bemelmans. When they give their friend Pepito a retired horse for his birthday, the horse, ridden by Madeline and Pepito, suddenly resumes his former position as leader of the Queen's Life Guards as they parade about the city. Unfortunately, the horse cannot remain with Pepito, so he is taken back to Paris to join the others in their old vine-covered house. Additional books about Madeline are described under France.

A book for the oldest children, Rumer Godden's *Fu-dog* is a chapter book which includes full- and double-page paintings as well as illustrations on pages of text. Li-la is fascinated by the satin Fu-dog that she receives from her Chinese great uncle, who lives in London. The tiny dog even talks to her. On their own, Li-la and her brother Malcolm take the train from their Devon home to visit their great uncle. Surprises await them: their great uncle's restaurant is not located in the Chinese setting Li-la expected, but he has created such a setting in his garden; Malcolm is injured while trying to rescue Fu-dog in a Chinese New Year celebration; and Li-la's lost Fu-dog is replaced by a real Fu, a Pekingese.

It is an earlier time, the mid-nineteenth century, which is the setting of *Little Kit*, by Emily Arnold McCully. Mistaken for a boy, Kit leaves her life on the street to work for the owner of a flea circus. However, she discovers that she was better off before as the owner is cruel and deceitful and she and the fleas have no freedom. Kit manages to escape with the now unburdened fleas and finds a home with a girl whom she had befriended at the flea circus.

The Princess and the Peacocks, a book for older children, by Linda Merrill and Sarah Ridley, takes place during the same time period, in 1876 and 1877. The princess of the title is the portrait of a princess and the peacocks are the birds which the American artist James McNeill Whistler paints all over the room in which her portrait is hanging. Although the owner of the London house does not like peacocks, he concedes that Whistler has made the room more fitting for the princess. Whistler's Peacock Room is now in the Freer Gallery of Art in Washington, D.C.

Ann Keay Beneduce's retelling, *Jack and the Beanstalk* is set even earlier than the preceding two books, in the Tudor England of Queen Elizabeth. In this tale Jack, who lives near London, finds his father's guardian fairy near the top of the beanstalk. She explains that she was unable to prevent Jack's father from being robbed and killed by the giant and that it is she who has made the beans grow into a towering beanstalk. To avenge his father, Jack takes back part of his father's fortune and then steals the giant's hen that lays golden eggs and his magic harp.

Two other versions of this tale, both entitled *Jack and the Beanstalk*, are described in the Fables... category.

Descriptions of *Dick Whittington and His Cat*, *The Yeoman's Daring Daughter and the Princes in the Tower*, and *A Visit to William Blake's Inn* are included under Historical figures.

Northumberland

Six books by Kim Lewis are set on a sheep farm.

In *First Snow* tiny Sara, her teddy bear, and her mother go out to feed the sheep. As they return to the house in the falling snow, Sara realizes that Teddy is missing. However, one of the dogs brings Teddy to her.

Through text and illustrations *The Shepherd Boy* presents a year of life on a sheep farm. From spring on into winter little James tends his toy lamb in imitation of his shepherd father. Finally, on Christmas, he receives the crook, cap, whistle, and collie puppy he needs to be a shepherd boy.

In *The Last Train* Sara and her brother James, with the help of their parents, fix up an old railroad hut on what was once a railroad line. Then, in a thunderstorm, the children see, or imagine they see, a steam train passing by.

Floss tells the story of a border collie who loves to play ball with children in a park. Taken by her owner to work with his son on a distant sheep farm, Floss learns how to be a sheepdog, but misses her playing times. Happily, after she does well in the dog trials, Floss is able to be both a working and a ball-playing dog.

In *Just Like Floss*, the farm's children are allowed to keep one of Floss's puppies. The smallest, Sam, proves that he should be chosen as he constantly follows Floss and then bravely stands up to a ewe. The brother and sister pictured in the two books about Floss look like the Sara and James of Lewis's other books.

When a little lost lamb is found in *Emma's Lamb*, Emma decides that she would like to take care of him. However, after temporarily losing him when playing hide-and-seek, Emma understands that he is better off with his own mother.

North Yorkshire

James Herriot, who has recounted his experiences as a country veterinarian in well-known books for adults, has also written picture books. The eight books described here, which are for older children, take place in North Yorkshire and, in some cases, in its fictional village of Darrowby. Three feature cats, two tell of dogs, and the others relate stories of a lamb, a cow, and a horse.

In *The Christmas Day Kitten*, a dying mother cat, who is a stray, brings her kitten to Mrs. Pickering who has been kind to her. The kitten becomes a retriever cat and Mrs. Pickering's best Christmas present.

It is a stray kitten found in the winter cold in some rushes who is the subject of *Moses the Kitten*. Appropriately named Moses, he finds his place on the farm, becoming part of a litter of piglets, even joining them as they suckle the sow.

Oscar, Cat-About-Town tells of a very social cat, who likes to turn up at town events, whether a rummage sale, a soccer game, or a band practice.

The Market Square Dog is noticed begging in the market square by Herriot and a policeman. Later that week the policeman brings the dog, who has been injured, to the Herriots to be tended. After spending time in the kennels at the police station with no one wanting to adopt him, the dog becomes a pet of the policeman's daughters.

Gyp, the sheepdog in *Only One Woof* is a silent dog, who barks only once in his life. That is when he sees his brother, from whom he has been separated for more than a year, win a sheepdog trial.

A farmer, needing the money, reluctantly sends his favorite old cow to market in *Blossom Comes Home*. However, escaping from a nearby village, Blossom trots back to her stall and the farmer decides to keep her.

Smudge, the Little Lost Lamb likes to explore and, going under the wire, gets out of his field and cannot find the way back to his mother. Encountering a dog, a bull, and then roadside traffic, Smudge almost freezes until he is found by a young girl and then finally reunited with the boy who owns him—and with his mother ewe.

In *Bonny's Big Day* everyone is surprised when old John Skipton enters one of his horses in a show's family pets class. However, Bonny has been retired for over a decade and, outfitted like an old carthorse, she wins first prize.

Shropshire

Marguerite Henry's *Five O'Clock Charlie* tells of an old workhorse who is retired to a small field. Feeling useless, lonely, and longing for the daily apple tart he used to get at the Boar's Head, Charlie escapes from the field and is first in line for the popular tarts. Thereafter, he not only appears daily for his tart, but becomes the bell ringer, who alerts the countryside that the tarts are ready.

Warwickshire

Hear, Hear, Mr. Shakespeare, which is set in Stratford-upon-Avon, is described under Historical figures.

General

Alphabet, counting, and word books

Alfie's ABC by Shirley Hughes is an alphabet book presenting Alfie; his little sister, Annie Rose; his parents; his grandmother; his cat; his special knitted elephant; his neighbors, the MacNallys; his best friend, Bernard; and his activities.

Alfie's family and friends are also featured in Hughes's

Alfie's 1 2 3. Other books about this English family are included under Celebrations; Poetry and songs; and Stories.

Another counting book by Hughes, *Lucy & Tom's 1.2.3.*, incorporates numbers into a look at a family Saturday spent at home, shopping, and going to Granny's birthday tea party.

An alphabet book, a counting book, and a word book, all featuring the British bear, Paddington, are described under Greater London.

Celebrations

It is not Alfie's birthday, but the fifty-second birthday of his neighbor, Bob MacNally, which is celebrated in Hughes's *Alfie and the Birthday Surprise*. Still mourning the death of his old cat, Bob is delighted by the surprise party given by his family and Alfie's family. He is especially pleased with his daughter Maureen's gift, a kitten. Additional Alfie books are found under Alphabet, counting, and word books; Poetry and songs; and Stories.

Fables, fairy tales, folktales, legends, myths, and proverbs (including original works)

In addition to the Beneduce retelling, *Jack and the Beanstalk*, described under the county of Greater London, Steven Kellogg and Richard Walker have retold this tale in books with the same title. In their versions there is no mention of Jack's father or of the father's guardian angel.

It is an ogre, not a giant, whom Jack encounters in the Kellogg retelling, which includes medieval knights in its paintings.

The English tale is given a more generic setting by Walker with no mention of an Englishman's blood. In this humorous version Jack brings back on the same day not only a bag of gold, a golden-egg-laying goose, and a magic harp, but also the giant's wife who wants to go with him.

Both Barbara Seuling in *The Teeny Tiny Woman* and Jill Bennett in *Teeny Tiny* retell the tale of the teeny tiny woman who takes a teeny tiny bone from a church graveyard. At night she hears a teeny tiny voice demanding its return and yells out for its owner to reclaim it.

Seuling's illustrations show the nightcap-wearing woman in bed with a nightcap-wearing duck.

In the Bennett version, Tomie dePaola's illustrations present a dog and a cat as the woman's companions as well as ghosts who watch the proceedings and then take back the bone.

It is the scary Hobyahs, not ghosts, who are the title characters of Robert D. San Souci's *The Hobyahs*, a book for older children. The old man and old woman with whom a little girl lives foolishly drive off the five dogs who protect them. The little girl is then captured by the Hobyahs, but the five dogs come to her rescue—and may still be living with her.

Because she has been kind to some bread, a cow, and an apple tree, a girl escapes from a witch and retrieves her family's stolen money in *Up the Chimney*, which is retold by Margaret Hodges. However, when her sister tries to duplicate the adventure, she refuses the requests of the bread, the cow, and the apple tree and returns penniless.

Thrice a witch captures Johnny Buttermilk in Jan Wahl's *Little Johnny Buttermilk.* Thrice Johnny Buttermilk gets free and tricks the witch. Finally, on the third occasion, the frustrated witch explodes with anger.

An old woman drags home what starts out as a kettle of gold coins in *Beware the Brindlebeast,* which is retold by Anita Riggio. On the way there it turns into a barrel of apples, a pumpkin, and finally the dreaded Brindlebeast. However, when the old woman shows no fear at the appearance of the terrible monster, it is revealed as a tiny little man who becomes her friend.

In Eric A. Kimmel's adaptation, *The Old Woman and Her Pig,* a different old woman has trouble getting the pig she has bought to go over a stile. In this cumulative tale, it is not until the woman gets hay for a cow, that the chain of events occurs that enables the old woman to get home with her pig.

The Old Woman Who Lived in a Vinegar Bottle, by Margaret Read MacDonald, tells of still another old woman, this time one who feels too confined in her vinegar bottle home. A fairy transforms her dwelling place into ever larger living quarters, but the ungrateful, demanding woman is never satisfied—and is finally returned to her vinegar bottle.

In Brian Alderson's *The Tale of the Turnip,* the king gives a farmer a wagonful of gold for his gigantic turnip. However, when his rich pompous neighbor attempts to secure a similar reward, he receives instead the turnip.

Historical figures

The legends of King Arthur and his knights may be

based on a leader of the Britons, who lived in the sixth century. Distinguished by its stained glass paintings, *Arthur and the Sword*, which is retold by Robert Sabuda, tells of the sword set in a stone which only the rightful king of England can remove and of the unsuccessful efforts of the knights to do so. However, young Arthur, having forgotten his brother's sword and urgently needing a substitute, pulls the sword out of the stone and takes it to his brother. Thereupon, it is revealed that Arthur is the son of the late King Uther and is indeed King Arthur.

Marcia Brown's *Dick Whittington and His Cat* tells another legend, how the cat bought for a penny by Dick is sent off for trade and, because of her mousing abilities, makes a fortune for her former master. Thence Richard Whittington, the once poor country boy, becomes Lord Mayor of London in 1397 and serves three separate terms in that position.

The fate of Prince Edward and Prince Richard, the young sons of King Edward IV of England, who were imprisoned in the Tower of London in 1483, remains a mystery. In Elaine Clayton's *The Yeoman's Daring Daughter and the Princes in the Tower*, Jane, whose father is a yeoman at the Tower of London, communicates with the brothers via her raven. When she hears of their uncle's plan to become king, she helps them escape. They eventually settle in an unspecified place.

Bruce Koscielniak's *Hear, Hear, Mr. Shakespeare*, a book for the oldest children, tells how a troupe of traveling players arrives at Shakespeare's house and garden in Stratford-upon-Avon in Warwickshire County. When the rain washes out the words of their play, Shakespeare writes them a new one. The troupe then sets off for London to perform the play before Queen Elizabeth I. The many small animals in the illustrations are shown reciting relevant Shakespearean quotations.

It is the imaginary London inn of another famous English writer, the poet William Blake, which is featured in the Newbery Medal winner, *A Visit to William Blake's Inn*, by Nancy Willard. Also a book for the oldest children, the poems tell the fanciful tale of a young boy's visit to the inn, which is occupied by dragons, a bear, a rabbit, a tiger, and other animals and of his meeting with William Blake, who tells a story to the tiger and leads a stroll upon the Milky Way.

My Dear Noel, by Jane Johnson, tells the story of Beatrix Potter and her friendship with the Moore family, who lived in London. Following a visit with the family on which she brings her rabbit named Peter, Miss Potter departs for Scotland and Noel, the eldest child, becomes ill. When he receives mail from Miss Potter, it is not a letter, but an illustrated story about Peter. Noel Moore kept the story for seven years before loaning it to Potter who revised it and then published it as *The Tale of Peter Rabbit*.

Alexandra Wallner's *Beatrix Potter* is a biography of Potter, which tells of her lonely childhood during which she enjoys drawing her pets; of her summers painting in Scotland; of her study of mushrooms; of her writing *The Tale of Peter Rabbit* and later books; and of her life in the Lake District.

Mary Anning was a fossil collector who lived in Lyme Regis in Dorset County from 1799 to 1847. Four books for older children, differing markedly in detail, present the story of the girl who thrilled the scientific world with her ichthyosaur fosssil. Three of the books, *Stone Girl, Bone*

Girl by Laurence Anholt, *Mary Anning and the Sea Dragon* by Jeannine Atkins, and *The Fossil Girl* by Catherine Brighton focus on this discovery.

In the Anholt story, Anning is pictured as an only child, very close to her father who dies shortly before her discovery. It is her father who introduces her to collecting fossils in the clay cliffs. She learns about fossils and the probable existence of a "sea monster" fossil from the Philpot sisters. Aided by a dog, Mary finds the ichthyosaur, which is excavated with the help of quarrymen.

Mary has brothers in the Atkins book, but it is she who finds the icthyosaur. She spends months, with little help, working with hammer and chisel to reveal its skeleton.

Mary goes fossil hunting with her brother Joe in the Brighton book, and it is he who finds the icthyosaur head, but Mary who works at removing it.

Rare Treasure, by Don Brown, is a biography of Mary Anning. In this account a skull is found by Joseph and a skeleton found a year later by Mary. This book also tells of Mary's discovery of the first complete plesiosaur fossil and of her other fossil discoveries.

Nonfiction

In a wordless picture book, *The Story of a Main Street*, John S. Goodall uses watercolor paintings to depict life outside and inside the buildings that front what begins as a medieval road and is now a busy urban street. The half-page inserts enrich the portrayal of each historical period.

Mick Manning's *A Ruined House* presents the attractions

of a broken-down sixteenth century stone farmhouse that has become home for countless animals and wild plants.

Poetry and songs

Melissa Sweet's illustrations of the carol, *On Christmas Day in the Morning*, show each of the animals mentioned, from the digging pig to the winnowing minnow, having its own farm. This is a book for the youngest children.

In Pat Hutchins's *The Wind Blew*, which is also for the youngest children, the blowing wind picks up an umbrella, a judge's wig, newspapers, and other objects and then drops them down before heading out to sea.

Toddler Annie Rose is the subject of her own book for the youngest children in Hughes's *Rhymes for Annie Rose*. Twenty-seven poems tell of Annie Rose: of her early awakening; of being in her house, in the town, and in the country; of her toys; of her pretending; and of her going to bed. Other books about Annie Rose and her older brother Alfie are described under Alphabet, counting, and word books; Celebrations; and Stories.

Two picture books presenting poems about Paddington Bear are included under Greater London.

Stories

In addition to *Alfie's ABC* and *Alfie's 1 2 3* (included under Alphabet, counting, and word books), *Alfie and the Birthday Surprise* (under Celebrations): and *Rhymes for Annie Rose* (under Poetry and songs), three books by Hughes about Alfie and his little sister are described below.

All about Alfie is a compilation of four previously published stories: "Alfie Gets in First" (Alfie locks himself in his house, but finally manages to open the door himself); "Alfie's Feet" (Alfie likes his new boots much better when he puts them on the correct feet); "Alfie Gives a Hand" (Alfie hangs on to his blanket when he attends a birthday party, but then puts it aside to hold the hand of a little girl more scared than he is); and "An Evening at Alfie's" (a water pipe bursts when Maureen is baby-sitting Alfie and Annie Rose).

Among the stories included in *The Big Alfie and Annie Rose Storybook* is one about Annie Rose surprising everyone when she says Bernard's name and another about Annie Rose's joining the wedding procession when Alfie is a page.

A pig sticks its snout into Alfie and his father's tent and Alfie's special stone gets lost at the seashore in two of the stories in *The Big Alfie Out of Doors Storybook*.

Hughes tells four stories of a different neighborhood in *Tales of Trotter Street*, a book for older children. Mae falls off her chair while performing in a Christmas play; the Patterson family and their neighbors work quickly to lay fast-setting concrete; Carlos gets a homemade birthday go-cart from his older brother; Sam manages to remove the message which would hurt the feelings of a difficult neighborhood lady;—and together the neighbors enjoy a non-bicycle race and an outdoor party.

In *Sorry, Miss Folio!* by Jo Furtado a boy borrows a book from Miss Folio, the librarian. Going to the library every month thereafter, he presents fantastic excuses for not returning the book. Finally, after twelve months, Santa Claus delivers the book to Miss Folio.

In Pat Hutchins's *The Doorbell Rang* Ma bakes a dozen cookies for tea. Her son and daughter figure that they will each get six cookies, but as the doorbell keeps ringing and more and more children arrive, the portions go down to one apiece. No one wants to heed the doorbell when it rings again, but happily it is Grandma with a whole tray of her special cookies.

A Sunday with Grandpa, by Philippe Dupasquier, tells of the happy day a young girl and her family spend on her grandfather's farm. Although her grandfather is very old and lives by himself, he is quite active and will not consider leaving his life as a country dweller.

British twins are cast overboard during an ocean liner accident in *Oh, Brother*, a book for older children by Arthur Yorinks. Landing in New York City, the quarrelsome boys manage to antagonize everyone they meet except for an elderly tailor who takes them in. When he dies, the brothers disguise themselves as his elderly relatives and continue his tailoring business. Taken to England by their customers, the Guggenheims, they discover that their parents are not dead, but are working for the Queen. She proclaims them tailors to her son, the Prince of Wales.

The Making of a Knight, a book by Patrick O'Brien for older children, recounts the process by which a fifteenth century boy becomes a knight. James is made a page at age seven; becomes a squire at fourteen; is knighted at twenty-one; and after several years rides off from the castle as a knight-errant.

Animals are featured in four of the stories.

Buddy, a cat, is the copycat in *Copycat*, Ruth Brown's book for even the youngest children. Buddy copies his mother, his sister, a dog, squirrels, and birds. Despite breaking teeth on a dog bone, Buddy remains a copycat.

In Graham Oakley's *The Church Mice and the Ring*, Sampson, the cat, and the numerous church mice try out several ingenious plans to get a home for the dog who is eating up their food. However, it is not until they successfully execute the wildest plan of all that the poorly-behaved dog is adopted.

Charlie's Checklist, by Rory S. Lerman, is also about a dog who wants a home, one in the city. Charlie the puppy and Chester, a boy from a nearby farm, read through the numerous responses from the personal ad Charlie runs in a London paper. Finally, Charlie realizes that it is Chester who best meets his criteria, and Charlie happily remains a country dog.

In a book for older children, Jane Yolen's *Piggins*, Piggins is a pig who is a butler to a fox couple, Mr. and Mrs. Reynard. At a dinner party which eight guests are attending, Mrs. Reynard's diamond necklace is stolen. In this case, it is not the butler who did it, but the butler who solves the crime.

Books

Alderson, Brian. *The Tale of the Turnip*. Illustrated by Fritz Wegner. Cambridge, MA: Candlewick Press, 1999.

Anholt, Laurence. *Stone Girl, Bone Girl: The Story of Mary Anning*. Illustrated by Sheila Moxley. New York: Orchard Books, 1999.

Atkins, Jeannine. *Mary Anning and the Sea Dragon*. Illustrated by Michael Dooling. New York: Farrar, Straus & Giroux, 1999.

Barber, Antonia. *The Mousehole Cat.* Illustrated by Nicole Bayley. New York: Simon & Schuster Children's Publishing, 1996.

Bemelmans, Ludwig. *Madeline in London.* Illustrated by author. New York: Viking Children's Books, 1961; Puffin, 1977, paperback.

Beneduce, Ann Keay, reteller. *Jack and the Beanstalk.* Illustrated by Gennady Spirin. New York: Philomel Books, 1999.

Bennett, Jill, reteller. *Teeny Tiny.* Illustrated by Tomie dePaola. New York: Paperstar, 1998, paperback.

Bond, Michael. *Paddington Bear.* Illustrated by R. W. Alley. New York: HarperCollins Publishers, 1998.

Bond, Michael. *Paddington Bear: My Scrapbook.* Illustrated by R. W. Alley. New York: Harper Festival, 1999.

Bond, Michael. *Paddington Bear All Day.* Illustrated by R. W. Alley. New York: HarperCollins Children's Books, 1998.

Bond, Michael. *Paddington Bear and the Busy Bee Carnival.* Illustrated by R. W. Alley. New York: HarperCollins Children's Books, 1998.

Bond, Michael. *Paddington Bear and the Christmas Surprise.* Illustrated by R. W. Alley. New York: HarperCollins Children's Books, 1997; 1999, paperback.

Bond, Michael. *Paddington Bear Goes to Market.* Illustrated by R. W. Alley. New York: HarperCollins Children's Books, 1998.

Bond, Michael. *Paddington Meets the Queen.* Illustrated by John Lobban. New York: Harper Festival, 1993.

Bond, Michael. *Paddington Rides On!* Illustrated by John Lobban. New York: Harper Festival, 1993.

Bond, Michael. *Paddington's ABC.* Illustrated by John Lobban. Devised by Carol Watson. New York: Viking Children's Books, 1991, paperback; Puffin Books, 1996, paperback.

Bond, Michael. *Paddington's Colors.* Illustrated by John Lobban. Devised by Carol Watson. New York: Viking Children's Books, 1991, paperback; Puffin Books, 1996, paperback.

Bond, Michael. *Paddington's First Word Book.* Illustrated by John Lobban. New York: Puffin Books, 1998, paperback.

Bond, Michael. *Paddington's 123.* Illustrated by John Lobban. Devised by Carol Watson. New York: Viking Children's Books, 1991, paperback; Puffin Books, 1996, paperback.

Bond, Michael. *Paddington's Opposites.* Illustrated by John Lobban. Devised by Carol Watson. New York: Viking Children's Books, 1991, paperback; Puffin Books, 1996, paperback.

Brighton, Catherine. *The Fossil Girl: Mary Anning's Dinosaur Discovery.* Illustrated by author. Brookfield, CT: Millbrook Press, 1999.

Brown, Don. *Rare Treasure: Mary Anning and Her Remarkable Discoveries.* Illustrated by author. Boston: Houghton Mifflin Company, 1999.

Brown, Marcia. *Dick Whittington and His Cat.* Illustrated by author. New York: Charles Scribner's Sons Books for Young Readers, 1988; Aladdin Paperbacks, 1997.

Brown, Ruth. *Copycat.* Illustrated by author. New York: Dutton Children's Books, 1994, paperback; Viking Penguin, 1999, paperback.

Clayton, Elaine. *The Yeoman's Daring Daughter and the Princes in the Tower.* Illustrated by author. New York: Crown Publishers, 1999.

Dupasquier, Philippe. *A Sunday with Grandpa.* Illustrated by author. London: Andersen Press (Distributed by Trafalgar Square), 1999.

Furtado, Jo. *Sorry, Miss Folio!* Illustrated by Frédéric Joos. Brooklyn, NY: Kane/Miller Publishers, 1992, paperback.

Garland, Sarah. *Seeing Red.* Illustrated by Tony Ross. Brooklyn, NY: Kane/Miller Book Publishers, 1996.

Godden, Rumer. *Fu-dog.* Illustrated by Valerie Littlewood. New York: N A L Dutton, 1999, paperback.

Goodall, John S. *The Story of a Main Street.* Illustrated by author. New York: Margaret K. McElderry Books, 1987.

Henry, Marguerite. *Five O'Clock Charlie.* Illustrated by Wesley Dennis. New York: Aladdin Paperbacks, 1995, paperback.

Herriot, James. *Blossom Comes Home.* Illustrated by Ruth Brown. New York: St. Martin's Press, 1993, paperback.

Herriot, James. *Bonny's Big Day.* Illustrated by Ruth Brown. New York: St. Martin's Press, 1991, paperback.

Herriot, James. *The Christmas Day Kitten.* Illustrated by Ruth Brown. New York: St. Martin's Press, 1993, paperback.

Herriot, James. *The Market Square Dog.* Illustrated by Ruth Brown. New York: St. Martin's Press, 1991, paperback.

Herriot, James. *Moses the Kitten.* Illustrated by Peter Barrett. New York: St. Martin's Press, 1991, paperback.

Herriot, James. *Only One Woof.* Illustrated by Peter Barrett. New York: St. Martin's Press, 1993, paperback.

Herriot, James. *Oscar, Cat-About-Town.* Illustrated by Ruth Brown. New York: St. Martin's Press, 1990; 1993, paperback.

Herriot, James. *Smudge, the Little Lost Lamb*. Illustrated by Ruth Brown. New York: St. Martin's Press, 1991; 1994.

Hodges, Margaret, reteller. *Up the Chimney*. Illustrated by Amanda Harvey. New York: Holiday House, 1998.

Hughes, Shirley. *Alfie and the Birthday Surprise*. Illustrated by author. New York: Lothrop, Lee & Shepard Books, 1998.

Hughes, Shirley. *Alfie's ABC*. Illustrated by author. New York: Morrow Junior Books, 1998.

Hughes, Shirley. *Alfie's 1 2 3*. Illustrated by author. New York: Lothrop, Lee & Shepard Books, 2000.

Hughes, Shirley. *All about Alfie*. Illustrated by author. New York: Lothrop, Lee & Shepard Books, 1997.

Hughes, Shirley. *The Big Alfie and Annie Rose Storybook*. Illustrated by author. New York: Lothrop, Lee & Shepard Books, 1989.

Hughes, Shirley. *The Big Alfie Out of Doors Storybook*. Illustrated by author. New York: Lothrop, Lee & Shepard Books, 1992.

Hughes, Shirley. *Lucy & Tom's 1.2.3.* Illustrated by author. New York: N A L Dutton, 1999, paperback.

Hughes, Shirley. *Rhymes for Annie Rose*. Illustrated by author. New York: Lothrop, Lee & Shepard Books, 1995.

Hughes, Shirley. *Tales of Trotter Street*. Illustrated by author. Cambridge, MA: Candlewick Press, 1997.

Hutchins, Pat. *The Doorbell Rang*. Illustrated by author. New York: Greenwillow Books, 1986; Mulberry Books, 1989, paperback.

Hutchins, Pat. *The Wind Blew*. Illustrated by author. New York: Aladdin Paperbacks, 1993.

James, Simon. *Leon and Bob*. Illustrated by author. Cambridge, MA: Candlewick Press, 1997.

Johnson, Jane. *My Dear Noel: The Story of a Letter from Beatrix Potter*. Illustrated by author. New York: Dial Books for Young Readers, 1999.

Kellogg, Steven, reteller. *Jack and the Beanstalk*. Illustrated by reteller. New York: Morrow Junior Books, 1991; Mulberry Books, 1997, paperback.

Kimmel, Eric A., adapter. *The Old Woman and Her Pig*. Illustrated by Giora Carmi. New York: Holiday House, 1992; 1992, paperback.

Koscielniak, Bruce. *Hear, Hear, Mr. Shakespeare: Story, Illustrations, and Selections from Shakespeare's Plays*. Illustrated by author. Boston: Houghton Mifflin Company, 1998.

Lerman, Rory S. *Charlie's Checklist*. Illustrated by Alison Bartlett. New York: Orchard Books, 1997.

Lewis, Kim. *Emma's Lamb*. Illustrated by author. Cambridge, MA: Candlewick Press, 1998.

Lewis, Kim. *First Snow*. Illustrated by author. Cambridge, MA: Candlewick Press, 1993; 1996, paperback.

Lewis, Kim. *Floss*. Illustrated by author. Cambridge, MA: Candlewick Press, 1992; 1994, paperback.

Lewis, Kim. *Just like Floss*. Illustrated by author. Cambridge, MA: Candlewick Press, 1998; 2000, paperback.

Lewis, Kim. *The Last Train*. Illustrated by author. Cambridge, MA: Candlewick Press, 1996, paperback.

Lewis, Kim. *The Shepherd Boy*. Illustrated by author. New York: Four Winds Press, 1990.

McCully, Emily Arnold. *Little Kit: or, The Industrious Flea Circus Girl*. Illustrated by author. New York: Dial Books for Young Readers, 1995, paperback.

MacDonald, Margaret Read. *The Old Woman Who Lived in a Vinegar Bottle: A British Fairy Tale.* Illustrated by Nancy Dunaway Fowlkes. Little Rock, AR: August House Publishers, 1995; Buccaneer Books, 1995.

Manning, Mick. *A Ruined House.* (Read and Wonder) Illustrated by author. Cambridge, MA: Candlewick Press, 1996, paperback.

Merrill, Linda, and Sarah Ridley. *The Princess and the Peacocks: or, The Story of the Room.* Illustrated by Tennessee Dixon. New York: Hyperion Books for Children in Association with the Freer Gallery of Art, Smithsonian Institution, 1993.

Oakley, Graham. *The Church Mice and the Ring.* Illustrated by author. New York: Atheneum Books for Young Readers, 1992.

O'Brien, Patrick. *The Making of a Knight: How Sir James Earned His Armor.* Watertown, MA: Charlesbridge Publishing, 1998.

On Christmas Day in the Morning: A Traditional Carol. Illustrated by Melissa Sweet. Foreword by John Langstaff. Cambridge, MA: Candlewick Press, 1999.

Potter, Beatrix. *Appley Dapply's Nursery Rhymes.* (Original Peter Rabbit Books: No. 22) Illustrated by author. New York: Frederick Warne & Co., 1987.

Potter, Beatrix. *The Tailor of Gloucester.* (Original Peter Rabbit Books: No. 3) Illustrated by author. New York: Frederick Warne & Co., 1987.

Potter, Beatrix. *The Tale of Benjamin Bunny.* (Original Peter Rabbit Books: No. 4) Illustrated by author. New York: Frederick Warne & Co., 1987.

Potter, Beatrix. *The Tale of Ginger and Pickles*. (Original Peter Rabbit Books: No. 18) Illustrated by author. New York: Frederick Warne & Co., 1987, paperback.

Potter, Beatrix. *The Tale of Jemima Puddle-duck*. (Original Peter Rabbit Books: No. 9) Illustrated by author. New York: Frederick Warne & Co., 1987; 1987, paperback.

Potter, Beatrix. *The Tale of Johnny Town-mouse*. (Original Peter Rabbit Books: No. 13) Illustrated by author. New York: Frederick Warne & Co., 1987.

Potter, Beatrix. *The Tale of Little Pig Robinson*. (Original Peter Rabbit Books: No. 19) Illustrated by author. New York: Frederick Warne & Co., 1987; 1987, paperback.

Potter, Beatrix. *The Tale of Mr. Jeremy Fisher*. (Original Peter Rabbit Books: No. 7) Illustrated by author. New York: Frederick Warne & Co., 1987.

Potter, Beatrix. *The Tale of Mr. Tod*. (Original Peter Rabbit Books: No. 14) Illustrated by author. New York: Frederick Warne & Co., 1987.

Potter, Beatrix. *The Tale of Mrs. Tiggy-winkle*. (Original Peter Rabbit Books: No. 6) Illustrated by author. New York: Frederick Warne & Co., 1987.

Potter, Beatrix. *The Tale of Mrs. Tittlemouse*. (Original Peter Rabbit Books: No. 11) Illustrated by author. New York: Frederick Warne & Co., 1987.

Potter, Beatrix. *The Tale of Peter Rabbit*. (Original Peter Rabbit Books: No. 1) Illustrated by author. New York: Frederick Warne & Co., 1987.

Potter, Beatrix. *The Tale of Pigling Bland*. (Original Peter Rabbit Books: No. 15) Illustrated by author. New York: Frederick Warne & Co., 1987; 1987, paperback.

Potter, Beatrix. *The Tale of Samuel Whiskers: or, The Roly-Poly Pudding.* (Original Peter Rabbit Books: No. 16) Illustrated by author. New York: Frederick Warne & Co., 1987; 1987, paperback.

Potter, Beatrix. *The Tale of Squirrel Nutkin.* (Original Peter Rabbit Books: No. 2) Illustrated by author. New York: Frederick Warne & Co., 1987.

Potter, Beatrix. *The Tale of the Flopsy Bunnies.* (Original Peter Rabbit Books: No. 10) Illustrated by author. New York: Frederick Warne & Co., 1987.

Potter, Beatrix. *The Tale of the Pie and the Patty-pan.* (Original Peter Rabbit Books: No. 17) Illustrated by author. New York: Frederick Warne & Co., 1987, paperback.

Potter, Beatrix. *The Tale of Tom Kitten.* (Original Peter Rabbit Books: No. 8) Illustrated by author. New York: Frederick Warne & Co., 1987; 1987, paperback.

Potter, Beatrix. *The Tale of Two Bad Mice.* (Original Peter Rabbit Books: No. 5) Illustrated by author. New York: Frederick Warne & Co., 1987.

Riggio, Anita, reteller. *Beware the Brindlebeast.* Illustrated by reteller. Honesdale, PA: Boyds Mills Press, 1997, paperback.

Sabuda, Robert, reteller. *Arthur and the Sword.* Illustrated by reteller. New York: Atheneum, 1995; Simon & Schuster Children's Publishing, 1998.

San Souci, Robert D. *The Hobyahs.* Illustrated by Alexi Natchev. New York: Bantam Doubleday Dell Books for Young Readers, 1993; Picture Yearling, 1996, paperback.

Seuling, Barbara, reteller. *The Teeny Tiny Woman: An Old English Ghost Tale.* Illustrated by reteller. New York: Puffin, 1978, paperback.

Wahl, Jan. *Little Johnny Buttermilk: After an Old English Folktale*. Illustrated by Jennifer Mazzucco. Little Rock, AR: August House Publishers, 1999.

Walker, Richard, reteller. *Jack and the Beanstalk*. Illustrated by Niamh Sharkey. New York: Barefoot Books, 1999.

Wallner, Alexandra. *Beatrix Potter*. Illustrated by author. New York: Holiday House, 1995; 1995, paperback.

Willard, Nancy. *A Visit to William Blake's Inn: Poems for Innocent and Experienced Travelers*. Illustrated by Alice and Martin Provensen. San Diego: Harcourt, 1981; Voyager Books, 1982, paperback.

Yolen, Jane. *Piggins*. Illustrated by Jane Dyer. San Diego: Harcourt, 1987; 1992, paperback.

Yorinks, Arthur. *Oh, Brother*. Illustrated by Richard Egielski. New York: Farrar, Straus & Giroux, 1989; Sunburst Books, 1991, paperback.

Zemach, Harve, reteller. *Duffy and the Devil: A Cornish Tale*. Illustrated by Margot Zemach. New York: Farrar, Straus & Giroux, 1973; 1986, paperback.

"Warning the birds of the coming of the snows, she showed them the special sky path to the warm lands."
—Moroney. *Elinda Who Danced in the Sky.*

Estonia (formerly Estonian Soviet Socialist Republic)

Estonia was formerly a constituent republic of the Union of Soviet Socialist Republics (U.S.S.R.), which was dissolved in December 1991. Estonia declared its independence in August 1991. Picture books set in the area of the former U.S.S.R. for which no other specific location is given are described under Russia (Russian Federation).

Elinda Who Danced in the Sky, which is adapted by Lynn Moroney, relates the folktale of Elinda, who turns down the North Star, the Moon, and the Sun as suitors and then plans to marry the Northern Lights. When he is unable to return to marry her, she is borne up into the sky by her friends, the birds, where she still guides their migrations. Her wedding veil is known as the Milky Way.

Book

Moroney, Lynn, adapter. *Elinda Who Danced in the Sky: An Estonian Folktale.* Illustrated by Veg Reisberg. San Francisco: Children's Book Press, 1990.

"Every evening as the sun is setting and the lights of Paris are turning the dusk into a twinkle, Minou can be seen crossing the bridge to the Île Saint Louis—to no one knows where."
—Bingham. *Minou.*

France
République française

Books set in the French overseas departments of French Guiana and Martinique are described in those two sections.

Specific Locations

Several regions of France are represented in the picture books described below.

Aquitaine

The Cave Painter of Lascaux by Roberta Angeletti, tells of a girl who visits Lascaux Cave near Montignac in the department of Dordogne. In addition to viewing the paintings, both she—and a guard—learn about Paleolithic people from a surprising stranger.

Île-de-France

A number of picture books are set in Paris, which is located in the department, Ville-de-Paris.

France's best known storybook child is undoubtedly Madeline, whose adventures are chronicled in the verses and illustrations of Ludwig Bemelmans.

In the first book, *Madeline*, the reader is introduced to this little girl who lives with eleven other girls and the ever-vigilant Miss Clavel in a house in Paris and whose appendectomy lands her in the hospital, much to the envy of the other children.

In *Madeline's Rescue*, a Caldecott Medal winner, the adventurous Madeline falls off a bridge and is rescued by a dog whom the girls name Genevieve. When Genevieve is dispatched from the house by the head of the board of trustees, the little girls unsuccessfully scour Paris in search of her. They are delighted when Genevieve returns that night—and then gives birth to a dozen puppies.

Everyone in the house but Madeline is abed with colds on Christmas Eve in *Madeline's Christmas*. She buys twelve rugs from a rug merchant who comes to the door and, then, when he returns half-frozen, she takes care of him. In gratitude he transforms the rugs into magic carpets which carry the little girls to their homes for Christmas.

The Ambassador of Spain, his wife, and their son Pepito move in next door in *Madeline and the Bad Hat*. Pepito taunts the girls and is cruel to animals until a frightening experience with a cat and a pack of dogs transforms him into an animal lover. In fact, his newly acquired love of animals prompts him to release the animals in the zoo.

In *Madeline and the Gypsies* Madeline and Pepito are left stranded at the top of a Ferris wheel operated by gypsies, who take the children with them as their carnival tours France. Despite being sewn into a lion suit, Madeline and Pepito are finally reunited with Miss Clavel and the eleven little girls and return with them to Paris. Although this book shows other parts of France as well as Paris, it is included under Île-de-France because of Madeline's close association with Paris.

Another book about Madeline, *Madeline in London*, is described under England.

Mirette, of Emily Arnold McCully's *Mirette on the High Wire*, a Caldecott Medal winner, is also a spirited little girl who lives in Paris, in this case the Paris of a century ago. Mirette learns from the famous Bellini how to walk a tightrope and then helps him to overcome his fear.

Hilda Louise is an orphan who has spent most of her life within the confines of a large orphanage in Paris in Olivier Dunrea's *The Tale of Hilda Louise*. Hilda Louise starts floating up into the air and one day is blown from an apple tree over the orphanage wall. She spends the day floating over Paris and then, descending, floats through a window into the garret of her long-lost uncle.

In *The Fantastic Drawings of Danielle*, by Barbara McClintock, both Danielle and her father enjoy recording what they see. However, Papa, who is a photographer, does not appreciate the imaginative pictures that Danielle draws until she proves the worth of her creativity.

A book for the oldest children, *Marguerite Makes a Book*, by Bruce Robertson, tells of another girl who is an artist, Marguerite who lives in the early fifteenth century. When her father is unable to meet the deadline for completing his illumination of a prayer book, Marguerite shops about Paris for the needed supplies; draws, prepares colors, and paints the manuscript margins; and then finishes the painting of his patron.

Diane Goode's book for the youngest children, *Where's Our Mama*, tells of a tiny girl and an even tinier boy who become separated from their mother in the original Gare d'Orsay train station. A most helpful gendarme takes them about Paris searching for their "most beautiful" mother who to them is always better in some aspect than each of the possibilities he points out. The little girl finally remembers that they were to wait at the train station, and they return there for a happy reunion.

The same children look about Paris for a birthday present for their mother in Goode's *Mama's Perfect Present*, which is also for the youngest children (as well as for those who are older). On the search their dachshund, observed only by the tiny boy, creates a disaster involving each potential gift. Finally, the children buy paints, paper, and brushes and paint a picture for their mother in which she has received all the gifts which they had earlier considered.

My Father is an illustrated song by Judy Collins about an Ohio miner who tells his daughters that they will live in France. The two oldest settle in the West, but the youngest moves to Paris where she tells her children of her life in Ohio.

Another American girl dreams of life in Paris in Marilyn Eisenstein's *Periwinkle Isn't Paris*. She and her best friend even set out on a bus for Paris, but homesick, she decides to postpone her trip until she is more grown up.

Harry and Lulu, by Arthur Yorinks, tells of Harry, a stuffed dog, and Lulu, a little girl who wishes that she had a real dog. One night Harry comes alive and they travel to France. After Harry saves Lulu from being hit by a car and, in the process, falls into the Seine River, Lulu finally acknowledges that he is a real dog.

It is hard to imagine a wilder visitor to Paris than Eloise of New York's Plaza Hotel. In Kay Thompson's *Eloise in Paris*, a book for older children, Eloise, together with her nanny, her dog, and her turtle, takes Paris by storm. Numerous drawings depict the exceedingly energetic and exuberant Eloise as she squirts pigeons with seltzer, captures gnats at the opera, and jumps into a fountain. Written for all ages, this book contains references directed at adults.

Another visitor to Paris who causes havoc is Pierre in Jay O'Callahan's *Tulips*. Pierre loves to play tricks on the household servants, but when he plays a trick on Grand Ma Mere, he finds the tables turned.

Bonjour, Lonnie, by Faith Ringgold, is a story for older children in which Lonnie, an orphan, is transported by the magical Love Bird to Paris where he meets his African-American grandfather, who tells him how he came to France as a soldier during World War I and later returned and married a French woman. Their son (Lonnie's father) was killed during World War II as was his Jewish wife, and Lonnie, taken to the United States by an American friend who became ill, was placed in an orphanage. Thanks to the Love Bird, Lonnie learns of his mixed racial heritage and is adopted by the aunt and uncle of the friend.

Paris is visited by the famous storybook elephant, Babar, in *Babar Loses His Crown*, a reader by Laurent de Brunhoff. When the suitcase containing Babar's crown is mistakenly picked up by a man with a mustache, Babar, his family, and Zephir the monkey search Paris for the Mustache-man. The situation is happily resolved at the opera house where Babar recovers his crown and the Mustache-man his flute.

The cows of Fontainebleau, which is in the department of Seine-et-Marne, decide to visit Paris in *The Cows Are Going to Paris*, by David Kirby and Allen Woodman. They board a train, don human clothes, and enjoy going to the top of the Eiffel Tower, dining at Maxim's, and shopping at the Galeries Lafayette. In the meantime the passengers who have fled the train enjoy the bovine life.

When Bonaparte's "boy" leaves to attend school, Bonaparte follows him to Paris to bring him back to their château. Unfortunately, the title character in Marsha Wilson Chall's *Bonaparte* is a dog and, despite disguising himself as Jean Claude's mother, a student, a band member, a lunchroom worker, and a janitor, Bonaparte is always discovered and expelled as dogs are not permitted in the school. Bonaparte finally finds Jean Claude returning to the château to be with him. Together the two return to the school, which decides to admit dogs, a decision which radically changes the school environment.

Paris Cat, by Leslie Baker, tells of the first day that Alice, a cat, spends in Paris. Chasing a mouse and then chased by a dog, the cat wanders around the city searching for her mistress, Annie. During the eventful day Alice tries to get a fish at an outdoor market, enjoys the paintings in the Louvre, falls into the Seine where she lands atop a boat, and then naps in a park where she is finally reunited with Annie.

Minou is a cat who lives in Paris in Mindy Bingham's *Minou*. Minou is unprepared for life in the city when the mistress who has always looked after her dies. Helped by a street-wise cat, she learns to care for herself and gets a job as a mouser at Notre Dame Cathedral. Large watercolor paintings present a number of Parisian landmarks.

It is not a cat, but the mouse Anatole, who is the subject of two picture books written by Eve Titus.

In *Anatole and the Cat* Anatole, who works as a cheese taster, is so terrified when the owner's cat comes to the factory that he writes misleading comments about the cheeses. However, thanks to his ingenuity, he manages to "bell" the cat and, thanks to pure luck, a new cheese is named Cheese Anatole.

Disaster strikes Anatole's family in *Anatole and the Toyshop*. A toyshop owner captures Anatole's wife and six children and forces the children to ride their bicycles around and around in the toyshop window in order to attract business. Anatole enlists carpenter mice to saw a hole in the window floor, and then, when his plans are temporarily thwarted, uses catnip to attract sixty-six cats to the store where they create havoc—and a major diversion.

Honk!, by Pamela Duncan Edwards, is the amusing story of how a swan comes to dance in Swan Lake at the Paris opera house.

In Jon Agee's *The Incredible Painting of Felix Clousseau*, Clousseau's paintings are incredible because the animals and objects in the paintings come alive. Unfortunately, the problems that this creates result in Clousseau being imprisoned—until a dog in one of his paintings catches a jewel thief.

Candace Fleming's *Madame LaGrande and Her So High, to the Sky, Uproarious Pompadour* is the amazing tale of Madame LaGrande's arrival at the Paris opera sporting an astoundingly high pompadour containing two pigeons and three calico cats and of how, when the king's monocle falls into her hair, the king too becomes attached to her pompadour. It is, thus, not surprising that the king outlaws pompadours in Paris.

A nonfiction book, *The Inside-Outside Book of Paris,* by Roxie Munro, uses large detailed paintings and an accompanying text filled with interesting facts to introduce children to the city. Besides covering the usual tourist attractions, e.g., the Arch of Triumph, the Eiffel Tower, this book for older children presents such lesser known places of interest as the Orsay Museum, the Paris subway system, the Shakespeare and Company bookstore, the carousel at the Tuileries Gardens, and a puppet theater.

Additional books set in Paris are described under Historical figures.

Patricia Polacco's *The Butterfly* is a book for the oldest children which is set in Choisy-le-Roi in the department of Val-de-Marne. It tells the story of the author's aunt, Monique, who as a girl discovers that her mother is secretly hiding Jews in their house. Monique and Sevrine, a Jewish girl, become friends. When Sevrine is spotted by a neighbor, Monique and her mother deliver her to the resistance worker who will take her to her next haven.

Versailles, which is in the department of Yvelines, is also in the Île-de-France Region.

Goode's *The Dinosaur's New Clothes* is a retelling of Hans Christian Andersen's "The Emperor's New Clothes" with a variety of dinosaurs as the characters and the palace of Versailles as the setting. By appealing to the fear of appearing stupid or incapable, the swindlers succeed in their deceit until it is exposed by a dinosaur child.

The King's Day and *Little Salt Lick and the Sun King,* books about King Louis XIV which are described under Historical figures, are also set in Versailles.

Haute-Normandie

Claude Monet's garden, immortalized in his paintings, is located in Giverny in the department of Eure. The Historical figures category includes two books about Monet, *A Blue Butterfly* and *Once upon a Lily Pad*, which are set in Giverny.

Provence-Alpes-Côte de Azur

Two former sea-faring rabbits are the proprietors of the Spinach Main restaurant in Provence in Judy Cox's *Rabbit Pirates*. They take great pains to curb their fighting nature even when they are threatened by a fox whose appetite extends beyond the menu items. Working together, the rabbits outwit the cunning fox.

Brave Martha and the Dragon, by Susan L. Roth, tells the tale of the young traveler who uses the sash of her dress to capture the terrible dragon which has been eating the animals of the town of Tarascon, located in the department of Bouches-du-Rhône.

Both *Camille and the Sunflowers* and *Painting the Wind* tell of the time Vincent van Gogh spent in Arles, which is also in Bouches-du-Rhône. Nice, in another department, Alpes-Maritimes, is the setting of *A Bird or Two*, which is a story about Henri Matisse. These three books are described under Historical figures.

General

Alphabet, counting, and word books

Count Your Way through France, by Jim Haskins and Kathleen Benson, is a book for older children which uses the numbers one through ten to provide an introduction to France, including its foods, its wines, its educational system, its flag, and several of its landmarks.

Fables, fairy tales, folktales, legends, myths, and proverbs (including original works)

Cynthia DeFelice and Mary DeMarsh's *Three Perfect Peaches* tells the tale of the lad who wins the hand of the ailing princess, not only by bringing three perfect peaches to heal her, but also by performing the seemingly impossible task of herding one hundred rabbits—and, in the process, embarrassing the demanding king.

A different version of the same tale appears in *Three Sacks of Truth*, which is adapted by Eric A. Kimmel. Here the king wants just one perfect peach so that he may enjoy all the peaches that the prospective suitors bring; the lad who brings him a perfect peach must tend ten thousand rabbits; and the king is both demanding and dishonest.

A book for older children, *The Acrobat and the Angel*, by Mark Shannon, tells of the boy Péquelé who is an acrobat. He agrees to give up his acrobatics so that he may live in a monastery. However, when he is asked to bless a small boy who has the plague, Péquelé breaks his promise in order to cheer up the tiny child. Told to leave the monastery Péquelé first performs his acrobatics before a statue of an angel—and a miracle occurs.

A Caldecott Medal winner, Charles Perrault's *Cinderella* which is illustrated by Marcia Brown, presents a French version of the familiar tale. Cinderella's fairy godmother changes a pumpkin, mice, a rat, and lizards into a coach, horses, a coachman, and footmen, respectively; Cinderella goes to the elegant ball twice; and on the second occasion leaves behind one of her glass slippers. After she marries the prince, the forgiving Cinderella arranges for her two condescending stepsisters to marry lords and live at the palace.

Three books entitled *Puss in Boots* retell Perrault's well-known story of the scheming cat.

In the versions illustrated by Giuliano Lunelli and by Fred Marcellino the "Marquis of Carabas" assumes ownership of the magician/ogre's castle where he entertains the king. Puss sports bright red boots in the clear, bold paintings by Lunelli, while the Marcellino version includes humor in its text and illustrations.

In the retelling by Lincoln Kirstein, which is illustrated by Alain Vaës, the Puss and his owner travel together as the cat executes his tricky plan. The Marquis of Carabas does not entertain the king in the ogre's castle, but instead Puss uses a magic feather from the deceased ogre's turban to revitalize the fields tended by hungry peasants and to change his cowhide boots into golden ones.

It is a far different cat who is the title character in *The White Cat*, a story for older children which is retold by Robert D. San Souci. The youngest prince enjoys the company of a lovely but mysterious white cat, the leader of a land of cats, who enables the prince to win two of his father's challenges. When the prince destroys the wizard who has cast a spell upon the cats, the white cat is revealed as a beautiful young woman, who then marries the prince.

Villagers hide all their food from three hungry soldiers in *Stone Soup*, by Marcia Brown. However, the soldiers trick the villagers by making delicious soup out of three stones and water, thanks to the carrots, the cabbage, and the other ingredients which the villagers add to make the stone soup even better. The foolish villagers then express gratitude to the soldiers for showing them that soup can be made out of stones.

A Basque folktale, *Nekane, The Lamiña & the Bear,* by Frank P. Arajuo, is described under Spain.

Historical figures

A number of picture books feature famous artists.

Camille and the Sunflowers, by Laurence Anholt, tells how Camille and his family befriend van Gogh when he comes to paint in Arles. Before being forced to leave by the villagers who fail to appreciate his talents, van Gogh paints pictures of the family—and the sunflowers which Camille has picked for him.

Michelle Dionetti's *Painting the Wind*, a book for older children, has the same setting. Young Claudine, who helps her mother clean van Gogh's Yellow House, sees all his canvases and witnesses both the animosity of the town's residents and his reaction to them. Thanks to van Gogh, she learns to see the world in her own personal colors. Paul Gauguin appears briefly in the story.

A Blue Butterfly, by Bijou Le Tord, presents another world-renowned artist, Monet, and his garden at Giverny. The brief text takes second place to Le Tord's watercolors that, with the same colors used by Monet, evoke the spirit of his painting.

Joan Sweeney's *Once upon a Lily Pad* also takes place at Giverny. A frog couple, Hector and Henriette, poses for Monet's paintings.

Marie in Fourth Position, by Amy Littlesugar, tells of a young ballet student who is in the chorus of the Paris Opera. Earning money for her family by modeling for Edgar Degas, she learns how to dance like a butterfly and he makes the drawings he needs to model his famous wax sculpture, "The Little Dancer".

Bijou, Bonbon & Beau, by Sweeney, tells of three kittens who romp around the theater while Degas draws the ballerinas and of how at an opening night performance they join in the dance.

In *A Bird or Two* Le Tord celebrates through text and illustration the painting of Matisse in Nice and especially his genius with colors.

In *Bonjour, Mr. Satie*, by Tomie dePaola, Mr. Satie, an anthropomorphic cat, is placed in the awkward position of having to judge between the works of two artists, Henri (Matisse) and Pablo (Picasso)—and diplomatically solves this dilemma. The characters depicted in the illustrations of Gertrude's Salon are well-known artists and writers of the Paris of the 1920s.

Young Pierre enjoys a remarkable visit with two surrealist artists, Salvador Dalí and René Magritte, in Michael Garland's *Dinner at Magritte's*, a book for older children.

Joan of Arc's life is presented in two biographies.

Joan of Arc, by Margaret Hodges, is for older children. It places more emphasis on her girlhood before she left to find the dauphin, is followed by an author's note giving historical information, and is illustrated with Robert Rayevsky's dry points and etchings.

Josephine Poole's *Joan of Arc* is for the oldest children. It is a longer version that presents more details, includes a map and a chronology, and is illustrated with Angela Barrett's large colorful paintings.

Two books introduce children to King Louis XIV.

The King's Day, by Aliki, is a book for older children which chronicles the king's daily routine that includes a two-hour getting-up period, two gigantic meals needed to satisfy his unusually large appetite, and an entertainment. The many detailed illustrations are accompanied by explanatory descriptions which elaborate upon the text.

Jennifer Armstrong's *Little Salt Lick and the Sun King* is a fictional story that tells of a boy dubbed Little Salt Lick because he sweats so much turning the rotisserie at Versailles that dogs try to lick him. When it is he who discovers the king's small missing dog, Louis XIV gives him a new job and the opportunity to be called by his real name, Paul.

In *I, Crocodile*, by Fred Marcellino, it is Napoleon Bonaparte who in 1799 brings the title character from Egypt to Paris. Always concerned about his diet, the crocodile achieves fleeting fame and then, to escape the cleaver, leaves his dwelling in a fountain in the Tuileries Gardens for life in the sewers where he dines on—people??

A book for the oldest children, *Seeker of Knowledge*, by James Rumford, is a biography of Jean-Françis Champollion, who lived from 1790 to 1832. At age 11 Jean-Françis decides that he wishes to be the first person to decipher Egyptian hieroglyphs. In 1822 Champollion discovers the key to the puzzle, thereby realizing his dream.

Hieroglyphs are incorporated in the text and on the page borders of this book.

A book for older children, *The King's Giraffe*, by Mary Jo and Peter Collier, is a story based on a true event, the gift of a giraffe in 1826 from Pasha Mehemet Ali of Egypt to King Charles X of France. Although the initial part of the story takes place in Egypt, the preponderance of the text and illustrations depicts France. The story tells of Abdul, a stable boy, who accompanies the giraffe on the ship, during its winter stay at Marseilles, and on the journey through Aix-en-Provence, Avignon, Lyon, Dijon and Saint-Cloud, the summer residence of the king, to Paris. Thanks to his appointment as keeper of the Royal Menagerie, Abdul is able to remain with his friend, the giraffe.

Nancy Milton's *The Giraffe That Walked to Paris* also tells the story of the unusual gift which the Egyptian pasha gave to the French king. This version does not focus on the stable boy (it mentions three attendants) and adds an ambassador, a professor, and an antelope to the account. Containing less detail on the towns through which the giraffe walks, it emphasizes King Charles X's impatience to see the giraffe and has the giraffe being taken to his residence at Saint-Cloud after its arrival in Paris. This book includes a lengthy historical note.

When the Prussian army surrounds Paris in 1870, Léon Gambetta escapes from the city by balloon and then raises a French army to fight the Prussians. The contrast between besieged Paris and Gambetta's experience amidst the tranquil horse-shaped clouds is emphasized in Dennis Haseley's *Horses with Wings*.

On July 25, 1909 Louis Blériot made the first airplane flight across the English Channel from Calais to a spot near

Dover. *The Glorious Flight*, a Caldecott Medal winner by Alice and Martin Provensen, describes the time in 1901 when Blériot first decides to make a flying machine; the development of seven of his aircraft, Blériot I through Blériot VII; and his successful flight in Blériot XI.

Poetry and songs

In Debbie Boon's *My Gran*, a girl extols the many characteristics of her grandmother through rhyming lines, each of which modifies the ending word "gran".

Wheels on the Bus uses the illustrations of Sylvie Kantorovitz Wickstrom to set this familiar children's song in a French town. Even the youngest children should enjoy not only singing this song, but also following the individual passengers as they board, ride, and then debark from the bus.

Stories

In *The Return of Freddy LeGrand*, by Agee, Freddy is unable to reach Paris on his transatlantic flight when his plane runs out of fuel. Parachuting, he and his plane land on a French farm where Freddy proves to be quite inept at farming. Later, however, when Freddy crashes in the Alps on the last leg of an around-the-world flight, it is his newly acquired farming skills and the French farm couple that save him.

Star of Fear, Star of Hope, by Jo Hoestlandt, is a book for the oldest children. Helen, an older woman, still regrets shouting angry words to her best friend, Lydia, when Lydia must leave her ninth birthday celebration in 1942 because police are rounding up the Jews in this northern French town. Helen never sees Lydia again, but hopes that she too is now a grandmother.

Two books by Satomi Ichikawa tell of a little girl, Nora, who lives in a French village with her dog, her doll, and her teddy bear.

In *Nora's Castle* the four of them explore a supposedly deserted castle and then host a joyful nighttime party for its inhabitants: an owl, a bat, a rabbit, a spider, and some bluebirds and toads.

Nora is ill and unable to go anywhere in *Nora's Roses*. That is until, after watching the passing people pick roses from the rose bush outside her window, she dreams that she and her three companions go via roses to a rose concert and rose parties.

Martine, a pig, cannot find truffles for the hotel's chef because she has no idea what one is. However, as related in Inga Moore's *The Truffle Hunter*, once a wild boar shows her how to dig truffles, she learns to appreciate both their taste and life away from the hotel in the forest.

Madame Bodot has an unusual pet, a boa constrictor, in *Crictor*, by Tomi Ungerer. Crictor accompanies Madame Bodot about her small French town, goes to school where he twists himself to form various letters and numbers, and catches a burglar.

Monsieur Racine acquires an even more unusual companion in Ungerer's *The Beast of Monsieur Racine*. In fact, the creature, who especially enjoys ice cream and its playground, is so unusual that he takes it to Paris to the Academy of Sciences where, to everyone's amazement, it turns out to be a girl and a boy in disguise.

Books

Agee, Jon. *The Incredible Painting of Felix Clousseau.* Illustrated by author. New York: Farrar, Straus & Giroux, 1988; Sunburst Books, 1990, paperback.

Agee, Jon. *The Return of Freddy LeGrand.* Illustrated by author. New York: Farrar, Straus & Giroux, 1992; 1994, paperback.

Aliki. *The King's Day: Louis XIV of France.* (Trophy Picture Book) Illustrated by author. New York: Harper Trophy, 1991, paperback.

Angeletti, Roberta. *The Cave Painter of Lascaux.* (A Journey through Time) Illustrated by author. New York: Oxford University Press, 1999.

Anholt, Laurence. *Camille and the Sunflowers: A Story about Vincent van Gogh.* Illustrated by author. Hauppauge, NY: Barron's Educational Series, 1994.

Armstrong, Jennifer. *Little Salt Lick and the Sun King.* Illustrated by Jon Goodell. New York: Crown Books for Young Readers, 1994.

Baker, Leslie. *Paris Cat.* Illustrated by author. New York: Little, Brown and Company, 1999.

Bemelmans, Ludwig. *Madeline.* Illustrated by author. New York: Viking Children's Books, 1958; Puffin, 1977, paperback; 1993, paperback; 1998, paperback; Buccaneer Books, 1995.

Bemelmans, Ludwig. *Madeline and the Bad Hat.* Illustrated by author. New York: Viking Children's Books, 1957; Puffin, 1977, paperback.

Bemelmans, Ludwig. *Madeline and the Gypsies.* Illustrated by author. New York: Viking Children's Books, 1959; Puffin, 1979, paperback.

Bemelmans, Ludwig. *Madeline's Christmas*. Illustrated by author. New York: Viking Children's Books, 1985; Puffin, 1988, paperback.

Bemelmans, Ludwig. *Madeline's Rescue*. Illustrated by author. New York: Viking Children's Books, 1953; Puffin, 1977, paperback.

Bingham, Mindy. *Minou*. Illustrated by Itoko Maeno. Santa Barbara, CA: Advocacy Press, 1987.

Boon, Debbie. *My Gran*. Illustrated by author. Brookfield, CT: Millbrook Press, 1998.

Brown, Marcia. *Stone Soup: An Old Tale*. Illustrated by author. New York: Charles Scribner's Sons Books for Young Readers, 1947.

Brunhoff, Laurent de. *Babar Loses His Crown*. Illustrated by author. New York: Beginner Books, 1967.

Chall, Marsha Wilson. *Bonaparte*. Illustrated by Wendy Anderson Halperin. New York: DK Ink, 2000.

Collier, Mary Jo, and Peter Collier. *The King's Giraffe*. Illustrated by Stéphane Poulin. New York: Simon & Schuster Books for Young Readers, 1996.

Collins, Judy. *My Father*. Illustrated by Jane Dyer. New York: Little, Brown and Company, 1997, paperback.

Cox, Judy. *Rabbit Pirates: A Tale of the Spinach Main*. Illustrated by Emily Arnold McCully. San Diego: Browndeer Press, 1999.

DeFelice, Cynthia, and Mary DeMarsh, retellers. *Three Perfect Peaches: A French Folktale Retold by The Wild Washerwomen Storytellers*. Illustrated by Irene Trivas. New York: Orchard Books, 1995.

dePaola, Tomie. *Bonjour, Mr. Satie*. Illustrated by author. New York: G. P. Putnam's Sons, 1991.

Dionetti, Michelle. *Painting the Wind*. Illustrated by Kevin Hawkes. New York: Little, Brown and Company, 1996.

Dunrea, Olivier. *The Tale of Hilda Louise*. Illustrated by author. New York: Farrar Straus & Giroux, 1996.

Edwards, Pamela Duncan. *Honk!* Illustrated by Henry Cole. New York: Hyperion Books for Children, 1998.

Eisenstein, Marilyn. *Periwinkle Isn't Paris*. Illustrated by Rudolf Stüssi. Plattsburgh, NY: Tundra Books of Northern New York, 1999.

Fleming, Candace. *Madame LaGrande and Her So High, to the Sky, Uproarious Pompadour*. Illustrated by S. D. Schindler. New York: Alfred A. Knopf Books for Young Readers, 1996.

Garland, Michael. *Dinner at Magritte's*. Illustrated by author. New York: Dutton Children's Books, 1995, paperback; Viking Penguin, 1999, paperback.

Goode, Diane. *The Dinosaur's New Clothes: A Retelling of the Hans Christian Andersen Tale*. Illustrated by author. New York: The Blue Sky Press, 1999.

Goode, Diane. *Mama's Perfect Present*. Illustrated by author. New York: N A L Dutton, 1996, paperback; Puffin, 1999, paperback.

Goode, Diane. *Where's Our Mama?* Illustrated by author. New York: Dutton Children's Books, 1991, paperback; Puffin Books, 1995, paperback.

Haseley, Dennis. *Horses with Wings*. (Laura Geringer Book) Illustrated by Lynn Curlee. New York: HarperCollins Children's Books, 1993.

Haskins, Jim, and Kathleen Benson. *Count Your Way through France*. (Count Your Way Books) Illustrated by Andrea Shine. Minneapolis: Carolrhoda Books, 1996; Lerner Publishing Group, 1996, paperback.

Hodges, Margaret. *Joan of Arc: The Lily Maid*. Illustrated by Robert Rayevsky. New York: Holiday House, 1999.

Hoestlandt, Jo. *Star of Fear, Star of Hope*. Illustrated by Johanna Kang. Translated from French by Mark Polizzotti. New York: Walker and Company, 1995.

Ichikawa, Satomi. *Nora's Castle*. Illustrated by author. New York: Paperstar, 1997, paperback.

Ichikawa, Satomi. *Nora's Roses*. Illustrated by author. New York: Paperstar, 1997, paperback.

Kimmel, Eric A., adapter. *Three Sacks of Truth: A Story from France*. Illustrated by Robert Rayevsky. New York: Holiday House, 1993.

Kirby, David, and Allen Woodman. *The Cows Are Going to Paris*. Illustrated by Chris S. Demarest. Honesdale, PA: Boyds Mills Press, 1991.

Kirstein, Lincoln, reteller. *Puss in Boots: Based on the Story by Charles Perrault*. Illustrated by Alain Vaës. New York: Little, Brown and Company, 1994, paperback.

Le Tord, Bijou. *A Bird or Two: A Story about Henri Matisse*. Grand Rapids, MI: Eerdmans Books for Young Readers, 1999.

Le Tord, Bijou. *A Blue Butterfly: A Story about Claude Monet*. Illustrated by author. New York, Doubleday Books for Young Readers, 1995.

Littlesugar, Amy. *Marie in Fourth Position: The Story of Degas' "The Little Dancer"*. Illustrated by Ian Schoenherr. New York: Philomel Books, 1996; Paperstar, 1999, paperback.

McClintock, Barbara. *The Fantastic Drawings of Danielle*. Illustrated by author. Boston: Houghton Mifflin Company, 1996.

McCully, Emily Arnold. *Mirette on the High Wire.* Illustrated by author. New York: G. P. Putnam's Sons, 1992; Paperstar, 1997, paperback.

Marcellino, Fred. *I, Crocodile.* (Michael di Capua Books) Illustrated by author. San Francisco: Harper San Francisco, 1999.

Milton, Nancy. *The Giraffe That Walked to Paris.* Illustrated by Roger Roth. New York: Random House Value Publishing, 1995.

Moore, Inga. *The Truffle Hunter.* (Cranky Nell Book) Illustrated by author. Brooklyn: Kane/Miller Book Publishers, 1987; 1999, paperback.

Munro, Roxie. *The Inside-Outside Book of Paris.* Illustrated by author. New York: Dutton Children's Books, 1992, paperback.

O'Callahan, Jay. *Tulips.* Illustrated by Debrah Santini. Atlanta, GA: Peachtree Publishers, 1996.

Perrault, Charles. *Cinderella: or The Little Glass Slipper.* Illustrated by Marcia Brown. Translated by illustrator. New York: Charles Scribner's Sons Books for Young Readers, 1971; Atheneum Books for Young Readers, 1997.

Perrault, Charles. *Puss in Boots.* Illustrated by Giuliano Lunelli. Translated by Anthea Bell. New York: North-South Books (Distributed by Chronicle Books), 1999.

Perrault, Charles. *Puss in Boots.* (Michael di Capua Books) Illustrated by Fred Marcellino. Translated by Malcolm Arthur. New York: Farrar, Straus & Giroux, 1990; 1998, paperback.

Polacco, Patricia. *The Butterfly.* Illustrated by author. New York: Philomel Books, 2000.

Poole, Josephine. *Joan of Arc*. Illustrated by Angela Barrett. New York: Alfred A. Knopf, 1998.

Provensen, Alice, and Martin Provensen. *The Glorious Flight: Across the Channel with Louis Blériot, July 25, 1909*. Illustrated by authors. New York: Viking Children's Books, 1983, paperback; Puffin, 1987, paperback.

Ringgold, Faith. *Bonjour, Lonnie*. Illustrated by author. New York: Hyperion Books for Children, 1996.

Robertson, Bruce. *Marguerite Makes a Book*. Illustrated by Kathryn Hewitt. Los Angeles: J. Paul Getty Museum, 1999.

Roth, Susan L. *Brave Martha and the Dragon*. Illustrated by author. New York: Dial Books for Young Readers, 1996, paperback.

Rumford, James. *Seeker of Knowledge: The Man Who Deciphered Egyptian Hieroglyphs*. Illustrated by author. Boston: Houghton Mifflin Company, 2000.

San Souci, Robert D., reteller. *The White Cat: An Old French Fairy Tale*. Illustrated by Gennady Spirin. New York: Orchard Books, 1990.

Shannon, Mark. *The Acrobat & the Angel*. Illustrated by David Shannon. New York: G. P. Putnam's Sons, 1999.

Sweeney, Joan. *Bijou, Bonbon & Beau: The Kittens Who Danced for Degas*. Illustrated by Leslie Wu. San Francisco: Chronicle Books, 1998.

Sweeney, Joan. *Once upon a Lily Pad: Froggy Love in Monet's Garden*. Illustrated by Kathleen Fain. San Francisco: Chronicle Books, 1995.

Thompson, Kay. *Eloise in Paris*. Illustrated by Hilary Knight. New York: Buccaneer Books, 1991; Simon & Schuster Books for Young Readers, 1999.

Titus, Eve. *Anatole and the Cat.* Illustrated by Paul Galdone. New York: Bantam Doubleday Dell Books for Young Readers, 1993.

Titus, Eve. *Anatole and the Toyshop.* Illustrated by Paul Galdone. New York: Bantam Doubleday Dell Books for Young Readers, 1991.

Ungerer, Tomi. *The Beast of Monsieur Racine.* (Sunburst Series) Illustrated by author. New York: Farrar, Straus & Giroux, 1986, paperback.

Ungerer, Tomi. *Crictor.* Illustrated by author. New York: HarperCollins Children's Books, 1958; Harper Trophy, 1983, paperback.

Wheels on the Bus. (Raffi Songs to Read Series) Illustrated by Sylvie Kantorovitz Wickstrom. New York: Crown Books for Young Readers, 1988; 1990, paperback.

Yorinks, Arthur. *Harry and Lulu.* Illustrated by Martin Matje. New York: Hyperion Books for Young Readers, 1999.

"Now the south side of Bremen lay along a river where many ships put in to trade, and the townsfolk were so hardworking and thrifty that the city had grown and grown until there was hardly room in which to turn around."
—Hodges. *The Hero of Bremen.*

<u>Germany</u> (formerly Federal Republic of Germany and German Democratic Republic)

Specific Locations

Eleven of the picture books described below are set in a specific state.

Baden-Württemberg

King of Magic, Man of Glass is a folktale retold by Judith Kintner, which is set in the Black Forest. Greedy young Rudolph is never satisfied with what he has, even the endless supply of coins supplied by his magical godfather, until he discovers the worth of what he already had, but never appreciated.

Also taking place in the Black Forest, J. Patrick Lewis's *Night of the Goat Children* is loosely derived from an incident which took place during the 1618-1648 Thirty Years War when the walled kingdom of Beda was under siege. Perched on the town wall, five goats seem impervious to the arrows that strike them. Unbeknownst to the invaders, they are in reality not goats, but children protectively clad in wool and covered with goatskins.

In *Kisses from Rosa* Petra Mathers recalls the months she spent in 1949 visiting her aunt and cousin in the Black Forest while her mother was being treated for tuberculosis. Rosa picks blueberries, shelves apples, plays pretend—and includes a kiss in each letter to her mother.

Bremen

There are really two heroes in *The Hero of Bremen*, by Margaret Hodges, which retells the legend of how the amount of land the over-crowded town is to acquire from a wealthy landowner is to be determined by the area which a man can walk around between sunrise and sunset. Because of the trickery of the landowner's nephew, the cobbler Hans, who can only drag himself, is chosen to set off the land. Thanks to the miraculous appearance of the knight Roland, the hero of Bremen, the sun delays its setting and Hans, the new hero of Bremen, manages to drag himself to the city gate by sundown.

Bremen is perhaps best known for the four musicians—a cat, a dog, a donkey, and a rooster—who never actually reach Bremen because on their journey they scare a bunch of robbers out of a house and then decide to stay there. Three versions of this Grimm folktale are included here.

In the retelling by Ilse Plume, *The Bremen-Town Musicians*, the animals all plan to sing as street musicians before deciding to remain in the comfy dwelling. This version features full-page colorful pictures.

The Bremen Town Band, by Brian Wildsmith, is illustrated with double-page paintings. In this version the animals all decide to sing in the Bremen band and the rooster is called a cockerel.

The Musicians of Bremen, which is retold by Jane Yolen, is a small book with less detailed illustrations. In this story the donkey plans to play a kettledrum and the dog a guitar while the others sing, and the animals are the recipients of the robbers' gold.

Lower Saxony

Two books for the oldest children, both entitled *The Pied Piper of Hamelin*, present the legend of the piper who rids Hamlyn (formerly Hamelin) from the rats that plague it, and then, after the town reneges on its bargain, pipes away Hamlyn's children.

The version by Barbara Bartos-Höppner presents a more sinister view of the piper, who initiates the offer to rid the town of its rats and returns after a number of weeks to lure away its children. Two children, one now deaf and one now blind, do return to Hamlyn and imply that the children have been taken to a place of towers and roofs.

The retelling by Sara and Stephen Corrin includes dramatic full-page paintings by Errol Le Cain. In this version the piper responds to an offer from the town council, the children are piped away the morning following the rats' drowning, all but one of the children go into a door in the Koppenberg hill, and no children return. A historical discussion at the end the book states that the disappearance of the 130 children is commemorated as taking place on June 26, 1284, that no one knows how they disappeared—perhaps kidnapped to become serfs or for the Children's Crusade, perhaps dying in the Black Death or warfare—and that the legend came later, with such a tale appearing in the 16th century.

Margaret Wild's *Let the Celebrations Begin!*, a book for the oldest children, takes place centuries later, in 1945. Miriam and the women of the Nazi concentration camp at Belsen cut off pieces of their clothes to make stuffed toys which they give to the children at the party celebrating the camp's liberation.

North Rhine-Westphalia

In Carol Chapman's *The Tale of Meshka the Kvetch*, Meshka, who constantly complains, lives in the town of Hemer. One day her complaints suddenly come true, e.g., her feet do become swollen melons, her house does become a box. It is not until Meshka learns to praise instead of complain that these misfortunes disappear.

General

Alphabet, counting, and word books

Count Your Way through Germany, a book by Jim Haskins for older children, was written just before the reunification of Germany and describes Germany as two countries. Its presentation of Germany as a counting book tells of the two towers of the Holsten Gate in Lübeck, three composers (Bach, Ludwig van Beethoven, Johannes Brahms), and the seven dwarfs of the Snow White tale.

Fables, fairy tales, folktales, legends, myths, and proverbs (including original works)

In *The Elves and the Shoemaker* Paul Galdone retells Jacob and Wilhelm Grimm's story of the shoemaker's leather which is transformed each night into expertly sewn shoes, of the shoemaker and his wife's discovery that it is two naked elves who craft the shoes, and of the joy and then disappearance of the elves when they receive clothes from the grateful couple.

The Grimm brothers' book by the same title which is retold by Bernadette Watts presents the same story. The Watts version is distinguished by its large full-page and double-page illustrations.

Two picture books retell the Grimm brothers' well-known tale of Snow White, the seven dwarfs, the mirror on the wall, the poisonous apple, and the prince.

Snow White, which is illustrated by Trina Schart Hyman, features warm double-page illustrations with embedded text.

In *Snow-White and the Seven Dwarfs*, illustrated by Nancy Ekholm Burkert, striking double-paged paintings are interspersed among double pages of text.

Historical figures

Jeanette Winter's *Sebastian* is a brightly-illustrated, clearly-told biography of Johann Sebastian Bach, who is born into a musical family; as a young person learns to play the violin, the clavichord, the organ, and the harpsichord; becomes the father of twenty children; serves as church school choirmaster and church music director; and composes the music (more than 1,000 compositions) that enriches us today.

Bach's Big Adventure, by Sallie Ketcham, tells of the time self-assured Sebastian walks thirty miles from his school in Lüneburg to Hamburg to hear the organist, Jan Adam Reincken, and discovers that as yet he is not the best organist in the world.

Nonfiction

A book for the oldest children, Holly Littlefield's *Colors of Germany* includes introductions to three famous Germans (Jacob and Wilhelm Grimm, Carl Benz), two legendary figures (Siegfried, Lorelei), one castle (Neuschwanstein Castle), and the Berlin Wall.

Stories

The Elisabeth of Claire A. Nivola's book, *Elisabeth*, is a treasured doll, left behind in 1933 when the child who loves her (the author's mother) must leave Germany because she is Jewish. Somehow Elisabeth travels to an American antique store where she is found by the child, now grown, who is seeking a doll for her daughter.

The Hand-Me-Down Horse, by Marion Hess Pomeranc, is set in post-World-War-II Germany. David and his family, who as Jews had been in hiding during the war, must wait a long time before they are able to resettle in the United States. The wait seems shorter when someone who has already left for America leaves David a rocking horse. When he leaves, David passes the horse on to a neighborhood girl who is also waiting to emigrate.

In Aliana Brodmann's *The Gift* a little girl in the Germany of the 1950s visits a number of stores trying to determine how best to spend the five-mark coin she has received for Hanukkah. Finally, moved by the beautiful music, she gives it to a sidewalk musician, and then, after he has shown her how, joins him in playing accordion tunes.

Books

Bartos-Höppner, Barbara. *The Pied Piper of Hamelin.* Illustrated by Annegert Fuchshuber. Translated by Anthea Bell. New York: J. B. Lippincott Children's Books, 1987.

Brodmann, Aliana. *The Gift.* Illustrated by Anthony Carnabuci. New York: Simon & Schuster Books for Young Readers, 1993; Aladdin Paperbacks, 1998.

Chapman, Carol. *The Tale of Meshka the Kvetch.* Illustrated by Arnold Lobel. New York: Dutton Unicorn Paperbacks, 1989, paperback.

Corrin, Sara, and Stephen Corrin, retellers. *The Pied Piper of Hamelin.* Illustrated by Errol Le Cain. San Diego: Harcourt, 1989.

Galdone, Paul, reteller. *The Elves and the Shoemaker, Based on Lucy Crane's Translation from the German of the Brothers Grimm.* Illustrated by reteller. New York: Clarion Books, 1986, paperback.

Grimm, Jacob, and Wilhelm Grimm. *The Elves and the Shoemaker*. Retold by Bernadette Watts. Illustrated by reteller. New York: North-South Books, 1986; 1997, paperback.

Grimm, Jacob, and Wilhelm Grimm. *Snow White*. Illustrated by Trina Schart Hyman. Translated from German by Paul Heins. Boston: Joy Street Books, 1979, paperback.

Grimm, Jacob, and Wilhelm Grimm. *Snow-White and the Seven Dwarfs*. Illustrated by Nancy Ekholm Burkert. Translated by Randall Jarrell. New York: Farrar, Straus & Giroux, 1972; Sunburst Books, 1987, paperback.

Haskins, Jim. *Count Your Way through Germany*. (Count Your Way Books) Illustrated by Helen Byers. Minneapolis: Carolrhoda Books, 1991, paperback; 1992.

Hodges, Margaret, reteller. *The Hero of Bremen*. Illustrated by Charles Mikolaycak. New York: Holiday House, 1993; 1993, paperback.

Ketcham, Sallie. *Bach's Big Adventure*. Illustrated by Timothy Bush. New York: Orchard Books, 1999.

Kintner, Judith, reteller. *King of Magic, Man of Glass: A German Folk Tale*. Illustrated by Dirk Zimmer. New York: Clarion Books, 1998.

Lewis, J. Patrick. *Night of the Goat Children*. Illustrated by Alexi Natchev. New York: Dial Books for Young Readers. 1999.

Littlefield, Holly. *Colors of Germany*. (Colors of the World Series) Illustrated by Andrea Shine. Minneapolis: Carolrhoda Books, 1997; 1997, paperback.

Mathers, Petra. *Kisses from Rosa*. Illustrated by author. New York: Alfred A. Knopf, 1995.

Nivola, Claire A. *Elisabeth*. Illustrated by author. New York: Farrar, Straus & Giroux, 1997.

Plume, Ilse, reteller. *The Bremen-Town Musicians*. Illustrated by author. New York: Picture Yearling, 1998, paperback.

Pomeranc, Marion Hess. *The Hand-Me-Down Horse*. Illustrated by Joanna Yardley. Morton Grove, IL: Albert Whitman & Company, 1996.

Wild, Margaret. *Let the Celebrations Begin!* Illustrated by Julie Vivas. New York: Orchard Books, 1991; 1996, paperback.

Wildsmith, Brian. *The Bremen Town Band*. Illustrated by author. New York: Oxford University Press, 2000.

Winter, Jeanette. *Sebastian: A Book about Bach*. Illustrated by author. San Diego: Harcourt, 1999.

Yolen, Jane, reteller. *The Musicians of Bremen: A Tale from Germany*. Illustrated by John Segal. New York: Simon & Schuster Books for Young Readers, 1995; 1996.

*"**Ten** animals featured in the fables of Greek storyteller Aesop...are a dog, camel, grasshopper, pig, stork, tortoise, fox, ant, hare, and monkey."*
—Haskins and Benson. *Count Your Way through Greece.*

Greece

Specific Locations

Three of the regions of Greece are represented in the picture books described below.

Attica

Bruce Coville's retelling for the oldest children, *William Shakespeare's A Midsummer Night's Dream,* is set in Athens and the nearby forest. The illustrations by Dennis Nolan help clarify the intricate plot in which magical flower juice complicates the love relationships of the humans, Hermia, Lysander, Helena, Demetrius, and Bottom, and of the fairies, Oberon and Titania.

My Uncle Nikos, by Julie Delton, is set in the village of Drossia. Helena's weekends with her uncle include enjoying a meal of lamb chops, bread, and salad with olives and spending time in his garden.

Southern Aegean

The illustrations in *Island Summer,* by Catherine Stock,

set this picture book on the island of Sifnos, which is in the Cyclades Department. When summer approaches, the deserted island awakens as the mainlanders come to prepare it for the imminent arrival of the summer people. There is then much swimming, playing, napping, and dancing until the season ends and the summer families return to their homes.

Thessaly

After telling how the earth and sky came to be and describing the early Greek gods and goddesses, Aliki's book for the oldest children, *The Gods and Goddesses of Olympus*, presents the thirteen Olympians who sat on the twelve thrones on Mt. Olympus (Hestia gave her throne to Dionysus) as well as Persephone, Eros, and Hades.

General

Alphabet, counting, and word books

A book for older children, *Count Your Way through Greece*, by Jim Haskins and Kathleen Benson, includes descriptions of the Greek Orthodox Church, the starting of the Olympics, the fishing business, Greek gods and goddesses, and the historical figures: Aesop, Aristotle, Euclid, Hippocrates, Leucippus, and Pythagoras. It should be noted that the regions listed as represented on the Greek flag are not the regions of today's Greece.

Fables, fairy tales, folktales, legends, myths, and proverbs (including original works)

Young children can be introduced to Greek myths, with a twist, in two books by Rosemary Wells in which the characters are anthropomorphic Greek rabbits.

In *Max and Ruby's First Greek Myth* Pandora disobeys her mother's order and opens her jewelry box, thereby releasing bees, fire ants, and Mexican jumping weevils.

In *Max and Ruby's Midas*, greedy Midas unintentionally turns his mother, father, and sister into, respectively, ice cream, Jell-O, and cake.

Charlotte Craft's *King Midas and the Golden Touch* relates the familiar King Midas myth in which everything that the king touches turns to gold, including his daughter. Fortunately, as in the Wells version, all works out in the end. This version has a stranger granting King Midas's wish and emphasizes the king's love of his daughter and her love of their rose garden. Although the King Midas tale is probably based on a Phrygian king, this book has no specific setting. Because it presents a well-known Greek myth, it is included under Greece.

On the other hand, Jan Mark's *The Midas Touch* and *King Midas* by John Warren Stewig are described under Turkey as they are set near the Pactolus River.

The Trojan Horse, a Greek legend which is retold by Warwick Hutton, is also described under Turkey, the location of the ancient city of Troy.

Although there are different theories as to the location of Atlantis, *Atlantis*, which is adapted and retold by Christina Balit, is included here because it is a Greek legend based on Plato's Timaeus and Critias. This book for older children describes how Poseidon, god of the seas, marries Cleito and then turns her island into the majestic and peaceful paradise known as Atlantis. However, when Poseidon discovers that its people have become corrupt and contentious, he causes the island to sink to the bottom of the sea.

It is a folktale, not a myth or legend, which Anthony L. Manna and Christodoula Mitakidou retell in *Mr. Semolina-Semolinus*. The enterprising Areti rescues the man whom she has made out of almonds, sugar, and semolina from the queen whose sailors have kidnapped him.

Stories

Yanni Rubbish, by Shulamith Levey Oppenheim, tells of Yanni, who, helping out the family's business by collecting trash, receives the dreadful nickname, Yanni Rubbish. However, using his ingenuity, Yanni, with his mother's help, spruces up the rubbish wagon, the donkey who pulls it, and his own appearance, and his former tormentors enjoy riding with him.

An olive tree in Greece is a birthday gift to Sophia from her grandfather in Eve Bunting's *I Have an Olive Tree*. A year later, after her grandfather has died, Sophia and her mother travel to the old Grecian homestead so that Sophia can hang her grandmother's beads on the olive tree that meant so much to her grandparents.

In *Seal*, by Judy Allen, tourist Jenny longs to be able to tell her parents and older brother something about Greece that they don't already know. However, when she discovers the hiding place of some rare monk seals, she wisely manages to keep it secret.

Books

Aliki. *The Gods and Goddesses of Olympus*. Illustrated by author. New York: HarperCollins Children's Books, 1994; Harper Trophy, 1997, paperback.

Allen, Judy. *Seal*. Illustrated by Tudor Humphries. Cambridge, MA: Candlewick Press, 1994.

Balit, Christina, adapter and reteller. *Atlantis: The Legend of a Lost City*. Illustrated by adapter. Note by Geoffrey Ashe. New York: Henry Holt and Company, 2000.

Bunting, Eve. *I Have an Olive Tree*. (Joanna Cotler Books) Illustrated by Karen Barbour. New York: HarperCollins Children's Books, 1999.

Coville, Bruce, reteller. *William Shakespeare's A Midsummer Night's Dream*. Illustrated by Dennis Nolan. New York: Dial Books for Young Readers, 1996, paperback.

Craft, Charlotte. *King Midas and the Golden Touch*. Illustrated by K. Y. Craft. New York: Morrow Junior Books, 1999.

Delton, Julie. *My Uncle Nikos*. Illustrated by Marc Simont. New York: T Y Crowell Junior Books 1983.

Haskins, Jim, and Kathleen Benson. *Count Your Way through Greece*. (Count Your Way Books) Illustrated by Janice Lee Porter. Minneapolis: Carolrhoda Books, 1996; 1996, paperback.

Manna, Anthony L., and Christodoula Mitakidou, retellers. *Mr. Semolina-Semolinus: A Greek Folktale*. Illustrated by Giselle Potter. New York: Simon & Schuster Children's Publishing, 1997.

Oppenheim, Shulamith Levey. *Yanni Rubbish*. Illustrated by Doug Chayka. Honesdale, PA: Boyds Mills Press, 1999.

Stock, Catherine. *Island Summer*. Illustrated by author. New York: Lothrop, Lee & Shepard Books, 1999.

Wells, Rosemary. *Max and Ruby's First Greek Myth: Pandora's Box*. Illustrated by author. New York: Dial Books for Young Readers, 1993, paperback; under title: *Max and Ruby in Pandora's Box*. New York: Puffin, 1998, paperback.

Wells, Rosemary. *Max and Ruby's Midas: Another Greek Myth*. New York: Dial Books for Young Readers, 1995, paperback.

"All day long the lad drove the sheep from place to place, always looking for the sweetest grass and clover, and playing a merry tune on his flute."
—Greene. *The Little Golden Lamb.*

Hungary
Republic of Hungary

In Judit Z. Bodnár's *A Wagonload of Fish* a peasant finally gives in to his wife's nagging and catches a wagonload of fish. They all disappear, thanks to a cunning fox, but all is not for naught as the peasant realizes how peaceful it was when he was out fishing.

Two Greedy Bears, which is adapted by Mirra Ginsburg, is written for even the youngest children and tells of two cubs, each concerned that the other will have more. Although the illustrations do not present a Hungarian setting, this book provides an introduction to Hungarian folktales.

The Little Golden Lamb, which is retold by Ellin Greene, is a Hungarian version of "The Golden Goose". The golden lamb, which a shepherd boy takes as payment from a farmer, enables him to cure the princess, whom he later marries.

Margaret Wise Brown's *Wheel on the Chimney* introduces the Hungarian custom of placing wheels on their chimneys so that the white storks returning from Africa in the spring will nest atop their houses—and bring them good fortune.

A naughty boy taunts his mother in *The Boy Who Stuck Out His Tongue*, by Edith Tarbescu. When his tongue gets stuck to a frozen fence rail, the villagers come to his aid, albeit in foolish ways. Finally freed by a traveling blacksmith, the grateful boy becomes his neighbors' helper.

The title character in *The Wise Shoemaker of Studena*, by Syd Lieberman, travels to Budapest to attend the wedding of a rich merchant's daughter. When he discovers that the merchant is more impressed by fine clothes than by wisdom, the shoemaker teaches him a lesson.

Lena's grandmother tells her the origin of the song she hums in *A Song for Lena*, by Hilary Horder Hippely. When her grandmother was a child in Hungary, her family and her friend's family shared some of their cherished apple strudel with a beggar, and he more than repaid them with the song of his violin. A recipe for making apple strudel is appended.

Books

Bodnár, Judit Z., adapter. *A Wagonload of Fish*. Illustrated by Alexi Natchev. Translated by adapter. New York: Lothrop, Lee & Shepard Books, 1996.

Brown, Margaret Wise. *Wheel on the Chimney*. Illustrated by Tibor Gergely. New York: Lippincott Children's Books, 1954.

Ginsburg, Mirra, adapter. *Two Greedy Bears: Adapted from a Hungarian Folk Tale*. Illustrated by Jose Aruego and Ariane Dewey. New York: Aladdin Paperbacks, 1998.

Greene, Ellin, reteller. *The Little Golden Lamb*. Illustrated by Rosanne Litzinger. New York: Clarion Books, 2000.

Hippely, Hilary Horder. *A Song for Lena*. Illustrated by Leslie Baker. New York: Simon & Schuster Books for Young Readers, 1996.

Lieberman, Syd. *The Wise Shoemaker of Studena*. Illustrated by Martin Lemelman. Philadelphia: Jewish Publication Society, 1994.

Tarbescu, Edith. *The Boy Who Stuck Out His Tongue: A Yiddish Folk Tale*. Illustrated by Judith Christine Mills. New York: Barefoot Books, 2000.

"In olden times, when Ireland's glens and woods were still filled with fairies and leprechauns, giants, too, lived on that fair Emerald Isle."
(dePaola. *Fin M'Coul.*)

Ireland

Books set in Ireland, unless they are specifically set only in Northern Ireland, are described here.

Specific Locations

Nine picture books are set in the provinces of Munster and Ulster.

Munster

The Irish Cinderlad, by Shirley Climo, is set in and near the town of Kinsale in county Cork. A Cinderella story, the protagonist in this version is a lad, Becan, who has a stepmother and three stepsisters. His magical helper is a bull he meets and whose tail, when the bull is killed by another bull, is worn by Becan as a magic belt. Becan acquires the boots of a vanquished giant and, after saving Princess Finola from a dragon, leaves one of them behind.

In Hudson Talbott's *O'Sullivan Stew*, a book for older children, Kate O'Sullivan tells the king who has captured the O'Sullivan family the supposedly tall tales that free her, her brothers, and her father. The stories also enable her to bring back the witch's wild stallion, thereby saving the lives of the residents of Crookhaven, which is in county Cork. This story contains two surprise twists: Kate's blarney in one case is proven to be true and Kate temporarily turns down the king's marriage offer to ride off for adventure.

Ulster

Donegal in county Donegal is the setting of Tim's cottage in *Tim O'Toole and the Wee Folk*, by Gerald McDermott. When Tim spies a group of wee folk, they give him first a magical goose and then a magical tablecloth, but he loses them both thanks to the trickery of the McGoons with whom he stays on his way home. However, when Tim is given a magical green hat, the trick is on the McGoons.

In Teresa Bateman's *The Ring of Truth* Patrick boasts so much about his blarney-telling ability that the king of the leprechauns, who are the experts at blarney, punishes Patrick by ensuring that henceforth he will speak only the truth. When Patrick tells of his true encounter with the leprechaun king, no one believes him, and he wins a pot of gold for the best blarney at the Donegal blarney contest.

Margaret of Robert D. San Souci's *Brave Margaret*, a book for older children, hails from county Donegal. She leaves her farm to travel to the north with Simon, a young prince. After besting a sea serpent and being entrapped by a sorceress, she goes forth with the sorceress's sword of light to slay a giant. Because of her actions, the sorceress is able to restore Simon's life.

A Symphony for the Sheep, which is written by C. M.

Millen and illustrated by Mary Azarian, describes through verse and woodcuts the work of the shearers, the spinners, the weavers, and the knitters who transform the wool of the sheep of Donegal.

Both *Fin M'Coul*, which is retold by Tomie dePaola, and *Finn MacCoul and His Fearless Wife*, which is retold by Robert Byrd, tell the tale of the clever giant Oonagh, who saves her scared giant husband Fin (or Finn) from the dreaded giant Cucullin. When Fin poses as a baby with apparently astounding power, Cucullin becomes discouraged at the prospect of fighting him and then has his strength-containing finger bitten off by the baby. The Byrd version features large, dramatic paintings, while the illustrations in the dePaola book are more humorous. This story takes place in the historical province of Ulster, which is now Northern Ireland and the province of Ulster in Ireland.

Also set in Ulster is Sheila MacGill-Callahan's *To Capture the Wind*. It is a different Oonagh in this story who sets out to save Conal, her betrothed, from a pirate king and ends up also reuniting the king's son with his beloved. In the process Oonagh successfully answers three of the pirate king's riddles and then, when escaping, demonstrates the answer to the fourth: the wind is captured by a sail.

General

Alphabet, counting, and word books

Jim Haskins and Kathleen Benson's *Count Your Way through Ireland* covers both Ireland and Northern Ireland. The counting proceeds from one Saint Patrick to ten handcrafted goods, including Waterford crystal and Irish lace.

Celebrations

When Patrick in Elizabeth Lee O'Donnell's *Patrick's Day* discovers that Patrick's Day is for Saint Patrick and not for him, he feels that he is not a special, but just an ordinary boy. After misbehaving like an ordinary boy and then apologizing, Patrick is greatly surprised by the town's holiday parade.

Fables, fairy tales, folktales, legends, myths, and proverbs (including original works)

Billy Beg and His Bull, a book for older children which is retold by Ellin Greene, is similar to Climo's *The Irish Cinderlad*, described under Munster. Here the magical bull has belonged to Billy Beg since early childhood; the bull kills the queen stepmother and fights three bulls before dying in a fight with the third one; Billy kills three giants; and he leaves behind a shoe, not a boot.

In dePaola's retelling, *Jamie O'Rourke and the Big Potato*, it would appear that Jamie gets the worst of a bargain with a leprechaun: a potato seed instead of a pot of gold. However, as this tale reveals, the lazy Jamie may have made the right choice.

Jamie is so lazy in the sequel, *Jamie O'Rourke and the Pooka*, that a pooka, an animal spirit, comes each night Jamie's wife is away to clean up their cottage. Unfortunately, when Jamie returns the favor, the pooka leaves, and Jamie's wife returns to a messy house.

Daniel O'Rourke, by McDermott, tells the tale of Daniel, who after much eating and dancing at a party, falls into a brook near a pooka spirit's tower. Subsequently, Daniel meets the man in the moon, is transported by an eagle and a gander, and bounces on a whale's waterspout—before being awakened by his mother.

The King of Ireland's Son, a book by Brendan Behan for older children, tells how the king's youngest son discovers that it is the captured daughter of the king of Greece who is making such glorious music and then, thanks to his stallion, is able to release her from a giant.

Historical figures

dePaola's *Patrick* presents not only an illustrated life story of Patrick, but also five of the legends told about this man who became the patron saint of Ireland.

Saint Patrick has no trouble in ridding Ireland of all but one snake in *The Last Snake in Ireland*, by MacGill-Callahan. That snake continues to torment him until finally, thanks to Saint Patrick's efforts to trap it and to an eagle's flying off with it, the snake becomes Scotland's Loch Ness Monster.

In *Saint Patrick and the Peddler*, by Margaret Hodges, Saint Patrick appears in dreams to a poor peddler who lives near Ballymena in Northern Ireland. Heeding Saint Patrick's advice, the peddler treks all the way to a bridge in Dublin (capital of not only Ireland, but also of county Dublin in the province of Leinster). There he discovers that there is a fortune in his cabin at home.

Saint Ciaran, by Gary D. Schmidt, tells of the life of an early Irish saint, who in childhood forms a special relationship with animals. Later, a deer, a fox, a wolf, a badger, and a boar work with Ciaran at his hermitage and even join him in prayer.

Grace (Grania) O'Malley was a famous Irish pirate who became a legend and who lived from 1530? to 1603?. A book for the oldest children, Emily Arnold McCully's *The Pirate Queen* tells of Grania's pirate fleets; of her six castles on Clew Bay in county Mayo in the province of Connacht; of her meeting with Elizabeth I, Queen of England and Ireland; and of her indomitable fighting spirit.

Poetry and songs

The Ballymara Flood, a humorous ballad by Chad Stuart, relates how, when a boy taking a bath is unable to turn off the faucets, the ensuing flood creates a town emergency that involves the mayor, the army, and the navy. The problem is solved when the boy secures a wrench and turns off the faucets.

Carole Gerber's *Hush!* presents a lullaby set during a storm on the Irish coast. The baby continues to cry despite being comforted by each of the family members and then finally falls asleep.

Compiled by Alice Taylor, *A Child's Treasury of Irish Rhymes* includes twenty-six poems that present Ireland: its physical features, its animals, its fairies, and the everyday life of its people.

Stories

Lorna Balian's *Leprechauns Never Lie* tells how a lazy girl, trying to find a leprechaun's gold, performs the much-needed chores which she has previously neglected—and how the leprechaun is able to keep his gold.

Dog, by Robert J. Blake, presents through story and oil

paintings a lonely, cranky old man who turns out a stray dog that has warmed his feet during the night. Then, feeling guilty, the man goes out in a storm to bring back his new companion whom he calls Dog.

Seven-year-old Tess and her friend enjoy the sights and activities of the monthly market day in Eve Bunting's *Market Day*. These include not only pigs, sheep, honey, and candy for sale, but also an organ grinder, a tinker, a fortune teller, and a sword swallower.

Books

Balian, Lorna. *Leprechauns Never Lie*. Illustrated by author. Shakopee, MN: Humbug Books, 1994.

Bateman, Teresa. *The Ring of Truth: An Original Irish Tale*. Illustrated by Omar Rayyan. New York: Holiday House, 1997; 1999, paperback.

Behan, Brendan. *The King of Ireland's Son*. Illustrated by P. J. Lynch. New York: Orchard Books, 1997.

Blake, Robert J. *Dog*. Illustrated by author. New York: Philomel Books, 1994; Paperstar, 1999, paperback.

Bunting, Eve. *Market Day*. Illustrated by Holly Berry. New York: HarperCollins Children's Books, 1996; Harper Trophy, 1999, paperback.

Byrd, Robert, reteller. *Finn MacCoul and His Fearless Wife: A Giant of a Tale from Ireland*. Illustrated by reteller. New York: Dutton Children's Books, 1999.

Climo, Shirley. *The Irish Cinderlad*. Illustrated by Loretta Krupinski. New York: HarperCollins Children's Books, 1996; 2000, paperback.

dePaola, Tomie, reteller. *Fin M'Coul: The Giant of Knockmany Hill*. Illustrated by reteller. New York: Holiday House, 1981; 1981, paperback.

dePaola, Tomie, reteller. *Jamie O'Rourke and the Big Potato: An Irish Folktale*. Illustrated by reteller. New York: G. P. Putnam's Sons, 1992; Paperstar, 1997, paperback.

dePaola, Tomie. *Jamie O'Rourke and the Pooka*. Illustrated by author. New York: G. P. Putnam's Sons, 2000.

dePaola, Tomie. *Patrick: Patron Saint of Ireland*. Illustrated by reteller. New York: Holiday House, 1992, paperback.

Gerber, Carole. *Hush! A Gaelic Lullaby*. Illustrated by Marty Husted. Dallas, TX: Whispering Coyote Press, 1997.

Greene, Ellin. *Billy Beg and His Bull: An Irish Tale*. Illustrated by Kimberly Bulcken Root. New York: Holiday House, 1994.

Haskins, Jim, and Kathleen Benson. *Count Your Way through Ireland*. (Count Your Way Books) Illustrated by Beth Wright. Minneapolis: Carolrhoda Books, 1996.

Hodges, Margaret. *Saint Patrick and the Peddler*. Illustrated by Paul Brett Johnson. New York: Orchard Books, 1993; 1997, paperback.

McCully, Emily Arnold. *The Pirate Queen*. Illustrated by author. New York: G.P. Putnam's Sons, 1995; Paperstar, 1998, paperback.

McDermott, Gerald. *Daniel O'Rourke: An Irish Tale*. (Viking Kestrel Picture Books) Illustrated by author. New York: Viking Children's Books, 1986, paperback; Puffin, 1988, paperback.

McDermott, Gerald. *Tim O'Toole and the Wee Folk: An Irish Tale*. Illustrated by author. New York: Puffin Books, 1992, paperback.

MacGill-Callahan, Sheila. *The Last Snake in Ireland: A Story about St. Patrick*. Illustrated by Will Hillenbrand. New York: Holiday House, 1999.

MacGill-Callahan, Sheila. *To Capture the Wind*. Illustrated by Gregory Manchess. New York: Dial Books for Young Readers, 1997, paperback.

Millen, C. M. *A Symphony for the Sheep*. Illustrated by Mary Azarian. Boston: Houghton Mifflin Company, 1996.

O'Donnell, Elizabeth Lee. *Patrick's Day*. Illustrated by Jacqueline Rogers. New York: Morrow Junior Books, 1994.

San Souci, Robert D. *Brave Margaret: An Irish Adventure*. Illustrated by Sally Wern Comport. New York: Simon & Schuster Books for Young Readers, 1999.

Schmidt, Gary D. *Saint Ciaran: The Tale of a Saint of Ireland*. Illustrated by Todd Doney. Grand Rapids, MI: Eerdmans Books for Young Readers, 2000.

Stuart, Chad. *The Ballymara Flood*. Illustrated by George Booth. San Diego: Harcourt, 1996.

Talbot, Hudson. *O'Sullivan Stew: A Tale Cooked up in Ireland*. Illustrated by author. New York: G. P. Putnam's Sons, 1999.

Taylor, Alice, compiler. *A Child's Treasury of Irish Rhymes*. Illustrated by Nicola Emoe. Brooklyn, NY: Barefoot Poetry Collections, 1999.

*"It was a beautiful day, and they left the roads and
followed winding paths—past sprouting vines, through
green and silver olive groves, skirting fields of freshly
sprung corn."*
(Mayo. *Brother Sun, Sister Moon.*)

Italy

Specific Locations

A number of Italy's autonomous regions are
represented in picture books.

Calabria

A village in the Calabrian hills is the setting of all but
one of Tomie dePaola's stories of Strega Nona and her
helper, Big Anthony.

Strega Nona: Her Story tells of the life of Strega Nona
from her birth until the arrival of Big Anthony when she is
an old woman. Nona and her friend Amelia learn how to be
witches from Nona's grandmother and attend a city witch
academy. However, unhappy at the academy, Nona leaves
and returns to her village where sometime later she
discovers her grandmother's secret ingredient.

Big Anthony: His Story is described under Stories as it
tells of his travels about Italy before reaching Calabria. In
Strega Nona: An Old Tale Big Anthony becomes Strega
Nona's assistant. He learns how Strega Nona's pot makes

pasta all by itself, but does not realize that it takes three kisses to stop its boiling. Fortunately, Strega Nona arrives in time to save the town from rapidly spreading pasta—and Big Anthony is directed to eat all of it.

It is Strega Nona's ring which Big Anthony appropriates in *Big Anthony and the Magic Ring*. Turned into a handsome ladies' man, the beau of the village dance, Big Anthony is unable to remove the ring when he is pursued by a pack of women who want him as their dance partner.

In *Strega Nona's Magic Lessons* Big Anthony disguises himself as a woman so he can join Bambolona, the baker's daughter, in learning Strega Nona's magic. Unfortunately, after secretly reading an off-limits magic book, his attempt at magic causes the sudden appearance of a toad where Strega Nona had been. Thanks to Bambolona, Strega Nona reappears.

It is Bambolona who causes the problem in *Strega Nona Takes a Vacation*. When Strega Nona sends presents from her vacation at the seashore, Bambolona decides she wants Big Anthony's candy, and Big Anthony ends up with the bubble bath. As a result it is not pasta, but bubble bath which covers the village.

Merry Christmas, Strega Nona tells how Big Anthony, apparently oblivious as usual, is in truth the organizer of a successful village Christmas feast for Strega Nona—and he doesn't even use magic.

Strega Amelia returns to the town with her scientific witch equipment in *Strega Nona Meets Her Match*. Strega Nona loses all her business to her competitor until Strega Amelia's new assistant, Big Anthony, takes over for a few days and unwittingly proves that Strega Nona is the only witch the town needs.

Campania

The province of Napoli is the source of the Rapunzel folktale which is retold in Diane Stanley's *Petrosinella*. Another version, *Rapunzel* is included in the Fables,... category. In Stanley's version, Petrosinella is taken at the age of seven by an ogress to whom she was promised before birth. Years later, thanks to her long hair, a prince is able to climb into the tower in which she is imprisoned and then, thanks to three acorns, they are able to escape from the ogress.

The Clown of God, by dePaola, begins and ends in Sorrento in Napoli. A poor orphan, Giovanni leaves Sorrento to juggle with a traveling company. Then, as an old man who is again destitute, he returns to Sorrento where he juggles once more, this time for a statue of the Christ Child.

Lazio

Three books are set in Rome in the province of Roma.

In *Androcles and the Lion*, an adaptation of the Aesop's fable by Janet Stevens, the slave Androcles befriends many forest animals; the lion covers its eyes with one paw so he will not have to look when Androcles removes the thorn from his injured other paw; and the lion purrs and licks Androcles in the Colosseum.

The Roman Twins, by Roy Gerrard, tells in verse how the young twin slaves, Maximus and Vanilla, escape from their demanding master and mistress in order to save the life of a horse. Then, after winning a chariot race and helping save Rome from the Ostrogoths, they are given their freedom by the emperor.

In *Rome Antics* David Macaulay presents a look at many of the city's landmarks through his distinctive detailed pen and ink drawings. It is a homing pigeon who will guide the oldest children readers on this city tour and who provides a bird's perspective. At the end of the book there are descriptions of the twenty-two places visited.

Lombardy

Set in the province of Milano, dePaola's *Tony's Bread* tells how the bread of Tony (pan di Toni) becomes the favorite flowerpot-shaped bread, panettone. It is when a nobleman from Milan falls in love with Tony's daughter that Tony transforms his plain bread and moves his bakery from a neighboring village into Milan near the Duomo.

The Genius of Leonardo, by Guido Visconti, which is also set in Milan, is described under Historical figures.

Piedmont

The town of Sabbia near Varallo-Sesio is the setting of *Days of the Blackbird*, by dePaola. A faithful white bird stays through the severe winter so that her beautiful song will help heal a seriously ill duke. She is warmed by a chimney whose soot turns her black.

The Canary Prince, by Eric Jon Nones, presents a folktale from the province of Torino, A young girl, like Petrosinella and Rapunzel, is imprisoned in a tower. However, the prince, transformed as a canary, flies into the tower and then returns to his human form. When the girl's evil stepmother sees the prince, she places needles in a cushion on the tower's windowsill, and the prince is almost mortally wounded. Once he discovers that it is the girl, in disguise, who has healed him, the two are married and the girl is reunited with her father.

Puglia

The Mysterious Giant of Barletta, which is adapted by dePaola, relates a folktale about the statue of a giant in Barletta, a town in the province of Bari. During the eleventh century Barletta is saved from an invading army by the brilliant plan of the town's oldest resident and by the giant, who comes to life to execute it.

Sardinia

Tony Johnston's *Pages of Music* tells of a small boy who accompanies his artist mother as she spends a spring painting on the island of Sardinia. Moved by the music of the shepherds' pipes, he returns as a man, a composer, who brings with him a symphony orchestra to play a Christmas concert for the shepherds whose music inspired him.

Tuscany

The title character of *Caterina*, by Julienne Peterson, proves to the king who becomes her husband that her cleverness can be an asset to him.

Michelango's Surprise, which is described under Historical figures, is set in the city of Florence in the province of Firenze.

Umbria

Assisi, which is so closely associated with Saint Francis, is located in the province of Perugia in Umbria. Two books about Saint Francis are described under Historical figures.

Veneto

Venice, in the province of Venezia, is the setting of *Gabriella's Song* by Candace Fleming. Young Gabriella incorporates the sounds she hears around her into a song that she hums—and it becomes a symphony.

The Piccolo of *Papa Piccolo* by Carol Talley is an independent Venetian tomcat. That is until he is adopted by two kittens and accepts his role as their father.

In *Mr. Lunch Borrows a Canoe*, by J. Otto Seibold and Vivian Walsh, a professional bird-chasing dog canoes to Venice where he chases all of the pigeons out of a plaza.

Bravo, Zan Angelo!, which is set in the Venice of the Renaissance, is described under Historical figures.

General

Alphabet, counting, and word books

Count Your Way through Italy, by Jim Haskins, introduces older children to Italy, including some of its foods and cities.

Celebrations

It appears that a village which has fallen upon hard times will not have their usual Christmas Eve circus show in dePaola's *Jingle, the Christmas Clown*. However, thanks to young Jingle and the baby circus animals, the villagers are treated to a memorable performance.

In *The Legend of Old Befana* dePaola retells a story of Twelfth Night: of the Feast of the Three Kings. Crotchety old Befana, who spends her days sweeping and baking, tries to catch up with the three kings who are following the star to the Child King. Carrying a broom and a gift basket of baked treats, she runs fast, even running in the sky. Although she never does find Bethlehem, she even now on January sixth visits sleeping children, sweeping their rooms and leaving them treats in case one of them might be the Child King.

Fables, fairy tales, folktales, legends, myths, and proverbs (including original works)

Rapunzel, a Caldecott Medal winner which is retold and illustrated by Paul O. Zelinsky, differs from Stanley's Petrosinella, which is described under Campania, in that Rapunzel is taken from her family at birth and imprisoned in the tower at age twelve. She marries the prince in the tower and, when the sorceress discovers that she is pregnant, is banished to the wilderness. Again climbing the hair to see his wife, the prince encounters the sorceress and falls off the tower. Blind, he wanders aimlessly until, discovered by Rapunzel, he returns with her and their twins to his kingdom. This is a book for older children, which is distinguished by its oil paintings patterned after those of artists of the Italian Renaissance.

Ilse Plume's retelling of the Brothers Grimm folktale, *The Shoemaker and the Elves*, is set in Italy. During the nighttime four elves secretly make shoes and boots for the elderly shoemaker Antonio. On Christmas Eve Antonio and his seamstress wife express their gratitude by making outfits for the elves, who, now well dressed, feel no need to continue their nocturnal work.

Another Grimm folktale, *Iron Hans* which is illustrated by Marilee Heyer, is also set in Italy, the Italy of the Renaissance. A book for older children, it tells the tale of a young prince who is taken off by a wild man, Iron Hans. After the boy's hair turns to gold, he is released by Iron Hans, but may return to have his wishes granted. The boy then works in a king's garden, secures a victory for the king, and weds the princess—whereupon Iron Hans is released from his spell and revealed as a mighty king.

Assunta comes to the rescue of her two younger sisters in *Count Silvernose*, which is retold by Eric A. Kimmel. She not only gets them out of a fiery pit, but also destroys the imps and goblins who are tormenting them and pushes Count Silvernose into the pit.

In Laura Cecil's retelling, *The Frog Princess*, three brothers shoot arrows and find their brides at the landing spots. Unfortunately, the youngest prince finds a frog near his arrow. However, after the frog has performed three miraculous tasks and he has agreed to marry her, she is transformed into a beautiful princess and he becomes king.

In *Papa Gatto*, retold by Ruth Sanderson, it is the industrious and warmhearted Beatrice, and not the beautiful and deceptive Sophia, who succeeds in caring for Papa Gatto's motherless kittens, in attracting the attentions of a prince, and in achieving her dream of going to live with Papa Gatto and his kittens.

Historical figures

A Boy Named Giotto, by Paola Guarnieri, tells a story involving two great artists. Eight-year-old Giotto loves to draw while tending sheep. Receiving colored powders from Giovanni Cimabue, he does a rock painting of a sheep that is so realistic that it attracts a lost lamb. Recognizing great talent, Cimabue later brings Giotto to Florence as his protégé.

Tony Parillo's *Michelangelo's Surprise* is based on a true event, the day in 1494 when Piero de' Medici celebrated a snowfall in Florence by summoning young Michelangelo to sculpt a snowman.

The Genius of Leonardo, by Guido Visconti, presents events in the life of Leonardo da Vinci as witnessed by the boy who is his assistant. Young Giacomo not only watches Leonardo paint the Mona Lisa and the Last Supper, but also admires Leonardo's buying caged birds and then freeing them and his work on a flying machine. This book for older children includes excerpts from Leonardo's notebooks as well as some of his sketches.

Saint Francis, by Brian Wildsmith, presents the life story of Saint Francis of Assisi told in the first person. A book for older children, the text is written on large double-page paintings and tells of the transformation of his life as a young man, his travels, his friend Clare, and his closeness to animals.

The first chapter of Margaret Mayo's *Brother Sun, Sister Moon*, an illustrated book for older children, tells of the life of Saint Francis. It is followed by chapters presenting eight legends about Saint Francis and a song that he wrote.

Starry Messenger, by Peter Sís, is also for older children. "The Starry Messenger" is the title of the book published by Galileo Galilei to present observations from his self-made telescope. This recent book presents Galileo's life through a brief, clear text, enhanced by more advanced commentary, including some of Galileo's writings, and by its remarkable graphic presentation.

Zan Polo was a masked clown in sixteenth century Venice. Niki Daly's *Bravo, Zan Angelo!* is the story of how Zan Polo's grandson convinces his grandfather that he can be a little rooster in Zan Polo's theater.

Stories

Big Anthony: His Story, by dePaola, describes Anthony's childhood on a farm in northern Italy where from infancy his inattentiveness causes problems. Sent to seek his fortune, he straightens the tower of Pisa, mixes together all of an artist's paints in Florence, charges the Cardinal for crossing the bridge into Rome, mixes up food orders in Naples—and then appears at Strega Nona's door in Calabria.

When Anna and her grandmother travel to the village of her grandmother's childhood, they are disappointed by the disappearance of the stone animals that Uncle Alfredo had found and made into a zoo. *Uncle Alfredo's Zoo*, by Judith Vigna, tells what happens when Anna places a stone shaped like Uncle Alfredo's sheepdog at the entrance to his land.

Books

Cecil, Laura, reteller. *The Frog Princess*. Illustrated by Emma Chichester Clark. New York: Greenwillow Books, 1995.

Daly, Niki. *Bravo, Zan Angelo!: A Commedia Dell'Arte Tale*. Illustrated by author. New York: Farrar, Straus & Giroux, 1998.

dePaola, Tomie. *Big Anthony: His Story*. Illustrated by author. New York: Putnam Publishing Group, 1998.

dePaola, Tomie. *Big Anthony and the Magic Ring*. Illustrated by author. San Diego: Harcourt, 1979; 1979, paperback.

dePaola, Tomie. *The Clown of God: An Old Story*. Illustrated by author. San Diego: Harcourt, 1986; Voyager Books, 1989, paperback.

dePaola, Tomie. *Days of the Blackbird: A Tale of Northern Italy*. Illustrated by author. New York: G. P. Putnam's Sons, 1997.

dePaola, Tomie. *Jingle, the Christmas Clown*. Illustrated by author. New York: Paperstar, 1998, paperback.

dePaola, Tomie, reteller. *The Legend of Old Befana: An Italian Christmas Story*. Illustrated by reteller. San Diego: Harcourt, 1980; Voyager Books, 1980, paperback.

dePaola, Tomie. *Merry Christmas, Strega Nona*. Illustrated by author. San Diego: Harcourt, 1986; 1991, paperback; Voyager Books, 1986.

dePaola, Tomie, adapter. *The Mysterious Giant of Barletta: An Italian Folktale*. Illustrated by adapter. San Diego: Harcourt, 1984; Voyager Books, 1988, paperback.

dePaola, Tomie, reteller. *Strega Nona: An Old Tale.* Illustrated by reteller. New York: Simon & Schuster Books for Young Readers, 1975; 1979, paperback; Little Simon, 1997.

dePaola, Tomie. *Strega Nona: Her Story.* Illustrated by author. New York: G. P. Putnam's Sons, 1996.

dePaola, Tomie. *Strega Nona Meets Her Match.* Illustrated by author. New York: G. P. Putnam's Sons, 1993; Paperstar, 1996, paperback.

dePaola, Tomie. *Strega Nona Takes a Vacation.* Illustrated by author. New York: G. P. Putnam's Sons, 2000.

dePaola, Tomie. *Strega Nona's Magic Lessons.* Illustrated by author. San Diego: Harcourt, 1982; Voyager Books, 1984, paperback.

dePaola, Tomie. *Tony's Bread: An Italian Folktale.* Illustrated by author. New York: G. P. Putnam's Sons, 1989; Paperstar, 1996, paperback.

Fleming, Candace. *Gabriella's Song.* (An Anne Schwartz Book) Illustrated by Giselle Potter. New York: Simon & Schuster Children's Publishing, 1997.

Gerrard, Roy. *The Roman Twins.* Illustrated by author. New York: Farrar, Straus & Giroux, 1998.

Grimm, Jacob, and Wilhelm Grimm. *Iron Hans.* Illustrated by Marilee Heyer. New York: Puffin, 1996, paperback.

Guarnieri, Paolo. *A Boy Named Giotto.* Illustrated by Bimba Landmann. Translated by Jonathan Galassi. New York: Farrar, Straus & Giroux, 1999.

Haskins, Jim. *Count Your Way through Italy.* (Count Your Way Books) Illustrated by Beth Wright. Minneapolis: Carolrhoda Books, 1990; 1991, paperback.

Johnston, Tony. *Pages of Music.* Illustrated by Tomie dePaola. New York: G. P. Putnam's Sons, 1988.

Kimmel, Eric A., reteller. *Count Silvernose: A Story from Italy*. Illustrated by Omar Rayyan. New York: Holiday House, 1996.

Macaulay, David. *Rome Antics*. Illustrated by author. Boston: Houghton Mifflin Company, 1997.

Mayo, Margaret. *Brother Sun, Sister Moon: The Life and Stories of St. Francis*. Illustrated by Peter Malone. New York: Little, Brown and Company, 2000.

Nones, Eric Jon. *The Canary Prince*. Illustrated by author. New York: Farrar, Straus & Giroux, 1991.

Parillo, Tony. *Michelangelo's Surprise*. Illustrated by author. New York: Farrar, Straus & Giroux, 1998.

Peterson, Julienne, reteller. *Caterina: The Clever Farm Girl: A Tale from Italy*. Illustrated by Enzo Giannini. New York: Dial Books for Young Readers, 1996, paperback.

Plume, Ilse, reteller. *The Shoemaker and the Elves*. Illustrated by reteller. San Diego: Harcourt, 1991.

Sanderson, Ruth, reteller. *Papa Gatto: An Italian Fairy Tale*. Illustrated by reteller. New York: Little, Brown and Company, 1995; 1999, paperback.

Seibold, J. Otto, and Vivian Walsh. *Mr. Lunch Borrows a Canoe*. Illustrated by J. Otto Seibold. New York: Viking Children's Books, 1994, paperback; Puffin Books, 1997, paperback.

Sís, Peter. *Starry Messenger: A Book Depicting the Life of a Famous Scientist, Mathematician, Astronomer, Philosopher, Physicist, Galileo Galilei*. Illustrated by author. New York: Farrar, Straus & Giroux, 1996.

Stanley, Diane, reteller. *Petrosinella: A Neapolitan Rapunzel*. Illustrated by reteller. New York: Dial Books for Young Readers, 1995, paperback; N A L Dutton, 1997, paperback.

Stevens, Janet, adapter. *Androcles and the Lion: An Aesop Fable*. Illustrated by adapter. New York: Holiday House, 1989; 1989, paperback.

Talley, Carol. *Papa Piccolo*. Illustrated by Itoko Maeno. Kansas City, MO: MarshMedia, 1992.

Vigna, Judith. *Uncle Alfredo's Zoo*. Illustrated by author. Morton Grove, IL: Albert Whitman & Company, 1994.

Visconti, Guido. *The Genius of Leonardo: With Quotations, Some Abridged, from the Notebooks of Leonardo da Vinci*. Illustrated by Bimba Landmann. New York: Barefoot Books, 2000.

Wildsmith, Brian. *Saint Francis*. Illustrated by author. Grand Rapids, MI: Eerdmans Books for Young Readers, 1996.

Zelinsky, Paul O., reteller. *Rapunzel*. Illustrated by reteller. New York: N A L Dutton, 1997.

"While the Germans approached from the west, the Soviets come from the east and took over Lithuania."
—Mochizuki. *Passage to Freedom.*

Lithuania (formerly Lithuanian Soviet Socialist Republic)

Lithuania was formerly a constituent republic of the Union of Soviet Socialist Republics (U.S.S.R.), which was dissolved in 1991. Lithuania declared its independence in 1990. Picture books set in the area of the former U.S.S.R. for which no other specific location is given are described under Russia (Russian Federation).

Passage to Freedom, by Ken Mochizuki, tells the true story of Chiune Sugihara, the Japanese consul to Lithuania, who in 1940, despite the disapproval of his government, issued visas to thousands of Polish Jewish refugees so that they would be able to escape the approaching Nazis and enter Japan (via Russia). This story for older children is based on the account of Sugihara's son and is set in the city of Kaunas.

Book

Mochizuki, Ken. *Passage to Freedom: The Sugihara Story.* Illustrated by Dom Lee. Afterword by Hiroki Sugihara. New York: Lee & Low Books, 1999.

"Papa bought raw herring from a little stand with a striped awning, and they dipped the small fish in chopped onions and ate them."
—Joosse. *The Morning Chair.*

Netherlands (The Netherlands, Holland)

Thomas Locker's landscape paintings evoke the seventeenth-century setting of *The Boy Who Held Back the Sea*, which is retold by Lenny Hort. Mischievous Jan as well as old Captain Blauvelt encounter disbelief when they report a hole in the dike. Thus, Jan spends a long uncomfortable night plugging the hole with his finger, thereby saving his town.

Moel Eyris is the painter in *The Painter Who Loved Chickens*, by Olivier Dunrea. City artist Moel makes money painting pictures of subjects he does not like, while painting pictures of chickens for his own pleasure. When a customer recognizes his true talent, he receives money to buy a small farm with chickens and becomes renowned for his chicken paintings.

The Lily Cupboard, by Shulamith Levey Oppenheim, a book for older children, tells a story of a little Jewish girl who during World War II is sent to live with a non-Jewish family where she will be safer. When the German soldiers come, she hides in a cupboard and protects the rabbit whom she has named after her father.

David A. Adler's book for the oldest children, *A Picture*

Book of Anne Frank, tells of her life from her birth in Frankfurt am Main, Germany, to her time at Westerbork concentration camp in the Netherlands, at Auschwitz in Poland, and at the Bergen-Belsen concentration camp in Germany where she died. However, the book focuses on Anne's life in Amsterdam.

The Morning Chair, by Barbara M. Joosse, takes place in 1950 when Bram and his parents move from the Netherlands to New York City. Bram is homesick for his seaside town until the family's furniture arrives and he can again enjoy mornings with his mother in the morning chair.

Written in verse, *Kinderdike*, by Leonard Everett Fisher, relates how the village of Kinderdike, just east of Rotterdam in the province of South Holland, came to be named after a baby.

Books

Adler, David A. *A Picture Book of Anne Frank.* Illustrated by Karen Ritz. New York: Holiday House, 1993; 1994, paperback.

Dunrea, Olivier. *The Painter Who Loved Chickens.* Illustrated by author. New York: Farrar, Straus & Giroux, 1995; 1998, paperback; Macmillan Books for Young Readers, 1995.

Fisher, Leonard Everett. *Kinderdike.* Illustrated by author. New York: Macmillan Books for Young Readers, 1994.

Hort, Lenny, reteller. *The Boy Who Held Back the Sea.* Illustrated by Thomas Locker. New York: Dial Books for Young Readers, 1987, paperback; Puffin Pied Piper, 1991, paperback; 1993, paperback.

Joosse, Barbara M. *The Morning Chair*. Illustrated by Marcia Sewall. New York: Clarion Books, 1995.

Oppenheim, Shulamith Levey. *The Lily Cupboard*. Illustrated by Ronald Himler. New York: Harper Trophy, 1995, paperback.

"Once upon a time, a long long time ago, way up in the mountains of Norway, there lived three goats and the names of all three were The Billy Goats Gruff."
—Lunge-Larsen. *The Troll with No Heart in His Body and Other Tales of Trolls from Norway.*

Norway

Janet Stevens (*The Three Billy Goats Gruff*) and Glen Rounds (*Three Billy Goats Gruff*) retell the classic tale of the three billy goats and the troll. The illustrations reveal more of the setting in the version by Stevens, while the text in the version by Rounds is more dramatic.

Two books entitled *The Man Who Kept House* present versions of another folktale.

The version by P. C. Asbjørnsen and J. E. Moe tells in direct simple language of the farmer who switches places with his wife and encounters a series of amusing mishaps with the butter churn, the beer barrel, the pig, the cow, and the well.

Kathleen and Michael Hague's retelling is written with a more advanced vocabulary and more detail and adds episodes involving the dishes, the baby, the sheets, the wash tub, and the cat (but omits the well).

The characters are cats clad in Norwegian clothing in *The Fisherman and His Wife,* by Rosemary Wells. Happy and content in their cottage, Ragmar and Ulla become increasingly self-centered and greedy as they receive more and more from the wish-granting fish—until they discover that they are happier with their earlier living.

In Eric A. Kimmel's retelling, *Boots and His Brothers*, it is the youngest of three brothers who is kind to an old woman and, heeding her advice, performs seemingly impossible tasks, thereby receiving his weight in gold.

Why the Sea Is Salt, which is retold by Vivian French, explains how Matilda acquires the churn which provides for her mother and sixteen siblings, how the churn is twice taken by her selfish uncle, and how when he cannot stop its churning, it falls into the sea where it continues to make salt.

In *The Troll with No Heart in His Body and Other Tales of Trolls from Norway* Lise Lunge-Larsen retells nine folktales, including the aforementioned "The Three Billy Goats Gruff". Illustrated with woodcuts, this is a book for older children.

Books

Asbjørnsen, P. C., and J. E. Moe. *The Man Who Kept House*. Illustrated by Svend Otto S. New York: Margaret K. McElderry Books for Young Readers, 1992.

French, Vivian, reteller. *Why the Sea Is Salt*. Illustrated by Patrice Aggs. Cambridge, MA: Candlewick Press, 1993.

Hague, Kathleen, and Michael Hague, retellers. *The Man Who Kept House*. Illustrated by Michael Hague. San Diego: Harcourt, 1981; Voyager Books, 1988, paperback.

Kimmel, Eric A., reteller. *Boots and His Brothers: A Norwegian Tale*. Illustrated by Kimberly Bulcken Root. New York: Holiday House, 1992.

Lunge-Larsen, Lise, reteller. *The Troll with No Heart in His Body and Other Tales of Trolls from Norway.* Illustrated by Betsy Bowen. Boston: Houghton Mifflin Company, 1999.

Rounds, Glen, reteller. *Three Billy Goats Gruff.* Illustrated by reteller. New York: Holiday House, 1993; 1993, paperback.

Stevens, Janet, reteller. *The Three Billy Goats Gruff.* Illustrated by reteller. San Diego: Voyager Books, 1990, paperback; Red Wagon Books, 1995, paperback.

Wells, Rosemary. *The Fisherman and His Wife: A Brand-New Version.* Illustrated by Eleanor Hubbard. New York: Dial Books for Young Readers, 1998, paperback.

"The people of Chelm were so proud of their Chanukkah tree that they decided to make one every year as a special present for their friends, the birds."
—Kimmel. *The Chanukkah Tree.*

Poland
Republic of Poland

Specific Locations

Four of Poland's provinces are represented in the picture books described below.

Chelm

The commune of Chelm is the capital of the province and a trade center. However, it has been immortalized in Jewish folklore as a village where foolishness is the norm. Five of the Polish books are set in this legendary town.

Yossel Zissel and the Wisdom of Chelm, by Amy Schwartz, tells of a butcher in Chelm who inherits money from his uncle in Warsaw. When he has difficulty bringing all the gold back to Chelm, he trades it for farm animals and then trades the animals for items filled with feathers. When he still has not solved his transportation problem, Yossel Zissel releases the feathers so that they will float to Chelm—where they never do arrive.

Ruth Gordon's *Feathers* explains that when the messenger was distributing wisdom and foolishness at the beginning of the world, he unintentionally spilled a bag of foolishness when he arrived at the place that Chelm would be. The book then tells a variation of the Schwartz tale, the story of Chelm's bathhouse which burns down one night while the town watchman watches. Traveling to other towns to raise money for a new bathhouse, a delegation of Chelmites fear that robbers will steal the money and, using it to buy feathers, set them loose to fly to Chelm. The residents are still waiting for the feathers which they plan to sell to build a much needed bathhouse.

A town watchman is the central character in *It Happened in Chelm*, retold by Florence B. Freedman. The watchman is unable to warn Chelm of nighttime bandits because, located away from the town, he doesn't know how to ride the horse provided him, doesn't run to Chelm because he fears his sheepskin coat will attract wolves, and doesn't yell for fear he'll wake the residents.

Just Stay Put, which is retold by Gary Clement, tells of the Chelmite named Mendel, who sets out to see the big city of Warsaw. While he is napping, a shepherd turns his boots around, causing Mendel unknowingly to walk back to Chelm. Despite the familiarity of the town and his family, Mendel remains convinced that he is in Warsaw.

In Eric A. Kimmel's *The Chanukkah Tree* a peddler tricks the townsfolk into believing that Chanukkah trees have become the rage in America. The Chelmites decorate the tree they buy with potato latkes, dreidels, candles, and the synagogue door with its Jewish star. Upset when they discover the trickery of the peddler, the residents come to appreciate their unique tree when it attracts a large bird population to Chelm.

Ciechanów

In *Escaping to America* Rosalyn Schanzer tells of the lives of her Jewish grandparents and their three small children during the time from 1918 to 1921 when they lived in Sochocin and of their escape via Plinsk (Plonsk) and Danzig to Knoxville, Tennessee. This book, which is for the oldest children, describes the dangers of living in a war zone, the family's perilous wagon ride to Plinsk, and the measles outbreak in the steerage section of their transatlantic ship.

Kraków

It is only the miller's youngest daughter who learns how to read in Janina Porazinska's folktale for older children, *The Enchanted Book*. Because she does, she is able to read the enchanted book and thereby rescue her two older sisters and eighteen other maidens from the enchanter who has imprisoned them and turned them into birds.

Warszawa

A moving book for the oldest children, Miriam Nerlove's *Flowers on the Wall* tells a story of Rachel, a little Jewish girl who lives in Warsaw. In 1938 Rachel's father loses his dry goods store because of a boycott against Jewish businesses. Confined during the winter to the cold apartment because the family cannot afford to buy her new shoes, Rachel spends her days brightening the apartment by painting flowers on the wall. When the Nazis invade Warsaw in 1939, Rachel and her family must move to the Warsaw ghetto and then, in 1942, to a concentration camp. Like her flowers, Rachel's aspirations fade.

General

Fables, fairy tales, folktales, legends, myths, and proverbs (including original works)

The Cinderella story related in Erica Silverman's *Raisel's Riddle* differs in many ways from the familiar one. Raisel is an orphan who acquires much learning from her scholarly grandfather. Forced to work as a cook's assistant once he dies, Raisel longs to attend the Purim play. Her wishes for a Purim costume and a wagon are granted by a beggar woman, and at the play she attracts the attention of the rabbi's son. Raisel leaves behind, not a glass slipper, but a wise riddle. Searching for the girl who told him the riddle, the rabbi's son finds Raisel, and, as he is able to answer the riddle, they are married.

Tsugele's Broom, by Valerie Scho Carey, is an original folktale about an independent-minded girl who does not wish to marry the suitors whom the matchmaker chooses for her. In fact, she wishes to marry only someone as dependable as the broom with which she does her work—and, lo and behold, she literally does when her broom is transformed into a man named Broom.

Joseph Had a Little Overcoat, written and illustrated by Simms Taback, is a winner of the Caldecott Medal. Adapted from a song which is appended, it tells the story of Joseph, who, as his overcoat wears out, converts it, in turn, into a jacket, a vest, a scarf, a necktie, a handkerchief, and finally a button which he loses. The book features holes in the pages through which children can view the coat's progressively smaller transformations.

Stories

It looks as if Hanukkah won't be the same this year in Barbara Diamond Goldin's *Just Enough Is Plenty*. Only two instead of a houseful of guests have been invited and there will probably be no Hanukkah money for Malka and her younger brother. Then, when the family shares their latkes with a peddler, surprising things happen.

In Nina Jaffe's *In the Month of Kislev* a peddler and his family are also poor. The three children have no latkes to eat, but do enjoy smelling the latkes of their wealthy neighbor. When the neighbor demands payment for the children's smelling, a wise rabbi demonstrates that all the payment he deserves is the jingling of coins.

Books

Carey, Valerie Scho. *Tsugele's Broom.* (Laura Geringer Book) Illustrated by Dirk Zimmer. New York: HarperCollins Children's Books, 1993.

Clement, Gary, reteller. *Just Stay Put: A Chelm Story.* Illustrated by reteller. Toronto: Groundwood-Douglas (Distributed by Publishers Group West), 1996.

Freeman, Florence B., reteller. *It Happened in Chelm: A Story of the Legendary Town of Fools.* Illustrated by Nik Krevitsky. New York: Sure Seller, 1990, paperback.

Goldin, Barbara Diamond. *Just Enough Is Plenty: A Hanukkah Tale*. Illustrated by Seymour Chwast. New York: Puffin, 1990, paperback.

Gordon, Ruth. *Feathers*. Illustrated by Lydia Dabcovich. New York: Macmillan Books for Young Readers, 1993.

Jaffe, Nina. *In the Month of Kislev: A Story for Hanukkah*. Illustrated by Louise August. New York: Viking Children's Books, 1992, paperback; Puffin Books, 1995, paperback.

Kimmel, Eric A. *The Chanukkah Tree*. Illustrated by Giora Carmi. New York: Holiday House, 1988.

Nerlove, Miriam. *Flowers on the Wall*. Illustrated by author. New York: Margaret K. McElderry Books, 1996.

Porazinska, Janina. *The Enchanted Book: A Tale from Krakow*. Illustrated by Jan Brett. Translated by Bozena Smith. San Diego: Harcourt, 1987.

Schanzer, Rosalyn. *Escaping to America: A True Story*. Illustrated by author. New York: HarperCollins Publishers, 2000.

Schwartz, Amy. *Yossel Zissel and the Wisdom of Chelm*. Illustrated by author. Philadelphia: Jewish Publication Society, 1986.

Silverman, Erica. *Raisel's Riddle*. Illustrated by Susan Gaber. New York: Farrar, Straus & Giroux, 1999.

Taback, Simms. *Joseph Had a Little Overcoat*. Illustrated by author. New York: Viking, 1999.

"The city of Constantsa stands on the shores of the Black Sea."
—Kimmel. *Gershon's Monster.*

Romania
(Rumania, Roumania)

In *Gershon's Monster*, which is retold by Eric A. Kimmel, Gershon, who lives in Constanta (Constantsa), is not only inconsiderate, but also unrepentant. It is not until his twin children are threatened by a monster that he sees the error of his ways.

Book

Kimmel, Eric A., reteller. *Gershon's Monster: A Story for the Jewish New Year.* Illustrated by Jon J. Muth. New York: Scholastic Press, 2000.

"Peter lived with his grandfather in a little house in the middle of one of the great Russian forests."
—Hastings. *Peter and the Wolf.*

Russia
Russian Federation

Russia was formerly a constituent republic of the Union of Soviet Socialist Republics (U.S.S.R.), which was dissolved in 1991. Picture books set in the area of the former U.S.S.R. for which no other specific location is given are described here.

Specific Locations

Six of the picture books are set in specific subdivisions.

Magadan Oblast

A Symphony of Whales, by Steve Schuch, is based on an event which took place in the 1984-1985 winter in the Senyavina Strait in the administrative district of Chukchi Autonomous Okrug. When the sled dogs of Glashka's parents discover thousands of beluga whales trapped in rapidly freezing water, the people of the Chukchi Peninsula keep the whales alive by chipping away ice and giving them food. Then, when the whales will not follow the icebreaker which has cleared a channel to the sea, it is Glashka who convinces the ship's captain to play different kinds of music until, finally, the whales sing in response to classical music and follow the ship to safety.

How Snowshoe Hare Rescued the Sun, which is retold by Emery Bernhard, is a folktale from the Yuit of Chukchi Autonomous Okrug. When the demons from the underground steal the sun from the sky, bear and wolf both fail in their attempts to get it back. However, snowshoe hare kicks the sun out of the demons' cave and then, kicking it into the sky, it breaks into the sun, the moon, and the stars of the Milky Way.

Novgorod Oblast.

In Celia Barker Lottridge's retelling for older children, *Music for the Tsar of the Sea*, the Tsar of the Sea so enjoys the harp music which Sadko, a minstrel in Novgorod, plays on the shore of Lake Ilmen that he gives the minstrel a valuable gift which enables him to become a prosperous merchant. When Sadko fulfills his promise to play at the tsar's palace, the resulting storm on the Caspian Sea causes major damage. Thanks to one of the tsar's daughters, further destruction is averted, and the city of Novgorod acquires a river, the Volkhov.

Another book for older children, *The Sea King's Daughter*, retold by Aaron Shepard, relates a somewhat similar story. However, Sadko attracts the attention of the King of the Sea while playing beside the Volkhov River; he immediately sets off to carry out his promise; the storm occurs on the Baltic Sea; and he weds Princess Volkhova, a daughter of the king, only to lose her so that he may return to his beloved Novgorod.

St. Petersburg Oblast

Much of the story, *The Impossible Riddle*, by Ellen Jackson, takes place in St. Petersburg. The tsar, who loves riddles, learns a valuable lesson from an old farmer, who turns out to be wiser than he is.

Vyatka Oblast

The path to the town of Vyatka is the setting of *Matreshka*, an original story by Becky Hickox Ayres. When Kata kindly gives food to a woman she meets, the woman gives her a wooden doll. The doll and the four smaller dolls nested within save Kata when she is held captive in the house of the witch, Baba Yaga. They not only keep Baba Yaga from turning Kata into a cooked goose, but turn Baba Yaga into a frog.

General

Alphabet, counting, and word books

Count Your Way through Russia, a book by Jim Haskins for older children, was written before the dissolution of the U.S.S.R. Its presentation of the numbers one through ten includes descriptions of the Kremlin, Russian nesting dolls, Women's Day, and Young Pioneers.

Fables, fairy tales, folktales, legends, myths, and proverbs (including original works)

Three picture books, all entitled *Peter and the Wolf*, relate Sergei Prokofiev's orchestral tale of the young boy who with the help of a distracting bird lassoes the wolf who has swallowed a duck and is threatening a bird and a cat. The three feature full- and double-page illustrations and differ only slightly in detail.

Michèle Lemieux prefaces her retelling by explaining that Prokofiev composed the piece with each musical instrument representing one of the characters.

In the retelling by Selina Hastings, Reg Cartwright's illustrations set the story in a snowy forest.

A summer meadow is the setting of the version by Prokofiev which is illustrated by Charles Mikolaycak.

In Demi's *The Firebird* the advice of Dimitri's Horse of Power enables him to perform the three seemingly impossible tasks which the tsar demands of him. Then, thanks once again to the horse and also to fairy magic, Dimitri is able to marry Vassilissa, the fairy princess whom he had earlier brought back to be the tsar's bride. The story is enhanced by the richness of Demi's illustrations.

Prince Ivan and the Firebird, which is retold by Laszlo Gal, tells a different, much more detailed version of the tale and is for the oldest children. Here too the prince brings back the firebird and marries the princess. However, in this story there are three tsars for whom Ivan must perform tasks; there is a grey wolf who constantly helps Ivan even though the prince disregards his advice; and Ivan's life is restored by the water of life.

A book for the oldest children, *The Little Humpbacked Horse*, which is adapted by Elizabeth Winthrop, tells of Ivan, who through the advice of a humpbacked horse, becomes the tsar's stablemaster and succeeds in fulfilling the tsar's demands. The last part of this story resembles the Demi version of the firebird folktale in that Ivan captures a princess by enticing her to a sumptuous feast and the tsar who plans to marry her is killed when he jumps into boiling liquid.

Rafe Martin's *The Language of Birds* tells of a different Ivan who is the son of a merchant. When he and his older brother are given some coins by their father, the brother squanders his money, while Ivan, instead of spending it, learns the language of birds. When the two brothers go out into the world, Ivan's amazing talent enables him to save a ship and the life of his brother and to win the hand of the czar's daughter.

In addition to *Matreshka*, which is described under Vyatka Oblast, six books tell the story of the witch Baba Yaga, who lives in a house on legs, and of how she is thwarted in her plans to eat the girl heroine.

In *Baba Yaga and Vasilisa the Brave*, by Marianna Mayer, the orphan Vasilisa, who is of marriageable age, is sent by her cruel stepmother to secure a light for their house. Thanks to the help of the doll her mother made her, Vasilisa is more than able to complete the witch's tasks and is sent home with a skull light when she mentions her mother's love. The skull lights her way and burns up the stepmother and her two stepsisters. Vasilisa later marries the tsar in this tale, which is illustrated with full-page paintings.

Vasilissa the Beautiful, by Winthrop, is quite similar to the Mayer version although Vasilissa's father does not die and is later reunited with his daughter. This book is illustrated with both full- and double-page illustrations and is for older children.

Baba Yaga and the Wise Doll, retold by Hiawyn Oram, differs from the Mayer and Winthrop tales in that the heroine is a child who is sent to secure a well-dressed toad. The toad consumes the two girls who had sent her to Baba Yaga in this book, which has double-page illustrations.

It is a needle which Tatia's stepmother sends her to secure from Grandma Chickenlegs in Geraldine McCaughrean's *Grandma Chickenlegs*. In this case Tatia is aided not only by her doll, but also by Grandma Chickenlegs' cat, dog, and elm tree to whom Tatia shows kindness. Thanks to them, Tatia escapes the pursuing Grandma Chickenlegs. In this story the offending stepmother and stepsisters are merely cast out of the house in their underclothes, and Tatia lives happily thereafter with her father, who has returned, and the cat and the dog.

It is not a doll, but a frog who gives Marina advice in Eric A. Kimmel's retelling, *Baba Yaga*. In this version the cat provides Marina with the towel and comb which enable her to escape from Baba Yaga. This story also differs from the other retellings in that Baba Yaga removes a horn which has grown from Marina's forehead and attaches it to the forehead of her stepsister.

Joanna Cole's *Bony-Legs* is a reader in which Sasha arrives at Bony-Legs' house by accident. Here again there is no doll, but Sasha's kindness to the gate, the dog, and the cat enable her to escape safely.

Two other Baba Yaga tales tell of how the witch plans to eat a boy rather than a girl.

In *The Black Geese*, which is retold by Alison Lurie, Elena is busy playing games and neglects to watch out for her little brother, who is taken by a goose to Baba Yaga's house. Thanks to the assistance of a fish, a squirrel, and a mouse whom she helps, Elena is able to rescue her brother.

A helpful goose comes to the rescue of Tishka in *Baba Yaga*, which is retold by Katya Arnold. Transformed from a piece of wood into a well-loved son, Tishka first saves his life by pushing Baba Yaga's daughter into the oven. The gosling, who then rescues Tishka from Baba Yaga, returns home with him and is cared for by his family.

In *The Frog Princess*, which is retold by Elizabeth Isele, the ugly frog which Prince Ivan must marry is later revealed as Vasilisa the Wise. However, no sooner does Ivan discover this than she disappears because he burns her frog skin. However, all turns out well thanks to a gold ball; a bird, a hare, and a fish whose lives he spares; and the information which the oldest Baba Yaga gives him.

Virtually the same tale is told in J. Patrick Lewis's retelling, *The Frog Princess*. However, in this version, which includes paintings by Russian artist, Gennady Spirin, Ivan is aided by not only Baba Yaga, but also by a ball of yarn, a bear, a falcon, and a pike.

Baba Yaga decides to be a babushka, a grandmother, in *Babushka Baba Yaga*, by Patricia Polacco. Disguised, she enjoys taking care of young Victor until the other babushkas tell him of the terrible Baba Yaga. Sadly Baba Yaga goes back into the forest until she rescues Victor from a pack of wolves and the other babushkas, realizing that appearances do not matter, accept Baba Yaga as one of them.

A conscientious housekeeper, Babushka does not immediately join the three men who come to her cottage in

Babushka, which is retold by Charles Mikolaycak. However, the next day when she smells the scent of cinnamon on her sleeve where one of them has touched her, she decides to join them on their journey to see the child king. Never catching up, she continues to leave a small gift and the scent of cinnamon with children for one of them may be the king whom she is seeking.

Baboushka and the Three Kings, by Ruth Robbins, presents a simpler version of this tale. This book includes the verses and music of the song, "Babushka", and with its illustrations by Nicolas Sidjakov is a Caldecott Medal winner.

The Magic Babushka, by Phyllis Limbacher Tildes, tells of the nature-loving girl Nadia who imagines the lovely designs with which she would decorate Easter eggs, but lacks the eyesight to create them. After rescuing a butterfly from a spider, the butterfly, who is in reality Baba Babochka, grants Nadia a wish. Foolishly not asking for good vision, Nadia suffers because of her wish—until she learns how to use the gifts that are already hers.

The Babushka of Polacco's *Rechenka's Eggs* lovingly tends to a goose, Rechenka, which has been wounded by a hunter. When Rechenka accidentally breaks the decorated eggs which Babushka planned to take to the Easter Festival in Moscow, she amends the accident by laying beautiful decorated eggs for Babushka. After sadly wishing good-bye to Rechenka who is ready to return to the wild, Babushka not only wins a prize at the festival, but also discovers that Rechenka has left her a most precious gift, a gosling who will always be her companion.

In *Babushka's Doll*, by Polacco, young Natasha discovers that her grandmother's doll is even more impatient and demanding than she is.

Babouschka brings a very special Christmas gift in *The Little Snowgirl* by Carolyn Croll. The snow girl which Pavel makes as a daughter for his wife and himself is alive, but must remain out in the cold and eat only crushed ice—until Babouschka grants her wish and turns her into a real girl.

First Snow, Magic Snow, by John Cech, tells of another snow child, Snowflake, whom a man makes out of the snow. In this instance, the snow baby quickly grows into a snow girl and, living with the man and his wife, enjoys sledding with the village children and even saves one from drowning. However, when spring comes, she disappears, and her parents must travel many days before reaching her and Grandfather Frost, who also wants to keep her. The situation is resolved when Snowflake returns to spend the winter with her parents.

It is not snow, but clay which an old man uses to make a son for himself and his wife in *Clay Boy*, which is adapted by Mirra Ginsburg. However, instead of becoming a beloved son, the clay boy, growing larger and larger, eats all their food, the old couple, the villagers, and the village animals. A goat rescues them all when he butts the clay boy, thereby shattering him. Adults should be aware that the illustrations of the giant may frighten some children.

The Turnip, which is illustrated by Pierr Morgan, relates how Dedouska together with his wife, Babouska, their granddaughter, the dog, the cat, and finally the field mouse succeed in pulling up a gigantic turnip. Bright, humorous pictures add to this tale, the text of which has been reprinted from *Once on a Time*, with Kathryn Milhous and Alice Dalgliesh as collectors.

Ethel Heins retells twelve fables by Ivan A. Krylov in *The Cat and the Cook and Other Fables of Krylov.* Pride, greed, and foolishness are among the traits addressed in these fables, most of which are accompanied by two large paintings, the first picturing the beginning of the fable and the second illustrating the moral.

It is the fool, Emelya, who is the main character in *At the Wish of the Fish*, a book for older children which is adapted by Lewis. Thanks to a pike who grants all of Emelya's wishes, Emelya gains the love of the tsarevna and a magnificent palace. Then Emelya makes his final wish: that he become wiser.

An old man aids the Fool of the World in Arthur Ransome's retelling, *The Fool of the World and the Flying Ship.* Thanks to the flying ship which the old man provides him and to his heeding of the old man's advice, the young foolish man weds the czar's daughter.

Salt, a retelling by Jane Langton of an A. N. Afanasyev folktale, tells of a youngest brother Ivan, who is thought to be foolish because he asks so many questions. However, Ivan not only finds the answers to his questions, but also wins a tsarevna as his bride and discovers a source of continuing wealth for his merchant father.

Another Ivan, this time in *Clever Katya* which is retold by Mary Hoffman, succeeds in a contest with his brother because of his keen-witted seven-year-old daughter. The tsar is so impressed with her intelligence that when she grows up he marries her.

In *Soldier and Tsar in the Forest*, which is illustrated by Uri Shulevitz, the older brother, who has become a general, refuses to acknowledge his younger brother, who is a lowly soldier. Hiding in the woods after running away, the soldier fails to recognize the tsar, who has become lost, and, treating the tsar like anyone else, saves him from robbers. In return, the tsar promotes the soldier to the rank of general and demotes his brother. This story has been translated from the folktale collected by Afanasyev.

Sergei Aksakov's *The Scarlet Flower* is a book for the oldest children. A devoted merchant succeeds in securing the gifts desired by his three daughters, but when he plucks the most beautiful scarlet flower for his youngest daughter, a monster informs him that he will live only if one of his daughters returns to the monster's magnificent palace. The youngest daughter chooses to go to the palace and, after an extended period, expresses her great love for the monster, thereby releasing him from a curse and revealing him as a most handsome prince whom she then weds.

In Alexander Pushkin's *The Tale of Tsar Saltan*, a book for older children, the jealous sisters and cousin of the tsarina cause her and her newborn son to be placed in a barrel and cast out to sea. The prince, who grows in the barrel, is then given his own city by a swan. Transformed into a gnat, the prince is able to at least view his father, the Tsar Saltan. At the end of this tale the prince marries the swan, who has turned into a beautiful maiden, and is reunited with his father.

The title character of *Bearhead*, which is adapted by Kimmel, has a bear's head and a human body. Responding literally to a witch's demands, he outwits her as well as a goblin. He then brings a wagonful of money to the human couple who has raised him and departs to the woods to lead a bear's life.

Historical figures

Vladimir I, also known as Vladimir the Great, ruled Russia from 980 to 1015 A.D. In *Vassilisa the Wise*, a book for older children which is retold by Josepha Sherman, Vassilisa disguises herself to free her boastful husband, who has been imprisoned by Vladimir. She succeeds in making Vladimir believe that she is not a woman, but a Tartar ambassador. Then, after cleverly gaining her husband's release, Vassilisa, her husband, and Vladimir joyfully decide to put the incident behind them.

A book for older children, *My Grandmother's Journey*, by Cech, is based on events in the life of his mother-in-law, Feodosia Ivanovna Belevtsov: her meeting gypsies as a child and as a young woman; losing everything during the civil war between the Mensheviks and Bolsheviks; walking westward with her husband and new baby during World War II; being taken as slave laborers to Germany; and finally journeying to the United States. Despite the trials described in the text, the colorful illustrations lend an upbeat feeling to this book.

Poetry and Songs

Even the youngest children may enjoy searching the pictures for the animals and people mentioned in the twenty verses and four tales of *Babushka's Mother Goose*, by Polacco.

Stories

Leo Tolstoy's *Shoemaker Martin* tells of the Russian shoemender who wonders how he would treat Jesus if he came to Martin's basement room and half expects his arrival. However, the next day the only ones who come by are a street sweeper, a poor mother and her baby, and a woman grasping a boy who has taken one of her apples—and Martin tends to all of them.

It is with a cabinet maker and his son that the dog Kashtanka lives in Anton Chekhov's *Kashtanka*, a book for older children. Becoming lost in the city, she is cared for by a stranger who teaches her to perform tricks with his goose, his cat and his sow. However, when she sees her former owners during a circus performance, she chooses to return to her old family.

The Wolfhound, by Kristine L. Franklin, tells of another dog, the wolfhound Tatiana, whom young Pavel saves from freezing. Only the tsar and the nobility are permitted to keep wolfhounds, but Pavel cannot bear to follow his father's instruction to let the dog loose into the cold. Instead, he takes Tatiana with him into the tsar's private dangerous forest. No one will believe that Pavel encounters the tsar who thanks him—until in the spring he receives Tatiana's puppy.

The duckling who is the title character of *Grey Neck*, by Marguerita Rudoph, cannot fly south with her family for the winter as she has a broken wing. Afraid because the only pool of water left is freezing and because of the threatening fox who had broken her wing, Grey Neck is saved at the last moment by a hunter, who takes her home to be a pet for his grandchildren.

Grusha, by Barbara Bustetter Falk, tells the story of a homesick circus bear. Thanks to his understanding trainer, he is allowed to return home to his forest, this time riding a bicycle.

In Elvira Woodruff's *The Memory Coat*, Grisha, Rachel's cousin, will not give up his tattered coat because his mother lined it with wool before she died. When the Jewish family emigrates to the United States to escape the cossacks, Grisha's eye is scratched as he and Rachel are playing their storytelling game, and an inspector at Ellis Island decides that he will be sent back to Russia. It is Rachel's idea and Grisha's coat which enable him to stay in the United States.

Books

Aksakov, Sergei. *The Scarlet Flower: A Russian Folk Tale.* Illustrated by Boris Diodorov. Translated from Russian by Isadora Levin. San Diego: Harcourt, 1989.

Arnold, Katya, reteller. *Baba Yaga: A Russian Folktale.* Illustrated by reteller. New York: North-South Books, 1996, paperback.

Ayres, Becky Hickox. *Matreshka.* Illustrated by Alexi Natchev. New York: Bantam Doubleday Dell Books for Young Readers, 1992.

Bernhard, Emery, reteller. *How Snowshoe Hare Rescued the Sun: A Tale from the Arctic.* Illustrated by Durga Bernhard. New York: Holiday House, 1993.

Cech, John. *First Snow, Magic Snow.* Illustrated by Sharon McGinley-Nally. New York: Macmillan Books for Young Readers, 1992.

Cech, John. *My Grandmother's Journey.* Illustrated by Sharon McGinley-Nally. New York: Bradbury Press, 1991.

Chekhov, Anton. *Kashtanka: Adapted from a New Translation by Ronald Meyer.* Illustrated by Gennady Spirin. San Diego: Gulliver Books, 1994.

Cole, Joanna. *Bony-Legs.* Illustrated by Dirk Zimmer. New York: Four Winds Press, 1984; Scholastic, 1986, paperback.

Croll, Carolyn, adapter. *The Little Snowgirl: An Old Russian Tale.* Illustrated by adapter. New York: Paperstar, 1996, paperback.

Demi. *The Firebird.* Illustrated by author. New York: Henry Holt and Company, 1995.

Falk, Barbara Bustetter. *Grusha.* (Laura Geringer Book) Illustrated by author. New York: HarperCollins Children's Books, 1993.

Franklin, Kristine L. *The Wolfhound.* Illustrated by Kris Waldherr. New York: Lothrop, Lee & Shepard Books, 1996.

Gal, Laszlo, reteller. *Prince Ivan and the Firebird: A Russian Folktale.* Illustrated by reteller. Plattsburgh, NY: McCland & Stewart/Tundra Books, 1991, paperback; Firefly Books, 1992.

Ginsburg, Mirra, adapter. *Clay Boy: Adapted from a Russian Folk Tale.* Illustrated by Jos. A. Smith. New York: Greenwillow Books, 1997.

Haskins, Jim. *Count Your Way through Russia.* (Count Your Way Books) Illustrated by Vera Mednikov. Minneapolis: Carolrhoda Books, 1987; 1987, paperback.

Hastings, Selina, reteller. *Peter and the Wolf: Based on the Orchestral Tale by Sergei Prokofiev.* Illustrated by Reg Cartwright. New York: Henry Holt and Company Books for Young Readers, 1995, paperback.

Heins, Ethel, reteller. *The Cat and the Cook and Other Fables of Krylov*. Illustrated by Anita Lobel. New York: Greenwillow Books, 1995.

Hoffman, Mary, reteller. *Clever Katya: A Fairy Tale from Old Russia*. Illustrated by Marie Cameron. New York: Barefoot Books, 1998.

Isele, Elizabeth, reteller. *The Frog Princess*. Illustrated by Michael Hague. New York: T Y Crowell Junior Books, 1984.

Jackson, Ellen. *The Impossible Riddle*. Illustrated by Alison Winfield. Dallas: Whispering Coyote Press, 1995.

Kimmel, Eric A., reteller. *Baba Yaga: A Russian Folktale*. Illustrated by Megan Lloyd. New York: Holiday House, 1991, paperback.

Kimmel, Eric A., adapter. *Bearhead: A Russian Folktale*. Illustrated by Charles Mikolaycak. New York: Holiday House, 1991, 1991, paperback.

Langton, Jane, reteller. *Salt: From a Russian Folktale by A. N. Afanasyev*. Illustrated by Ilse Plume. Translated by Alice Plume. New York: Hyperion Books for Children, 1992.

Lemieux, Michèle, reteller. *Peter and the Wolf: Story by Sergei Prokofiev*. Illustrated by reteller. New York: Mulberry Books, 1996, paperback.

Lewis, J. Patrick, adapter. *At the Wish of the Fish: A Russian Folktale*. Illustrated by Katya Krénina. New York: Athenium Books for Young Readers, 1999.

Lewis, J. Patrick, reteller. *The Frog Princess: A Russian Folktale*. Illustrated by Gennady Spirin. New York: Dial Books for Young Readers, 1994, paperback.

Lottridge, Celia Barker, reteller. *Music for the Tsar of the Sea: A Russian Wonder Tale*. Illustrated by Harvey Chan. Toronto: Groundwood-Douglas (Distributed by Publishers Group West), 1998.

Lurie, Alison, reteller. *The Black Geese: A Baba Yaga Story from Russia*. Illustrated by Jessica Souhami. New York: DK Ink, 1999.

McCaughrean, Geraldine. *Grandma Chickenlegs*. Illustrated by Moira Kemp. Minneapolis: Carolrhoda Books, 2000.

Martin, Rafe. *The Language of Birds*. Illustrated by Susan Gaber. New York: G. P. Putnam's Sons, 2000.

Mayer, Marianna. *Baba Yaga and Vasilisa the Brave*. Illustrated by K. Y. Craft. New York: Morrow Junior Books, 1994.

Mikolaycak, Charles, reteller. *Babushka: An Old Russian Folktale*. Illustrated by reteller. New York: Holiday House, 1984; 1988, paperback.

Oram, Hiawyn, reteller. *Baba Yaga and the Wise Doll: A Traditional Russian Folktale*. Illustrated by Ruth Brown. New York: N A L Dutton, 1998.

Polacco, Patricia. *Babushka Baba Yaga*. Illustrated by author. New York: Philomel Books, 1993; Putnam Publishing Group, 1999, paperback.

Polacco, Patricia. *Babushka's Doll*. Illustrated by author. New York: Simon & Schuster Books for Young Readers, 1990; Aladdin Paperbacks, 1995, paperback.

Polacco, Patricia. *Babushka's Mother Goose*. Illustrated by author. New York: Philomel Books, 1995.

Polacco, Patricia. *Rechenka's Eggs*. Illustrated by author. New York: Philomel Books, 1988; Paperstar, 1996, paperback.

Prokofiev, Sergei. *Peter and the Wolf.* (Picture Puffins Series) Illustrated by Charles Mikolaycak. Translated by Maria Carlson. New York: Puffin, 1986, paperback.

Pushkin, Alexander. *The Tale of Tsar Saltan.* Illustrated by Gennady Spirin. New York: Dial Books for Young Readers, 1996, paperback.

Ransome, Arthur, reteller. *The Fool of the World and the Flying Ship: A Russian Tale.* Illustrated by Uri Shulevitz. New York: Farrar, Straus & Giroux, 1968; 1987, paperback.

Robbins, Ruth, adapter. *Baboushka and the Three Kings: Adapted from a Russian Folk Tale.* Illustrated by Nicolas Sidjakov. Boston: Houghton Mifflin Company, 1960; 1986, paperback.

Rudolph, Marguerita, adapter. *Grey Neck: Adapted from the Russian Tale of D. N. Mamin-Sibiryak.* Illustrated by Leslie Shuman Kronz. Ownings Mills, MD: Stemmer House Publishers, 1988.

Schuch, Steve. *A Symphony of Whales.* Illustrated by Peter Sylvada. San Diego: Harcourt, 1999.

Shepard, Aaron, reteller. *The Sea King's Daughter: A Russian Legend.* Illustrated by Gennady Spirin. New York: Atheneum Books for Young Readers, 1997; Simon & Schuster Children's Publishing, 1999.

Sherman, Josepha, reteller. *Vassilisa the Wise: A Tale of Medieval Russia.* Illustrated by Daniel San Souci. San Diego: Harcourt, 1988; American Printing House for the Blind, 1993.

Soldier and Tsar in the Forest: A Russian Tale. Illustrated by Uri Shulevitz. Translated by Richard Lourie. New York: Farrar, Straus & Giroux, 1972.

Tildes, Phyllis Limbacher. *The Magic Babushka: An Original Russian Tale*. Illustrated by author. Watertown, MA: Charlesbridge Publishing, 1998.

Tolstoy, Leo. *Shoemaker Martin*. Adapted by Birgitte Hanhart. Illustrated by Bernadette Watts. Translated by Michael Hale. New York: North-South Books, 1986; 1997, paperback.

The Turnip: An Old Russian Folktale. Illustrated by Pierr Morgan. New York: Paperstar, 1996, paperback.

Winthrop, Elizabeth, adapter. *The Little Humpbacked Horse: A Russian Tale*. Illustrated by Alexander Koshkin. New York: Clarion Books, 1997.

Winthrop, Elizabeth, adapter. *Vasilissa the Beautiful: A Russian Folktale*. Illustrated by Alexander Koshkin. New York: HarperCollins Children's Books, 1991.

Woodruff, Elvira. *The Memory Coat*. Illustrated by Michael Dooling. New York: Scholastic, 1999.

"When wishes were horses and beggars could ride, in a stone castle by the sea there lived a rich laird."
—Del Negro. *Lucy Dove*.

Scotland

Picture books whose setting embraces Scotland and one or more other parts of the United Kingdom are described in the United Kingdom section.

Specific Locations

Five of Scotland's regions are represented in the picture books.

Borders

Jane Yolen retells a Scottish ballad in her picture book, *Tam Lin*, which is for the oldest children. Seeking to win back the old family castle, Carterhaugh, which has been taken over by fairies, Jennet meets Tam Lin, a young-appearing man who had been captured by the fairies three generations previously and is scheduled to die. Following Tam Lin's advice, Jennet rescues him from the fairies and regains the castle. The tale sets the story near Selkirk, and appended information notes that there is in actuality a plain of Carterhaugh close to Selkirk, which, according to one old source, was noted for fairies. Another book entitled *Tam Lin* is described under Fables....

Grampian

A bakerwoman also bests the fairies in *The Woman Who Flummoxed the Fairies*, which is retold by Heather Forest and originates in a tale from Durris near Aberdeen. The bakerwoman, whose cakes are fit for royalty, fears that she will have to stay permanently, baking fine cakes for the fairies. However, she wisely arranges for her dog, her cat, and her baby to join the proceedings, and the fairies, who cannot abide the ensuing noise, release her.

Highland

The Last Snake in Ireland, by Sheila MacGill-Callahan, is described under Ireland, as it is Saint Patrick whose efforts result in the snake's becoming the Loch Ness Monster.

Lothian

Ruth Brown's *The Ghost of Greyfriar's Bobby* tells of the faithful dog who lived for fourteen years, from 1858 to 1872, in the Greyfriar's Churchyard near his master's grave. A fountain in Edinburgh commemorates his fidelity.

Strathclyde

Mairi Hedderwick's *Katie Morag and the New Pier* is set on a fictional isle near the island of Coll in the Inner Hebrides. The residents are excited that the pier being built will enable boats to come from the mainland three times a week. However, Katie is concerned that the ferryman will lose his job and that her grandmother will no longer be his substitute. To her relief, when the pier is completed, ferryboat rides become an attraction for tourists.

General

Fables, fairy tales, folktales, legends, myths, and proverbs (Including original works)

Tam Lin, a book for older children which is retold by Susan Cooper, contrasts with the Yolen book of the same title, which is described under Borders, in that Margaret goes out, not to reclaim a castle, but because she wants adventure. In this book Tam Lin has been kidnapped as a child. In rescuing Tam Lin, Margaret must hang onto him as he turns into a wolf, a snake, a deer, and a hot iron bar as opposed to a serpent, a lion, and burning wood in the Yolen version.

The title character in *Lucy Dove*, by Janice Del Negro, is a seamstress and a courageous one in this scary tale for the oldest children. Despite the presence of a monster in a nighttime graveyard, Lucy continues to sew the trousers that will earn her a cottage for her old age.

Kate's mother makes an unfortunate bargain with a fairy in Carolyn White's *Whuppity Stoorie*. In exchange for healing their pig, the fairy is to take Kate unless the mother can guess her name. Thanks to the pig and Kate, the fairy is the loser.

Poetry and songs

Dominic Catalano's retelling, *Frog Went A-Courting*, places the familiar song in a Scottish setting, complete with kilts, a drummer, golf clubs—and bagpipes which are taken away from the groom by the disapproving tomcat.

A Caldecott Medal winner, *Always Room for One More*, by Sorche Nic Leodhas, presents the Scottish folk song about a hospitable man with a wife and ten children who welcomes so many persons into his little house that the crowding and noise cause it to fall down. However, thanks to his guests, he ends up with a larger house.

Stories

Jane Duncan's *Brave Janet Reachfar* is set in the Scottish Highlands. It relates how Janet disobediently goes onto the East Hill in a winter storm to find a lost sheep, also discovers a newborn lamb, and is rescued by her dog and by Tom and George, who work on the farm. Further, much to her relief, Janet is not chastised by her sometimes stern grandmother.

Laura Jean Allen's reader, *Rollo and Tweedy and the Ghost of Dougal Castle*, tells of an American mouse detective and his assistant who travel to Scotland to catch the castle's ghost. Despite misleading clues, they discover that the ghost is the housekeeper, who wants the castle's treasure.

It is the ducktective Miss Mallard who solves the mystery in Robert Quackenbush's *Stairway to Doom*, a book for older children. By figuring out the clues, Miss Mallard determines that it is the lawyer who is trying to scare relatives away from the castle by posing as the ghost of its former resident, Count Kisscula.

Books

Allen, Laura Jean. *Rollo and Tweedy and the Ghost at Dougal Castle*. (An I Can Read Book) Illustrated by author. New York: HarperCollins Children's Books, 1992; Harper Trophy, 1994, paperback.

Brown, Ruth, reteller. *The Ghost of Greyfriar's Bobby*. Illustrated by reteller. New York: Dutton Children's Books, 1996, paperback.

Catalano, Dominic, reteller. *Frog Went A-Courting: The Highland Minstrel Players Proudly Present a Musical Play in Six Acts*. Illustrated by reteller. Honesdale, PA: Boyds Mills Press, 1998.

Cooper, Susan, reteller. *Tam Lin*. Illustrated by Warwick Hutton. New York: Margaret K. McElderry Books, 1991.

Del Negro, Janice. *Lucy Dove*. Illustrated by Leonid Gore. New York: DK Ink, 1998.

Duncan, Jane. *Brave Janet Reachfar*. Illustrated by Mairi Hedderwick. New York: Clarion Books, 1975.

Forest, Heather, reteller. *The Woman Who Flummoxed the Fairies: An Old Tale from Scotland*. Illustrated by Susan Gaber. San Diego: Harcourt, 1990; 1996, paperback.

Hedderwick, Mairi. *Katie Morag and the New Pier*. Illustrated by author. London: Bodley Head (Distributed by Trafalgar Square), 1994.

Nic Leodhas, Sorche. *Always Room for One More*. Illustrated by Nonny Hogrogian. New York: Henry Holt Books for Young Readers, 1995; 1995, paperback.

Quackenbush, Robert. *Stairway to Doom: A Miss Mallard Mystery*. Illustrated by author. Paramus, NJ: Prentice-Hall, 1983; Simon & Schuster Books for Young Readers, 1998, paperback.

White, Carolyn. *Whuppity Stoorie: A Scottish Folktale*. Illustrated by S. D. Schindler. New York: G. P. Putnam's Sons, 1997.

Yolen, Jane, reteller. *Tam Lin: An Old Ballad*. Illustrated by Charles Mikolaycak. San Diego: Voyager Books, 1998, paperback.

"The setting sun cast a golden glow upon the simple whitewashed house as three brothers—Santiago, Tomás, and Matías—returned home from the fields."
—Ada. *The Three Golden Oranges.*

Spain

Eric A. Kimmel's *Bernal & Florinda* is set in Seville. Bernal wishes to marry the mayor's daughter, but he possesses only a field of grasshoppers. This is the story of how he cleverly parlays the grasshoppers into a fortune and the hand of his beloved Florinda.

Squash It, which is adapted by Kimmel, is indeed, as described in its subtitle, a ridiculous tale, although hardly a true one. With the help of a flea, a peasant solves the riddle of the king's louse guitar and returns home wealthy from Madrid. The flea remains and, like the louse, gets royal blood by biting the king, thereby offering the opportunity for another ridiculous story.

The title character marries a mouse in *The Beautiful Butterfly*, which is retold by Judy Sierra. When her groom is swallowed by a fish, her friends all help her out, including the king, who by running in his underwear, causes the fish to laugh out the mouse.

In *The Girl, the Fish & the Crown*, a book for older children which is adapted by Marilee Heyer, the girl can transform herself and other fish back to human form only by securing an undersea queen's crown from the giant who keeps it. The girl must turn into a deer, an ant, a monkey, a parrot, an eagle, and a toad in order to retrieve the crown—

and then she not only becomes a young woman, but also marries the now-human queen's son.

Another heroine comes to the rescue in John Warren Stewig's *Princess Florecita and the Iron Shoes*. In this case it is the Princess Florecita, who, wearing heavy iron shoes, travels beyond the homes of the West Wind, the East Wind, and the North Wind to save a bewitched prince.

In *Nekane, the Lamiña & the Bear*, by Frank P. Araujo, a little Basque girl saves herself and a bottle of olive oil from a bear and a forest spirit by setting them against each other.

The three golden oranges are in reality bewitched sisters in *The Three Golden Oranges*, which is retold by Alma Flor Ada and is for older children. It is Matías, a youngest brother, who releases the sisters and their mother from the spell and then marries the youngest sister.

Ferdinand the bull has been immortalized in *The Story of Ferdinand*, by Munro Leaf. Ferdinand, who prefers smelling the flowers to fighting, enrages the bullfighters when he just sits down in the bullfighting ring in Madrid.

In Ann Zamorano's *Let's Eat* it takes almost two weeks, but finally all of Antonio's large family are able to share a meal together—and there are now eight rather than seven at the table.

Books

Ada, Alma Flor, reteller. *The Three Golden Oranges*. Illustrated by Reg Cartwright. New York: Athenium Books for Young Readers, 1999.

Araujo, Frank P. *Nekane, the Lamiña & the Bear: A Tale of the Basque Pyrenees.* (Toucan Tales) Illustrated by Xiao Jun Li. Windsor, CA: Rayve Productions, 1993.

Heyer, Marilee, adapter. *The Girl, the Fish & the Crown: A Spanish Folktale.* Illustrated by adapter. New York: Puffin Putnam, 1997, paperback.

Kimmel, Eric A. *Bernal & Florinda: A Spanish Tale.* Illustrated by Robert Rayevsky. New York: Holiday House, 1994.

Kimmel, Eric A., adapter. *Squash It! A True and Ridiculous Tale.* Illustrated by Robert Rayevsky. New York: Holiday House, 1997.

Leaf, Munro. *The Story of Ferdinand.* Illustrated by Robert Lawson. New York: Viking Children's Books, 1936; 1985, paperback; Puffin, 1977, paperback; Buccaneer Books, 1989.

Sierra, Judy, reteller. *The Beautiful Butterfly: A Folktale from Spain.* Illustrated by Victoria Chess. New York: Clarion Books, 2000.

Stewig, John Warren. *Princess Florecita and the Iron Shoes: A Spanish Fairy Tale.* Illustrated by K. Wendy Popp. New York: Alfred A. Knopf Books for Young Readers, 1995.

Zamorano, Ana. *Let's Eat.* Illustrated by Julie Vivas. New York: Scholastic, 1997; 1999, paperback.

"In faraway Sweden, there is a pretty yellow house with green shutters and green doors."
—Lindman. *Flicka, Ricka, Dicka and the Little Dog.*

Sweden

Specific Locations

The province of Kopparberg is represented in one of the picture books.

Kopparberg

Dala horses, small carved and painted toy horses made in Sweden's Dalarna region, were the inspiration for and are featured in Ursula K. Le Guin's book for older children, *A Ride on the Red Mare's Back*. A Dala horse comes alive as a full-sized horse to help a brave young girl rescue her little brother from trolls.

General

Fables, fairy tales, folktales, legends, myths, and proverbs (including original works)

In Flavia Weedn and Lisa Weedn Gilbert's *The Magic Cap* a young boy refuses to give up the cap his mother has made him even when offered the king's crown. Then, thanks to a wise woman, he discovers why only he can feel the magic of the cap.

A picture book for older children, *The Queen's Necklace* is retold by Jane Langton from a fairy tale by Helena Nyblom. It tells of the laughing Blanzeflor, who becomes a cruel king's wife. When she is about to be killed because she has given the individual pearls of her necklace to the needy, the birds she has befriended rescue both her and the king's nephew.

Stories

First published in 1901 in Sweden, Elsa Beskow's *Peter in Blueberry Land* tells how Peter enters the world of tiny people: picking blueberries with the sons of the King of Blueberry Land, picking cranberries with the daughters of Mrs. Cranberry, riding a mouse, and swinging on a cobweb.

Pelle's New Suit by Beskow, which was originally published in 1919, shows through its paintings and brief text how Pelle performs chores for his two grandmothers, a painter, his mother, and the tailor as his lamb's wool is transformed into a new suit.

From 1932 to 1960 Maj Lindman wrote books about two sets of triplets: three boys named Snipp, Snapp, and Snurr and three girls named Flicka, Ricka, and Dicka.

In *Snipp, Snapp, Snurr and the Red Shoes* Snipp, Snapp, and Snurr earn enough money to buy red shoes for their mother's birthday and in the process return home with red, gray, and white suits, respectively, instead of the blue suits they had worn when they left.

Snipp, Snapp, Snurr and the Gingerbread relates the story of how, when the triplets fall into gingerbread batter, they create havoc in the town and are then taken by a princess to have a party in her palace.

The rocking horse which the Swedish boys receive for their birthday takes them on a magical trip to Candy Land in *Snipp, Snapp, Snurr and the Magic Horse*.

When the three boys want butter for their bread in *Snipp, Snapp, Snurr and the Buttered Bread*, they have to wait for the sun to shine so that the grass grows so that the cow, once again happy, gives the milk with the cream that their mother churns into butter.

Snipp, Snapp, Snurr and the Yellow Sled tells how the triplets help their mother for two weeks so that they can buy the yellow sled they've been wanting—and then, because of their generosity, work two more weeks.

In *Snipp, Snapp, Snurr and the Big Surprise* the surprise is a chair made for the boys' mother. To pay for it the triplets do chores for the frame maker, the upholsterer, the cloth salesman, and the woman who sews the cover.

The three boys visit their aunt, uncle, and small cousin in *Snipp, Snapp, Snurr and the Big Farm*. They enjoy riding in the hay wagon, fishing, and picking berries, but not being trapped in a tree by an angry bull.

Snipp, Snapp, Snurr, and their parents go to northern Sweden in *Snipp, Snapp, Snurr and the Reindeer*. When the triplets get lost in the snow, they are saved by their new friends, a Laplander boy and his dog and reindeer.

Snipp, Snapp, Snurr Learn To Swim tells of another trip, a visit to the seashore. After two escapes from drowning, the boys become swimmers.

In *Snipp, Snapp, Snurr and the Seven Dogs* a frightened dog rescues a dachshund from deep water and then accepts the meat scraps the boys have brought him.

Flicka, Ricka, and Dicka get lost when they go on a picnic and pick wild strawberries in *Flicka, Ricka, Dicka and the Strawberries*. When they return home, they use the money they have earned to buy presents for the family which helped them and in the process befriend the family's little girl.

The triplets make a different friend in *Flicka, Ricka, Dicka and Their New Friend*. This friend is an old man, a retired geography teacher, who ends up going tobogganing with the girls.

In *Flicka, Ricka, Dicka and the New Dotted Dresses* the girls' dresses don't stay new very long when they spend the day helping out still another new friend whom they call Aunt Helma.

In *Flicka, Ricka, Dicka and the Three Kittens* the triplets are very upset when they lose the cat that they are tending. However, all works out well when not only the cat, but her three newborn kittens, are found. On their birthday each girl receives one of the kittens.

The girls get a dog of their own, the dog who has chosen them as his family, in *Flicka, Ricka, Dicka and the Little Dog*.

Flicka, Ricka, Dicka Bake a Cake explains why the girls had to make two cakes so that they could have a birthday cake for their mother.

The triplets take care of Aunt Lotta's seven chickens in *Flicka, Ricka, Dicka and the Big Red Hen*. The big red hen disappears, but then returns—accompanied by six chicks.

Lotta, an appealing, irrepressible little girl, is the subject of three books by Astrid Lindgren.

In *Lotta's Bike* Lotta is so disappointed that she doesn't get a bike for her fifth birthday that she steals a large bicycle from a neighbor, Mrs. Berg. After a terrifying ride, she ends up injured in a rosebush, loses the bracelet Mrs. Berg has given her, and regrets that she is having such an awful birthday—until her father brings a small bike just for her.

It appears that the Easter bunny will come a day late in *Lotta's Easter Surprise*. But thanks to Lotta, it is the Christmas bunny who brings candy for Easter. This delightful story may not be appropriate for those children who still believe in Santa Claus and the Easter bunny.

Lotta's Christmas Surprise tells how, after accidentally throwing her beloved stuffed animal, a pig named Teddy, and Mrs. Berg's bread into the garbage can, Lotta has a great day as she is able to recover them—and to bring her family a Christmas tree.

Pippi Longstocking, another irrepressible child created by Lindgren, is featured in *Pippi Longstocking's After-Christmas Party*. Pippi's party includes hot chocolate and cream cake in her igloo, a Christmas tree bedecked with goodies and presents, sledding on the roof of her house, and three unexpected visitors.

In *Stina* by Lena Anderson, the little girl Stina learns from her fisherman grandfather the way to watch a storm.

David M. Schwartz's *Supergrandpa* is based on a real incident which occurred in 1951. In that year sixty-six year old Gustaf Håkansson became the unofficial winner of the 1,094 mile Tour of Sweden, the bicycle race he was not allowed to enter because of his age.

In Lindgren's *The Day Adam Got Mad*, Adam is a normally calm bull, who for some inexplicable reason gets angry one Easter day. Family and neighbors come to watch his spectacular outburst until a small boy proves that he is indeed a Swedish bullfighter.

Lindgren is also the adapter of two books about the Tomten, a troll who has lived on an old farm for centuries.

In *The Tomten* the troll speaks in tomten language to his friends, the farm animals, as he makes his nightly rounds.

Tomten gives porridge to a fox, thereby protecting the farm's hens in *The Tomten and the Fox*.

Books

Anderson, Lena. *Stina*. Illustrated by author. New York: Greenwillow Books, 1989.

Beskow, Elsa. *Pelle's New Suit*. Illustrated by author. Translated by Marion Letcher Woodburn. Edinburgh: Floris Books (Distributed by Gryphon House), 1989.

Beskow, Elsa. *Peter in Blueberry Land*. Illustrated by author. Edinburgh: Floris Books (Distributed by Gryphon House), 1988.

Langton, Jane, reteller. *The Queen's Necklace: A Swedish Folktale*. Illustrated by Ilse Plume. New York: Hyperion Books for Children, 1994.

Le Guin, Ursula K. *A Ride on the Red Mare's Back*. Illustrated by Julie Downing. New York: Orchard Books, 1992; 1996, paperback.

Lindgren, Astrid. *The Day Adam Got Mad*. Illustrated by Marit Törnqvist. Translated by Barbara Lucas. Stockholm: R & S Books (Distributed by Farrar, Straus & Giroux), 1993.

Lindgren, Astrid. *Lotta's Bike*. Illustrated by Ilon Wikland. Stockholm: R & S Books (Distributed by Farrar, Straus & Giroux), 1989.

Lindgren, Astrid. *Lotta's Christmas Surprise*. Illustrated by Ilon Wikland. Stockholm: R & S Books (Distributed by Farrar, Straus & Giroux), 1990.

Lindgren, Astrid. *Lotta's Easter Surprise*. Illustrated by Ilon Wikland. Translated by Barbara Lucas. Stockholm: R & S Books (Distributed by Farrar, Straus & Giroux), 1991.

Lindgren, Astrid. *Pippi Longstocking's After-Christmas Party*. Illustrated by Michael Chesworth. Translated from Swedish by Stephen Keeler. New York: Viking Penguin, 1996; Puffin Books, 1998.

Lindgren, Astrid, adapter. *The Tomten: Adapted from a Poem by Viktor Rydberg*. Illustrated by Harald Wiberg. New York: Paperstar, 1997, paperback.

Lindgren, Astrid, adapter. *The Tomten and the Fox: Adapted from a Poem by Karl-Erik Forsslund*. Illustrated by Harald Wiberg. New York: Paperstar, 1997, paperback.

Lindman, Maj. *Flicka, Ricka, Dicka and the Big Red Hen*. Illustrated by author. Morton Grove, IL: Albert Whitman & Company, 1995, paperback.

Lindman, Maj. *Flicka, Ricka, Dicka and the Little Dog*. Illustrated by author. Morton Grove, IL: Albert Whitman & Company, 1995, paperback.

Lindman, Maj. *Flicka, Ricka, Dicka and the New Dotted Dresses*. Illustrated by author. Morton Grove, IL: Albert Whitman & Company, 1994, paperback.

Lindman, Maj. *Flicka, Ricka, Dicka and the Strawberries.* Illustrated by author. Morton Grove, IL: Albert Whitman & Company, 1996, paperback.

Lindman, Maj. *Flicka, Ricka, Dicka and the Three Kittens.* Illustrated by author. Morton Grove, IL: Albert Whitman & Company, 1994, paperback.

Lindman, Maj. *Flicka, Ricka, Dicka and Their New Friend.* Illustrated by author. Morton Grove, IL: Albert Whitman & Company, 1995, paperback.

Lindman, Maj. *Flicka, Ricka, Dicka Bake a Cake.* Illustrated by author. Morton Grove, IL: Albert Whitman & Company, 1995, paperback.

Lindman, Maj. *Snipp, Snapp, Snurr and the Big Farm.* Illustrated by author. Cutchogue, NY: Buccaneer Books, 1993.

Lindman, Maj. *Snipp, Snapp, Snurr and the Big Surprise.* Illustrated by author. Cutchogue, NY: Buccaneer Books, 1993; Albert Whitman & Company, 1996, paperback.

Lindman, Maj. *Snipp, Snapp, Snurr and the Buttered Bread.* Illustrated by author. Cutchogue, NY: Buccaneer Books, 1993; Albert Whitman & Company, 1995, paperback.

Lindman, Maj. *Snipp, Snapp, Snurr and the Gingerbread.* Illustrated by author. Cutchogue, NY: Buccaneer Books, 1991, paperback; Albert Whitman & Company, 1994, paperback.

Lindman, Maj. *Snipp, Snapp, Snurr and the Magic Horse.* Illustrated by author. Cutchogue, NY: Buccaneer Books, 1993.

Lindman, Maj. *Snipp, Snapp, Snurr and the Red Shoes.* Illustrated by author. Cutchogue, NY: Buccaneer Books, 1993; Albert Whitman & Company, 1994, paperback.

Lindman, Maj. *Snipp, Snapp, Snurr and the Reindeer.* Illustrated by author. Cutchogue, NY: Buccaneer Books, 1993; Albert Whitman & Company, 1995, paperback.

Lindman, Maj. *Snipp, Snapp, Snurr and the Seven Dogs.* Illustrated by author. Cutchogue, NY: Buccaneer Books, 1993.

Lindman, Maj. *Snipp, Snapp, Snurr and the Yellow Sled.* Illustrated by author. Cutchogue, NY: Buccaneer Books, 1991; Albert Whitman & Company, 1995, paperback.

Lindman, Maj. *Snipp, Snapp, Snurr Learn to Swim.* Illustrated by author. Cutchogue, NY: Buccaneer Books, 1993; Albert Whitman & Company, 1995, paperback.

Schwartz, David M. *Supergrandpa.* Illustrated by Bert Dodson. New York: Lothrop, Lee & Shepard Books, 1991.

Weedn, Flavia, and Lisa Weedn Gilbert. *The Magic Cap.* (Flavia Dream Maker Stories) Illustrated by Flavia Weedn. New York: Hyperion Books for Children, 1995.

"They decided to call their new country Switzerland and, to this day, the Swiss people have never forgotten the brave deeds of their hero, William Tell."
—Early. *William Tell.*

Switzerland
Swiss Confederation

Two picture books with large colorful paintings tell the legend of William Tell.

Leonard Everett Fisher's *William Tell* relates how Tell and his son travel through Altdorf and discover that the residents are required to kneel before the hat of the cruel governor Hermann Gessler. When Tell refuses to do so, Gessler tells him that he can avoid imprisonment and the homage of kneeling will be discontinued if he shoots an arrow through an apple placed atop his son's head. Tell successfully meets this challenge, but when Gessler discovers why Tell has a second arrow, he is taken off for prison. Tell later escapes and kills Gessler.

William Tell, which is retold by Margaret Early, is written for older children and includes more details. This account tells how Austria controlled the countries of Uri (the site of Altdorf), Schwytz and Unterwalden and of the oath taken by the leaders of these countries to secure their freedom.

Books

Early, Margaret, reteller. *William Tell*. Illustrated by
   reteller. New York: Harry N. Abrams, 1991.
Fisher, Leonard Everett. *William Tell*. Illustrated by author.
   New York: Farrar, Straus & Giroux, 1996.

"They tucked birds inside their coats, hats, and mittens."
—Kimmel. *The Birds' Gift.*

<u>Ukraine</u> (the Ukraine, formerly Ukrainian Soviet Socialist Republic)

Ukraine was formerly a constituent republic of the Union of Soviet Socialist Republics (U.S.S.R.), which was dissolved in 1991. Picture books set in the area of the former U.S.S.R. for which no other specific location is given are described under Russia (Russian Federation).

Two books entitled *The Mitten* present the folktale of a little boy's mitten, which he drops in the snow and which then becomes a shelter for a number of large and small animals.

In the version retold by Alvin Tresselt and illustrated by Yaroslava, when a cricket joins the animals in the mitten, the mitten comes apart. The boy, who has been out gathering wood, is not concerned when he discovers the mitten's pieces because his grandmother is knitting him new mittens.

The version retold and illustrated by Jan Brett is distinguished by its Ukrainian-style paintings, which include border pictures of the boy, who is completely oblivious to what is happening to his mitten. In this story the last arrival is a mouse, who inadvertently causes the bear to sneeze. The mitten then sails up into the air where it is caught by the little boy, who is happy to recover his brand new white mitten.

In *One Eye, Two Eyes, Three Eyes*, which is retold by Eric A. Kimmel, Larissa becomes the slave of a witch and her two daughters. However, even though the witch manages to kill Larissa's goat companion, the goat's magic enables Larissa to return home and marry a prince.

The Birds' Gift, another story retold by Kimmel, relates how a great number of birds are saved from an early freezing storm by villagers, who take them into their homes, their barns, and their church and keep them there until the birds are ready to be released. On Easter the grateful birds return with beautifully decorated eggs. It is in remembrance of the birds' gift that Ukrainians developed their distinctive egg decorating, which is known as pysanky.

In *The Naughty Crow*, by Irina Hale, Constantine and Marina go with their parents from their home in Kiev to spend the summer at their country home. There they find an injured crow, who as their pet is the cause of much havoc. When the children are required to release their crow in a forest, they become lost, but are able to follow the crow's feathers to their house. Then, because of the crow's good deed, he is allowed to remain with the family.

Books

Brett, Jan, adapter. *The Mitten: A Ukrainian Folktale*. Illustrated by adapter. New York: G. P. Putnam's Sons, 1989.

Hale, Irina. *The Naughty Crow*. Illustrated by author. New York: Margaret K. McElderry Books, 1992.

Kimmel, Eric A., reteller. *The Birds' Gift: A Ukrainian Easter Story*. Illustrated by Katya Krenina. New York: Holiday House, 1999.

Kimmel, Eric A., reteller. *One Eye, Two Eyes, Three Eyes: A Hutzul Tale*. Illustrated by Dirk Zimmer. New York: Holiday House, 1996.

Tresselt, Alvin, reteller. *The Mitten: An Old Ukranian Folktale, Adapted from the Version by E. Rachev*. Illustrated by Yaroslava. New York: Lothrop, Lee & Shepard Books, 1964; Mulberry Books, 1989, paperback.

"Still she headed south into the dales of Yorkshire, into the dead of February."
—Wells. *Lassie Come-Home.*

United Kingdom
United Kingdom of Great Britain and Northern Ireland

Because a great number of picture books are set in the United Kingdom, only those books which embrace two or more parts of the United Kingdom or are not set in a specific part are described here. Books set in each of the three parts of Great Britain are described in the separate sections, England, Scotland, and Wales. None of the picture books included in *Faraway Places* is set specifically only in Northern Ireland. Books with an Irish setting and those set in both Northern Ireland and Ireland are described under Ireland. Picture books set in the British crown colonies of Montserrat and the Turks and Caicos Islands are described in those two sections.

Lassie Come-Home, by Rosemary Wells, presents Eric Knight's well-loved story in a picture-book format for older children. After escaping several times from the duke who has bought her from Joe's poverty-stricken father, Lassie is taken to the duke's estate in the Scottish Highlands. It is from there that the collie makes the difficult thousand mile trek home, past the Scottish lochs, through Glasgow, and thence to her Yorkshire family.

In *Mr. Horrox and the Gratch*, by James Reeves, Mr. Horrox, an English landscape painter, heeds the advice of his art dealer and travels to Scotland to paint some new subjects. It is there that the Gratch, an invisible spirit, introduces him to the abstract painting that enables Mr. Horrox to have a successful London exhibit.

Books

Reeves, James. *Mr. Horrox and the Gratch*. Illustrated by Quentin Blake. Chicago: Wellington Publishing, 1991.

Wells, Rosemary. *Lassie Come-Home: Eric Knight's Original 1938 Classic in a New Picture-Book Edition Written for Young Readers*. Illustrated by Susan Jeffers. New York: Henry Holt and Company, 1995; 2000; Owlet Paperbacks for Young Readers, 1998, paperback.

*"Up on the mountain alone, Huw played his harp beside
the lake, while the black Welsh cattle chewed away at the
grass and paid him no attention."*
—Cooper. *The Silver Cow*.

Wales

The Silver Cow, which is retold by Susan Cooper, has its
origin in the village of Aberdovey. The silver cow is a gift
from the magic beings of the lake beside which Huw grazes
his father's cattle. It and its silver calves give rich and
copious amounts of milk for Huw's family until the time the
first cow gives no more milk and Huw's selfish, uncaring
father decides to butcher it. Then all the family's silver cows
jump into the lake and for each, a lily blossom appears.

Book

Cooper, Susan, reteller. *The Silver Cow: A Welsh Tale*.
Illustrated by Warwick Hutton. New York: Aladdin
Paperbacks, 1991.

North America

"So it was we lost our lands to the strangers from the sky."
—Yolen. *Encounter.*

Bahamas (the Bahamas, The Bahamas) Commonwealth of the Bahamas

The House in the Sky, with Robert D. San Souci as reteller, relates the folktale of two brothers who dislike work. One brother succeeds in providing for his family by stealing from a spirit-folks' well-stocked house, but when his greedy brother tries to emulate him, the venture fails—and both brothers decide to make an honest living.

In Jane Yolen's *Encounter*, a book for older children, a young Taino boy has a dream that the Christopher Columbus expedition should not be welcomed to his island of San Salvador. However, his elders do not heed his warning.

Books

San Souci, Robert D., reteller. *The House in the Sky: A Bahamian Folktale.* Illustrated by Wil Clay. New York: Dial Books for Young Readers, 1996, paperback.
Yolen, Jane. *Encounter.* Illustrated by David Shannon. San Diego: Harcourt, 1992; 1996, paperback.

*"Tucked in the middle were the sun-bleached cow bones
Dad and I had found on the prairie walk and the tiny
tractor he'd given me—just like his."*
—Spalding. *Me and Mr. Mah.*

Canada

Specific Locations

Thirty-one of the picture books described below are set in a specific province or in the Northwest Territories.

British Columbia

In *The Loon's Necklace* William Toye retells the Tsimshian legend that explains how the loon got its distinctive markings and its often cheerful song. Collage illustrations by Elizabeth Cleaver illustrate this tale of the loon who restores a blind old man's sight.

Mary of Mile 18, by Ann Blades, takes place forty-five miles from Fort St. John on a remote farm that has no electricity, running water, or indoor plumbing. The family's middle daughter, Mary, spends one frigid February day hoping that something special will happen, but it is not until she has gone to bed for the night that her wish is granted—and she gets to keep the part-wolf pup she found earlier that day.

Julie Lawson's *Emma and the Silk Train* is a story based on the 1927 derailment of a silk-carrying train that was speeding alongside the Fraser River. Catching a piece of the dumped silk, Emma is swept into the river, but, after climbing onto a tiny island, she uses the silk to secure her rescue.

Manitoba

In W. D. Valgardson's *Winter Rescue* a young boy, who is visiting his grandparents in Manitoba, reluctantly gives up watching his TV cartoon heroes to help his grandfather with his fishing nets—and ends up being a real life hero. Older children should be especially intrigued by the way the Icelandic-Canadian fishermen of Gimli set their nets under the ice of Lake Winnipeg.

Full-page paintings by the artist William Kurelek illustrate his two accounts for the oldest children of growing up on a Manitoba farm in the 1930s.

A Prairie Boy's Winter covers the period from the departure of the crows to the south to their return in the spring. In between there are chores, games of fox and geese, hockey, skiing behind a hayrack, and making apartments in snowdrifts.

A Prairie Boy's Summer describes the many chores that William performs, including fence-mending, haying, plowing, and milking cows, and also his swimming with friends in the swimming hole and finding a sport in which he excels: archery.

Northwest Territories

In Will Hobbs's *Howling Hill* Hanni, an appealing wolf pup can't seem to learn how to howl with her family.

However, after being swept down the Nahanni River on a log and guided back by a sleepy bear, she finally howls: howls of loneliness that lead her family to her.

Nova Scotia

Silent Observer, by Christy MacKinnon, relates through watercolors and text the story of the author's childhood, first in Boisdale on Cape Breton Island and then in Halifax as a student at the Halifax School for the Deaf. Her early experiences include falling down a well, bringing in the cows, going to a one-room school, getting to know Alexander Graham Bell, and meeting Helen Keller.

Turn-of-the-twentieth-century Cape Breton, a county on Cape Breton Island, is the setting of Ian Wallace's *Boy of the Deeps*. On James's first day working with his father in a coal mine beneath the Atlantic Ocean, the two are temporarily trapped when the ceiling collapses.

Brave Highland Heart, by Heather Kellerhals-Stewart, is also set in Cape Breton, among the descendants of its Scottish Highlander settlers. Told that she is too little to stay up all night for the ceilidh party, a little girl hides in the hay of the hayloft where she enjoys her father's bagpipe playing and then, discovered, joins in the dancing.

Nunavut

The setting of Michael Arvaarluk Kusugak's *Baseball Bats for Christmas* is on the Arctic Circle in Repulse Bay where he grew up. The six trees flown into this remote location in 1955 are the first trees the children have seen, and they are unsure as to how they should be used—until they discover that they can be made into baseball bats.

Arctic Stories, a book for older children by Kusugak, tells three stories about Agatha, an Inuit girl who also lives in Repulse Bay. Agatha defiantly yells at the airship which in 1958 caused panic among the villagers, comes to like the ugly raven which follows her grandmother everywhere, and, homesick and unhappy at the school in Chesterfield Inlet to which she is taken with two of her friends, nevertheless enjoys skiing—and rescues a priest who has fallen through the ice.

Kusugak's *My Arctic 1, 2, 3* is a counting book set in and around Rankin Inlet where Kusugak currently lives (as of 1996). The text and illustrations go from one polar bear to ten lemmings and then depict the numbers 20, 100, and 1,000,000. At the end of the book Kusugak tells how the animals and the berries relate to his family's experiences.

Kusugak's *Northern Lights: The Soccer Trails* is a story for older children about an Inuit family. Although no setting is specified, the story and Kusugak's other works make it likely that it is set in the largely Inuit province of Nunavut. Kataujaq greatly misses her mother, who has died, but is comforted when her grandmother tells her that just as she and the other villagers play soccer on the sea ice, so also the souls of those who have died play soccer in the sky. You can see them if you watch the northern lights.

Jeanne Bushey's *A Sled Dog for Moshi* tells of a little Inuit girl who lives in the village of Iqaluit on Baffin Island. Moshi longs for a pet dog, but it is not until she and her friend are lost in a whiteout that her father decides to give her a puppy—and that she decides it will be a sled dog.

Ontario

Children can take an armchair tour of Toronto as they peruse Allan Moak's *A Big City ABC*. Focusing on places of interest to children, this alphabet book also includes information on the settings of its twenty-six paintings.

A Chinese-Canadian girl is determined to go to Kapuskasing in Robert Munsch's *Where Is Gah-Ning?* When all else fails, she floats there by hanging on to three hundred balloons.

It is a family farm in Haliburton County which is the setting of Margaret Carney's *At Grandpa's Sugar Bush*. A boy spends his spring vacation helping his grandfather get sap from his maple trees, boiling the sap to get syrup—and finally enjoying maple syrup on pancakes.

In Barbara Smucker's *Selina and the Bear Paw Quilt* Waterloo is the destination of a Mennonite girl and her family who must flee their Pennsylvania home during the Civil War because they will not take sides in the conflict. Although Selina leaves her grandmother behind, she finds that her grandmother is still close because of the quilt Selina has brought with her and because of the quilt that she finds in her cousins' Ontario home.

Selina and the Shoo-Fly Pie, by Smucker, continues the story of Selina, this time one year later. Living in a new house in nearby St. Jacobs, Selina welcomes the visit of her grandmother and a cousin, Henry, who has left Virginia to escape the enmity displayed towards the neutral Mennonites. Selina's grandmother shows her how to bake shoo-fly pie, Henry's favorite.

Quebec

Children can learn about the different areas of Quebec from the many picture books set in this predominantly French–Canadian province.

Two books by Stéphane Poulin are set in east–end Montreal and feature a young boy who is constantly chasing his cat—through the neighborhood trying to find out where she spends her Saturdays (*Have You Seen Josephine?*) and through his school building when, unbeknownst to him, she comes to school in his book bag (*Can You Catch Josephine?*).

In Poulin's third book about Josephine, *Could You Stop Josephine?*, the cat hides in the car and goes with the family to spend a Sunday in the country. As might be imagined, the boy, his cousin, and his cousin's dog are kept busy chasing Josephine around the farm. These amusing stories will appeal to even very young children who will enjoy looking for Josephine in the full-page illustrations.

In Jonathan London's *The Sugaring-off Party* Paul's grandmother tells the story of her first maple sugar celebration held near the village of Mont-Saint-Hilaire, just east of Montreal. Enduring the antics of her twin cousins and tasting la tire (a "maple-taffy snowsicle") are among the memories recorded in the narrative and paintings.

The village of Ste. Justine near the Quebec-Maine border is the setting for three childhood recollections by author Roch Carrier.

In *The Boxing Champion* Roch, who hates boxing, spends the winter developing muscles for the boxing matches held in a neighbor's summer kitchen.

The Longest Home Run recounts the story of a traveling

magician's daughter who sets a record when her towering home run breaks Sergeant Bouton's window.

The third book, *A Happy New Year's Day*, is for the oldest children. The text and colorful illustrations present the author's memories of the New Year's Day when he was four (1941) and of the events which preceded it.

Set in the late 1700's, Natalie Kinsey-Warnock's *Wilderness Cat* tells of Serena and her family (minus her cat Moses), who move from Vermont to a Quebec cabin fifty miles away. The cat somehow manages to journey to the hungry family, bringing with him some much needed food.

In Marie Killilea's *Newf*, another cat—a kitten—and a Newfoundland dog become best friends as they live in a deserted cottage on the Gaspe Peninsula.

In *The Fiddler of the Northern Lights*, by Kinsey-Warnock, Henry and his grandfather skate up the St. Maurice River trying to find the fiddler who makes the Northern Lights dance.

When the tide is out, an Inuit girl goes by herself beneath the ice and collects mussels from the bottom of Ungava Bay in *Very Last First Time*, by Jan Andrews.

General

Alphabet, counting, and word books

The prairies found in Alberta, Manitoba, and Saskatchewan and a number of states in the United States come to life in paintings by Yvette Moore in Jo Bannatyne-Cugnet's *A Prairie Alphabet*. It presents for each letter a full-page painting, a one sentence description that includes words starting with that letter, and, at the end of the book, both a paragraph (written for adults or older children) explaining the painting and a list of objects starting with the letter that children may find in the picture.

The Yukon Territory, Northwest Territory, and the very northern part of Quebec lie above the 60th parallel. This area is the primary focus of Ted Harrison's *A Northern Alphabet*. The page for each letter includes a picture and the names of northern locations starting with (or for X and Z including) that letter. The book also includes a listing of letter-related objects depicted in each picture.

In Jim Haskins's *Count Your Way through Canada* the numbers are presented in both French and English and the objects counted include a beaver, hockey players, and articles of Inuit clothing.

Fables, fairy tales, folktales, legends, myths, and proverbs (including original works)

Rabbit and the Moon, by Douglas Wood, retells a legend of the Cree of Saskatchewan and Manitoba. It tells how Rabbit achieved his dream of riding on the moon and how the helpful Crane got his long legs and a red forehead.

The First Red Maple Leaf is an original story by Ludmila Zeman, a refugee from Czechoslovakia, who wished to explain why the maple leaf is Canada's national symbol. Thanks to Branta the goose and a young boy, maple tree leaves bring shelter to the early people and, in turn, birds restore color to the trees.

Historical figures

Drawing upon accounts in the explorer Alexander Mackenzie's journal, *A Dog Came, Too* by Ainslie Manson tells of the dog who accompanied the Mackenzie party on its 1793 journey across Canada.

Nonfiction

O Canada, by Ted Harrison, a book for the very oldest children, presents each Canadian province and territory with a page of text and a full-page painting.

Stories

A 1953 Caldecott Medal winner, *The Biggest Bear*, by Lynd Ward, is based partially on his memories of Canadian boyhood summers. When Johnny's bear cub grows up and becomes a nuisance, Johnny has a hard time getting him to return to the woods, but then finds a home for him in a zoo.

Teddy Jam's *The Year of Fire* is a chapter book illustrated with double-page, full-page, and smaller pictures of the big forest fire of 1919 and its aftermath. A grandfather tells his granddaughter of his experiences during the fire, now evident only in some cedar stumps rooted in rocks.

Saoussan, a little girl from Lebanon, finds it difficult to adjust to life in a Canadian town in Munsch and Saoussan Askar's *From Far Away*. She is relieved when she learns that the scariness of Halloween does not signal the shooting which she encountered in her homeland.

Ian also finds it hard to adjust to city life in Andrea Spalding's *Me and Mr. Mah*. Moving away from his prairie home and his father because of an impending divorce, Ian is lonely until he meets the Chinese-Canadian man who likes to garden next door. Together they share their special boxes and their memories of the prairie and China.

Munsch and Kusugak's *A Promise Is a Promise*, is the story of a young Inuit girl who disobeys her mother and goes ice fishing in Hudson Bay. It is only her mother's ingenuity that saves her and her brothers and sisters from the Qallupilluit, the imaginary creatures who live in the bay.

Paddle-to-the-Sea by Holling Clancy Holling is now a classic. Although the text is long and more advanced, children can spend hours poring over the book: finding the little canoe in the full-page paintings, looking at the sketches which accompany the text, and tracing on the maps Paddle's four-year journey from an Indian boy's cabin down the Nipigon River and then through the Great Lakes, the St. Lawrence River, and the Gulf of St. Lawrence to his intended destination: the sea.

Books

Andrews, Jan. *Very Last First Time*. Illustrated by Ian Wallace. New York: Margaret K. McElderry Books, 1986; Simon & Schuster Children's Publishing, 1988.

Bannatyne-Cugnet, Jo. *A Prairie Alphabet*. Illustrated by Yvette Moore. Plattsburgh, NY: Tundra Books of Northern New York, 1992; 1994, paperback.

Blades, Ann. *Mary of Mile 18*. Illustrated by author. Plattsburgh, NY: Tundra Books of Northern New York, 1996, paperback.

Bushey, Jeanne. *A Sled Dog for Moshi*. Illustrated by Germaine Arnaktauyok. New York: Hyperion Books for Children, 1994.

Carney, Margaret. *At Grandpa's Sugar Bush*. Illustrated by Janet Wilson. Toronto: Kids Can Press (Distributed by General Distribution Services), 1998.

Carrier, Roch. *The Boxing Champion*. Illustrated by Sheldon Cohen. Translated from French by Sheila Fischman. Plattsburgh, NY: Tundra Books of Northern New York, 1991; 1993, paperback.

Carrier, Roch. *A Happy New Year's Day*. Illustrated by Gilles Pelletier. Plattsburgh, NY: Tundra Books of Northern New York, 1991.

Carrier, Roch. *The Longest Home Run*. Illustrated by Sheldon Cohen. Translated and adapted from French by Sheila Fischman. Plattsburgh, NY: Tundra Books of Northern New York, 1993.

Harrison, Ted. *A Northern Alphabet*. Illustrated by author. Plattsburgh, NY: Tundra Books of Northern New York, 1996, paperback.

Harrison, Ted. *O Canada*. Illustrated by author. New York: Ticknor & Fields Books for Young Readers, 1993.

Haskins, Jim. *Count Your Way through Canada*. (Count Your Way Books) Illustrated by Steve Michaels. Minneapolis: Carolrhoda Books, 1989; 1989, paperback.

Hobbs, Will. *Howling Hill*. Illustrated by Jill Kastner. New York: Morrow Junior Books, 1998.

Holling, Holling Clancy. *Paddle-to-the-Sea*. Illustrated by author. Boston: Houghton Mifflin Co., 1941; 1980, paperback.

Jam, Teddy. *The Year of Fire*. Illustrated by Ian Wallace. New York: Margaret K. McElderry Books, 1993.

Kellerhals-Stewart, Heather. *Brave Highland Heart.* Illustrated by Werner Zimmerman. New York: Stoddart Kids (Distributed by General Distribution Services), 1999.

Killilea, Marie. *Newf.* Illustrated by Ian Schoenherr. New York: Philomel Books, 1992; Paperstar, 1996, paperback.

Kinsey-Warnock, Natalie. *The Fiddler of the Northern Lights.* Illustrated by Leslie W. Bowman. New York: Cobblehill Books, 1994; 1996; 1996, paperback.

Kinsey-Warnock, Natalie. *Wilderness Cat.* Illustrated by Mark Graham. New York: Cobblehill Books, 1992, paperback.

Kurelek, William. *A Prairie Boy's Summer.* Illustrated by author. Boston: Houghton Mifflin Company, 1975; Tundra Books of Northern New York, 1996, paperback.

Kurelek, William. *A Prairie Boy's Winter.* Illustrated by author. Boston: Houghton Mifflin Company, 1984, paperback.

Kusugak, Michael Arvaarluk. *Arctic Stories.* Illustrated by Vladyana Krykorka. Toronto: Annick (Distributed by Firefly Books), 1998; 1998, paperback.

Kusugak, Michael Arvaarluk. *Baseball Bats for Christmas.* Illustrated by Vladyana Krykorka. Toronto: Annick (Distributed by Firefly Books), 1990; 1993, paperback.

Kusugak, Michael Arvaarluk. *My Arctic 1, 2, 3.* Illustrated by Vladyana Krykorka. Toronto: Annick (Distributed by Firefly Books), 1996; 1996, paperback.

Kusugak, Michael Arvaarluk. *Northern Lights: The Soccer Trails.* Illustrated by Vladyana Krykorka. Toronto: Annick (Distributed by Firefly Books), 1993; 1993, paperback.

Lawson, Julie. *Emma and the Silk Train*. Illustrated by Paul Mombourquette. Toronto: Kids Can Press (Distributed by General Distribution Services), 1998.

London, Jonathan. *The Sugaring-Off Party*. Illustrated by Gilles Pelletier. New York: Dutton Children's Books, 1995, paperback; Viking Penguin, 1999, paperback.

MacKinnon, Christy. *Silent Observer*. Illustrated by author. Washington, D.C.: K. Green Publications (Distributed through Gallaudet University Press), 1993; Forest House Publishing Co., 1997.

Manson, Ainslie. *A Dog Came Too: A True Story*. Illustrated by Ann Blades. New York: Margaret K. McElderry Books, 1993.

Moak, Allan. *A Big City ABC*. Illustrated by author. Plattsburgh, NY: Tundra Books of Northern New York, 1989, paperback.

Munsch, Robert. *Where Is Gah-Ning?* Illustrated by Hélène Desputeaux. Toronto: Annick (Distributed by Firefly Books), 1994; 1994, paperback.

Munsch, Robert, and Michael Kusugak. *A Promise Is a Promise*. Illustrated by Vladyana Krykorka. Toronto: Annick (Distributed by Firefly Books), 1988; 1998, paperback.

Munsch, Robert, and Saoussan Askar. *From Far Away*. Illustrated by Michael Martchenko. Toronto: Annick (Distributed by Firefly Books), 1995.

Poulin, Stéphane. *Can You Catch Josephine?* Illustrated by author. Plattsburgh, NY: Tundra Books of Northern New York, 1988; 1988, paperback.

Poulin, Stéphane. *Could You Stop Josephine?* Illustrated by author. Plattsburgh, NY: Tundra Books of Northern New York, 1988; 1988, paperback.

Poulin, Stéphane. *Have You Seen Josephine?* Illustrated by author. Plattsburgh, NY: Tundra Books of Northern New York, 1988; 1988, paperback.

Smucker, Barbara. *Selina and the Bear Paw Quilt.* Illustrated by Janet Wilson. New York: Crown Publishing Group, 1999, paperback.

Smucker, Barbara. *Selina and the Shoo-Fly Pie.* Illustrated by Janet Wilson. New York: Stoddart Kids (Distributed by General Distribution Services), 1999.

Spalding, Andrea. *Me and Mr. Mah.* Illustrated by Janet Wilson. Custer, WA: Orca Book Publishers, 2000.

Toye, William, reteller. *The Loon's Necklace.* Illustrated by Elizabeth Cleaver. New York: Oxford University Press, 1990, paperback.

Valgardson, W. D. *Winter Rescue.* Illustrated by Ange Zhang. New York: Margaret K. McElderry Books, 1995.

Wallace, Ian. *Boy of the Deeps.* Illustrated by author. New York: DK Ink, 1999.

Ward, Lynd. *The Biggest Bear.* Illustrated by author. Boston: Houghton Mifflin Company, 1952; Sandpiper, 1973, paperback.

Wood, Douglas. *Rabbit and the Moon.* Illustrated by Leslie Baker. New York: Simon & Schuster Books for Young Readers, 1998.

Zeman, Ludmila. *The First Red Maple Leaf.* Illustrated by author. Plattsburgh, NY: Tundra Books of Northern New York, 1998, paperback.

"Here in the cloud forests of Costa Rica, you can find three hundred different kinds of birds."
—Collard. *The Forest in the Clouds.*

Costa Rica

And Sunday Makes Seven, retold by Robert Baden, tells the tale of two cousins, one poor and one rich, and how the poor one received gold from twelve witches when he helped them add to their poem, but the rich one received nothing but another mole on his nose when he added a nonrhyming line. Children enjoying this story can learn the days of the week in Spanish, as well as the rhyming tres (three) and seis (six) and the trouble-causing siete (seven).

Lynn Reiser's *Tortillas and Lullabies*, which is written in both English and Spanish, can be enjoyed by even very young children and especially by those interested in the concept of same and different. Slightly older children will appreciate the continuity of the daily experiences of grandmother, mother, daughter—and doll. A group of six Costa Rican women, the "Corazones Valientes", cooperated in painting the colorful illustrations.

A book for the oldest children, *The Forest in the Clouds*, by Sneed B. Collard III, presents the cloud forest near Monteverde. The text describes the forest and its birds, plants, and animals, while the accompanying paintings by Michael Rothman place them, with identifying labels, in their forest setting.

Books

Baden, Robert, reteller. *And Sunday Makes Seven.* Illustrated by Michelle Edwards. Morton Grove, IL: Albert Whitman & Company, 1990.

Collard, Sneed B., III. *The Forest in the Clouds.* Illustrated by Michael Rothman. Watertown, MA: Charlesbridge Publishing, 2000.

Reiser, Lynn. *Tortillas and Lullabies/Tortillas y cancioncitas.* Illustrated by "Corazones Valientes". Translated by Rebecca Hart. New York: Greenwillow Books, 1998.

"It was fiercely hot in the tropical sun."
—Howard. *Papa Tells Chita a Story.*

Cuba
Republic of Cuba

In Elizabeth Fitzgerald Howard's *Papa Tells Chita a Story* the tall tale that Chita's father relates is about an experience he had as an African-American soldier in the Spanish-American War. While carrying a secret message across Cuba, he fools a snake, swims under an alligator, and sleeps in an eagle's nest.

Book

Howard, Elizabeth Fitzgerald. *Papa Tells Chita a Story.* Illustrated by Floyd Cooper. New York: Simon & Schuster Books for Young Readers, 1995; Aladdin Paperbacks, 1998, paperback.

"Early morning is the best time to climb a tree because the sun has not yet had time to bake the earth until it is hot and steamy like a roasted plantain."
—Appelbaum. *Cocoa Ice.*

Dominican Republic

In Diana Appelbaum's *Cocoa Ice*, which is set in the late 1800s, a little girl in Maine and a little girl living on the island of Hispaniola can both enjoy chocolate ice, thanks to the work of their families and the schooner which carries cocoa beans to Maine and blocks of ice to the Dominican Republic.

The ciguapas are legendary creatures of the Dominican Republic who live secretly underwater and have backwards feet. In *The Secret Footprints*, by Julia Alvarez, a curious ciguapa girl is found by a human family. She manages to escape, but discovers from her encounter that humans can be caring.

Books

Alvarez, Julia. *The Secret Footprints*. Illustrated by Fabian Negrin. New York: Alfred A. Knopf, 2000.

Appelbaum, Diana. *Cocoa Ice*. Illustrated by Holly Meade. New York: Orchard Books, an imprint of Scholastic Inc., 1997.

"From that day on there has been peace on the volcanoes of El Salvador."
—Argueta. *Magic Dogs of the Volcanoes.*

El Salvador

Elaine Marie Alphin's *A Bear for Miguel* is set during the 1980s when there was guerrilla warfare in El Salvador. However, this book should be appropriate for children as young as age four, who will empathize with María, who makes the painful decision to trade her beloved stuffed bear for food for her family. The illustrations in this easy reader picture María's home and the village market.

Magic Dogs of the Volcanoes, by Manlio Argueta, is an original tale featuring cadejos, the magic dogs of El Salvadoran folklore. When lead soldiers try to destroy the magic dogs, the cadejos seek—and receive—the help of two volcanoes. The text is written in English and Spanish.

Books

Alphin, Elaine Marie. *A Bear for Miguel.* (An I Can Read Book) Illustrated by Joan Sandin. New York: Harper Trophy, 1997, paperback.

Argueta, Manlio. *Magic Dogs of the Volcanoes/Los perros mágicos de los volcanes.* Illustrated by Elly Simmons. Translated into English by Stacey Ross. San Francisco: Children's Book Press, 1990; 1995, paperback.

"I remember only the cold Arctic days when I sat for centuries, freezing cold and half buried in the hard and bitter earth."
—Conrad. *Call Me Ahnighito.*

Greenland

Greenland is a self-governing entity of Denmark.

Pam Conrad's *Call Me Ahnighito* is the account of the enormous meteorite named Ahnighito which was brought from Greenland to New York City by Robert E. Peary's expedition. The story is told by Ahnighito, who twice sadly watches the expedition sail away because of approaching winter and then finally leaves for a new home in 1897.

Book

Conrad, Pam. *Call Me Ahnighito.* Illustrated by Richard Egielski. (A Laura Geringer Book) New York: HarperCollins Children's Books, 1995.

"Esperanza's mother fed the chickens and pigs behind the main thatch hut while her father was off with her brothers in the field of corn, beans and coffee."
—Castañeda. *Abuela's Weave.*

Guatemala

Two picture books reveal the contrast between modern urban and traditional village life.

In Amy Glaser Gage's *Pascual's Magic Pictures* Pascual travels from Tikal in northern Guatemala to busy Guatemala City where he buys a hard-earned disposable camera. However, upon his return, it is thieving howler monkeys, not Pascual, who use his camera to take pictures.

Abuela's Weave, by Omar S. Castañeda, shows how young Esperanza feels overwhelmed by the noise, crowds, and pollution of Guate (Guatemala City). However, she discovers that despite all the manufactured products being sold at the city's fiesta, there is a great demand for the goods she and her grandmother have so painstakingly woven.

In *Gracias, Rosa*, by Michelle Markel, an American girl named Kate learns about Guatemala from her baby-sitter. When Rosa goes back to Guatemala to join her daughter Juana, Kate sends her favorite store-bought doll to Juana—and treasures the cloth Guatemalan doll Rosa has given her.

The diversity of Guatemala's culture is reflected in Amelia Lau Carling's *Mama & Papa Have a Store*. Too young to join her siblings at school, a little girl spends her day at her parents' store in Guatemala City where she listens to her parents and a friend reminisce about life in China, watches a Mayan family carefully select threads for weaving clothing patterns, hears business being conducted in Spanish, and enjoys playing with her siblings at lunchtime and after school in the store building which is also their home.

The Sleeping Bread, by Stefan Czernecki and Timothy Rhodes, tells of villagers who force a beggar to leave town so that he won't be an embarrassment at the upcoming festival. Upon his departure, the baker's bread stops rising—and it is only when the beggar returns that the bread is awakened.

The origin of the quetzal, the national bird of Guatemala, is the legend told in *The Hummingbird King*, written and adapted by Argentina Palacios.

The origin of the chirimia, a musical pipe, is the topic of Jane Anne Volkmer's *Song of the Chirimia*, which is written in both English and Spanish. When Black Feather plays the chirimia, its music is so beautiful that the Mayan princess agrees to marry him.

Books

Carling, Amelia Lau. *Mama & Papa Have a Store*. Illustrated by author. New York: Dial Books for Young Readers, 1998.

Castañeda, Omar S. *Abuela's Weave*. Illustrated by Enrique O. Sanchez. New York: Lee & Low Books, 1995, paperback.

Czernecki, Stefan, and Timothy Rhodes. *The Sleeping Bread*. Illustrated by Stefan Czernecki. New York: Hyperion Books for Children, 1992.

Gage, Amy Glaser. *Pascual's Magic Pictures*. Illustrated by Karen Dugan. Minneapolis: Carolhoda Books, 1996.

Markel, Michelle. *Gracias, Rosa*. Illustrated by Diane Paterson. Morton Grove, Illinois: Albert Whitman & Company, 1995.

Palacios, Argentina, writer and adapter. *The Hummingbird King: A Guatemalan Legend*. (Legends of the World) Illustrated by Felipe Davalos. Mahwah, NJ: Troll Communications, 1993, paperback; 1997.

Volkmer, Jane Anne, reteller. *Song of the Chirimia: A Guatemalan Folktale/La musica de la chirimia: Folklore Guatemalteco*. Illustrated by reteller. Translated by Lori Ann Schatschneider. Minneapolis: First Avenue Editions, 1992, paperback.

"They sped past mud huts with green and pink doors and shutters, and pretty houses with gingerbread trim."
—Williams. *Tap-Tap.*

Haiti

Two stories tell of little girls who go with their mothers to market.

In *Tap-Tap*, by Karen Lynn Williams, Sasifi uses the money her mother has given her for a treat to buy them a ride home to Deschapelles on the tap-tap, a truck crowded with people and their fruit, furniture, and animals.

Another little girl, Ti Marie, helps increase her mother's sales. In Williams's *Painted Dreams*, Ti Marie paints colorful pictures on the wall behind her mother's tomato and onion stall.

The paintings in *Mama Rocks, Papa Sings*, by Nancy Van Laan, illustrate the rhythmic story of a small girl whose parents acquire more and more babies as they help out their friends and neighbors. Children can learn to count in Creole as well as English as the number of people in the house grows from three to ten and then, when the babies depart, drops back to three.

Running the Road to ABC, by Denizé Lauture, describes through poetic writing and acrylic landscapes the daily morning run of three boys and three girls who in the dark and across hilly terrain race to their schoolhouse.

Melanie Hope Greenberg's *Aunt Lilly's Laundromat* is set in Brooklyn, but the laundromat is decorated with pictures Aunt Lilly has painted of her native Haiti. The paintings and the text's descriptions provide an introduction to this Caribbean country.

Diane Wolkstein relates two Haitian folktales.

One, *The Banza*, tells of two friends, a small goat and a small tiger, and of how the tiger's gift to the goat protects her when she is confronted by ten big tigers.

The other folktale, *Bouki Dances the Kokioko*, describes how the king outwits the country's dancers—until Malice outwits both the king and his friend Bouki.

Books

Greenberg, Melanie Hope. *Aunt Lilly's Laundromat.* Illustrated by author. New York: Dutton Children's Books, 1994, paperback.

Lauture, Denizé. *Running the Road to ABC.* Illustrated by Reynold Ruffins. New York: Simon & Schuster Books for Young Readers, 1996.

Van Laan, Nancy. *Mama Rocks, Papa Sings.* (An Apple Soup Book) Illustrated by Roberta Smith. New York: Alfred A. Knopf Books for Young Readers, 1995.

Williams, Karen Lynn. *Painted Dreams.* Illustrated by Catherine Stock. New York: Morrow Junior Books, 1998.

Williams, Karen Lynn. *Tap-Tap.* Illustrated by Catherine Stock. New York: Clarion Books, 1994.

Wolkstein, Diane. *The Banza: A Haitian Story.* (Pied Piper Books) Illustrated by Marc Brown. New York: Dial Books for Young Readers, 1984, paperback; N A L Dutton, 1992, paperback.

Wolkstein, Diane, reteller. *Bouki Dances the Kokioko: A Comical Tale from Haiti.* Illustrated by Jesse Sweetwater. San Diego: Harcourt, 1997.

"Raindrops beating the metal roof of her house sounded like a hundred drums."
—Hanson. *The Face at the Window.*

Jamaica

Trees play a role in two picture books by Regina Hanson.

In *The Tangerine Tree*, when Ida's father leaves to find work in wintry New York, Ida bottles some of the sun from the tangerine tree to keep him warm.

It is a mango tree which creates a problem for Dora in *The Face at the Window*. Frightened by her schoolmates' tales of what will happen to her because she has seen scary Miss Nella's face, Dora discovers the truth and becomes Miss Nella's friend.

The Chalk Doll, by Charlotte Pomerantz, tells of an American girl who learns about her mother's childhood in Jamaica and decides that she too would like a homemade rag doll.

Two books relate Jamaican folktales having their origin in Africa.

In *The Magic Feather*, retold by Lisa Rojany, a Jamaican girl uses compliments to trick half-human–half-bird Mancrow—and light returns to the island.

As retold by Frances Temple, *Tiger Soup* shows how Anansi the spider steals Tiger's soup and manages to place the blame on some gullible monkeys.

Doctor Bird is Jamaica's national bird. In Gerald Hausman's *Doctor Bird* he manages to teach lessons to both Mouse and Brother Owl, but the lesson he teaches Mongoose is short-lived.

Colorful double-page pictures of Jamaica in *Island in the Sun* illustrate the calypso song of that title which was written by Harry Belafonte and Lord Burgess (Irving Burgie) and sung by Belafonte. The book includes the song's music.

Books

Belafonte, Harry, and Lord Burgess. *Island in the Sun*. Illustrated by Alex Ayliffe. New York: Dial Books for Young Readers, 1999.

Hanson, Regina. *The Face at the Window*. Illustrated by Linda Saport. New York: Clarion Books, 1997.

Hanson, Regina. *The Tangerine Tree*. Illustrated by Harvey Stevenson. New York: Clarion Books, 1995.

Hausman, Gerald. *Doctor Bird: Three Lookin' Up Tales from Jamaica*. Illustrated by Ashley Wolff. New York: Philomel Books, 1998.

Pomerantz, Charlotte. *The Chalk Doll*. Illustrated by Frané Lessac. New York: Lippincott Children's Books, 1989; Harper Trophy, 1993, paperback.

Rojany, Lisa, reteller. *The Magic Feather: A Jamaican Legend*. (Legends of the World) Illustrated by Philip Kuznicki. Mahwah, NJ: Troll Communications, 1997; 1998, paperback.

Temple, Frances, reteller. *Tiger Soup: An Anansi Story from Jamaica*. Illustrated by author. New York: Orchard Books, 1994; 1998, paperback.

"Everywhere vivid blossoms blazed against the bright green of sugarcane and banana and pineapple fields and the deeper green of distant mountains."
—San Souci. *The Faithful Friend.*

Martinique

Martinique is an overseas department of France.

Nineteenth century Martinique is the setting for two books by Robert D. San Souci.

In *Cendrillon: A Caribbean Cinderella* the washerwoman, who has loved Cendrillon since birth, assumes the role of fairy godmother, using the magic wand her mother had left her.

The Faithful Friend tells the tale of a young man who saves his friend and his friend's betrothed from the evils plotted by her father. Paintings of the Caribbean island convey the foreboding mood of the story.

Books

San Souci, Robert D. *Cendrillon: A Caribbean Cinderella.* Illustrated by Brian Pinkney. New York: Simon & Schuster Books for Young Readers, 1998.

San Souci, Robert D. *The Faithful Friend.* Illustrated by Brian Pinkney. New York: Four Winds Press, 1995; Simon & Schuster Children's Publishing, 1999.

"Her tree glowed in the night, dripping with lemons as big and round as baby moons."
—Fine. *Under the Lemon Moon.*

Mexico
Estados Unidos Mexicanos

Specific Locations

Many of the picture books described below are set in the Federal District or in specific Mexican states.

Federal District (Mexico City)

Tomie dePaola's *The Lady of Guadalupe* tells the legend of Mexico's patron saint, the Lady of Guadalupe, who spoke to an Indian farmer in 1531 and sent a sign to convince the church's bishop to build a church at the spot of her appearance. This site is within the city limits of Mexico City.

The 1702 welcoming of the newest viceroy to be sent from Spain is presented in a book for older children, *When the Viceroy Came*, by Claudia Burr, Krystyna Libura, and Maria Cristina Urrutia. Details from a painted screen together with the text depict the festivities that took place at Chapultepec, the summer home of the viceroys. Children can search the double-page illustration of the screen to find the settings of individual pictures.

Written in Spanish and English, *Mediopollito*, by Alma Flor Ada, tells of a half chicken who, because of the favors he has performed for a stream, a fire, and the wind, escapes a cooking pot and becomes a weather vane atop a palace in Mexico City.

Guerrero

In this story from the town of Ayutla, *Borreguita and the Coyote* retold by Verna Aardema, a little lamb repeatedly tricks the coyote who wants to eat her until the coyote decides it would be better to coexist.

Hidalgo

Domitila, a book for older children which is adapted by Jewell Reinhart Coburn, tells of Domitila, who has learned from her mother to add love to whatever she does. When the governor's son sets out to search for the girl who has made a tasty dish from cacti and transformed leather into a work of art, he is given wrong directions by the woman who becomes Domitila's stepmother. Nevertheless, there is a happy ending to this Mexican Cinderella story.

Jalisco

In Emery Bernhard's retelling of a Huichol Indian myth, *The Tree That Rains*, the hardworking farmer builds a boat out of a fig tree to escape the coming flood and fills it, not with pairs of animals, but with different types of seeds, all in portions of five, and with his hardworking dog.

When the flood subsides, the dog turns into a woman, the couple's descendants people the earth, the seeds are planted, and a fig tree, which stands beside Lake Chapala, provides water for the crops.

Jeanette Winter's *Josefina*, which tells of Josefina Aguilar, a resident of Ocotlán, is included under Historical figures.

Michoacán

Thomas P. Lewis's *Hill of Fire* tells the story of the Parícutin volcano which erupted in 1943. A Tarascan Indian farmer who complains of the boredom of his routine receives an astounding surprise when his plow slides into the ground and the volcano is born.

The Hummingbirds' Gift, by Stefan Czernecki and Timothy Rhodes, is set in the Tarascan village of Tzintzuntzan. When a drought turns a farmer's wheat into straw and destroys the flowers from which the hummingbirds get nectar, a family provides them with little clay pots filled with sugar water. In return, the hummingbirds show the family how to weave straw into figures, which the family sells for their sustenance.

Erandi's Braids, by Antonio Hernández Madrigal, is set in another Tarascan village, Pátzcuaro. When her mother's hair is not long enough to sell so that their fishing net can be replaced, Erandi bravely sells her own long braids, bringing enough money both for the net and for a birthday doll for Erandi.

Oaxaca

The Oaxaca market in Patricia Grossman's *Saturday*

Market comes alive through the descriptions and paintings of the individual vendors, who sell such varied products as chile peppers, sandals, rugs with Mayan designs, parrots, breads, and Zapotec figurines.

Tony Johnston's *The Tale of Rabbit and Coyote* is based on a story from Juchitán. Rabbit so infuriates Coyote with his tricks that Coyote is still howling at the moon where he sees the fugitive Rabbit.

Alberto Blanco's *Angel's Kite* is inspired by the early life of the book's illustrator, Rodolfo Morales, who lived in Ocotlán de Morelos. This book, which is written in both English and Spanish, tells how much the kite maker misses the town's church bell, which has disappeared. He illustrates his most magnificent kite with a picture of his town, including the missing bell. The kite flies off into the sky, and, when it is recovered, the bell depicted on the kite has vanished, but the bell in the church has reappeared.

The Woman Who Outshone the Sun is the retelling of an Alejandro Cruz Martinez' poem, which is based on a Zapotec story. It tells of Lucia Zenteno, who was driven from the village by those who disliked her special powers and her dignity. When she leaves, the river who loves her comes along and does not return until the villagers agree to show tolerance.

Two of the picture books are original folktales by Matthew Gollub.

Uncle Snake explains the origin of lightning in its account of a boy who enters a forbidden cave and after twenty years becomes a snake with a man's head. The light flashes caused by his sprints across the sky signal the coming of a rainstorm.

Having never seen a cat, the villagers fear and then turn

against the healer's cats in *The Twenty-Five Mixtec Cats*. However, after the cats help heal the butcher and then save the healer himself, they become honored members of the community.

Veracruz

Lucha Corpi's bilingual book, *Where Fireflies Dance*, tells of her childhood in Jáltipan: of going at night with her brother to the haunted house once occupied by a revolutionary soldier and of listening to her grandmother's stories, the music from a jukebox, and her father's singing.

Yucatan

In Michelle McCunney's *Mario's Mexican Journey* a boy in Mexico City dreams that, accompanied by Mayan-speaking children, he visits the magnificent Mayan city, Chichén Itzá, and then sleeps in the nearby jungle.

General

Alphabet, counting, and word books

The first of the two counting books can be enjoyed by even the youngest children. *Uno, Dos, Tres: One, Two, Three* by Pat Mora shows two little girls buying birthday gifts for their mother in a Mexican market.

In Jim Haskins's *Count Your Way through Mexico* older children can learn much about Mexico's history and culture. The numbers are written in both Spanish and English.

Celebrations

Twelve books on Mexico tell of celebrations.

In James Flora's *The Fabulous Firework Family* the firework family's village celebrates the birthday of its patron saint, Santiago, with a fireworks fiesta. The parents, the son, the daughter, the burro, and the parrot all participate in the making of a magnificent firework castle which is lit during the fiesta.

Johnston's *Day of the Dead*, Janice Levy's *The Spirit of Tío Fernando*, and Kathleen Krull's *Maria Molina and the Days of the Dead* tell of the celebration of the Day of the Dead which extends from October 31 through November 2.

In Johnston's story, in which a number of Spanish words are introduced, two children find it difficult not to sample all the food which their family is preparing for the holiday. However, after the procession to the cemetery to remember their loved ones and after singing and dancing, it is finally time to eat.

Levy's book is a bilingual book for older children. During the Day of the Dead Nando experiences many fond memories of his uncle, Fernando.

A book for older children, *Maria Molina and the Days of the Dead* tells how Maria and her family honor her deceased baby brother and grandmother and then enjoy the fiesta. When the family moves to the United States, Maria celebrates a different holiday, Halloween—and discovers that she can still honor those who have died.

It is Christmas which is celebrated in five of the books.

The Legend of the Poinsettia, retold by dePaola, and *The Gift of the Poinsettia*, by Mora and Charles Ramírez

Berg, provide different versions of the origin of the poinsettia as a Christmas plant.

In dePaola's book, Lucida helps her mother weave a new blanket for the manger at the village church, but when her mother takes ill, she hopelessly tangles the yarn. Without a gift for the Baby Jesus on Christmas Eve, Lucida decides to bring some weeds to the church—and they suddenly blossom into red stars.

Written in both English and Spanish, *The Gift of the Poinsettia* tells how Carlos celebrates the nine days of Christmas, happily relating his experiences to his aunt, but worrying about what gift he can bring to the Baby Jesus on Christmas Eve. Heeding his aunt's advice, he sadly brings a wild plant to the manger and his tears turn the leaves red.

James Rice's *La Nochebuena South of the Border* also is a Christmas Eve story, an adaptation of the familiar "Night before Christmas". Written in both Spanish and English, with Spanish words interspersed into the English version, the text and the illustrations provide a Mexican setting for Papá Noel, his cart drawn by eight burros, and the piñata which he fills.

Pancho's Piñata, by Czernecki and Rhodes, relates how an old man creates a Christmas piñata for his village to repay the gift of happiness which a Christmas star had given him when he was a little boy.

It is a piñata which Ceci wants most when she has her first posada in *Nine Days to Christmas*, a Caldecott Medal winner by Marie Hall Ets and Aurora Labastida, which is illustrated by Ets. Upset when the children break the beautiful star piñata she has chosen, Ceci watches it become a real star.

Three girls have very personal celebrations in three other books.

Manuela celebrates a birthday in *Manuela's Gift* by Kristyn Rehling Estes. Initially disappointed when she does not get the new party dress she has hoped for, Manuela comes to appreciate the dress which her mother and grandmother have made her out of one of her mother's dresses.

In Loretta Lopez's *The Birthday Swap*, Lori goes across the border to her Mexican relatives, presumably to celebrate her much older sister's birthday. However, the party turns out to be a surprise birthday party for Lori.

In Nancy Riecken's *Today Is the Day*, Yesenia is confident that her father will be returning after six months away looking for work. She meets each bus to no avail, but then her father appears, making it a very special day.

Fables, fairy tales, folktales, legends, myths, and proverbs (including original works)

Collages illustrate *Cuckoo*, Lois Ehlert's bilingual adaptation of a Mayan tale. The vain and lazy cuckoo displays real courage when fire threatens the vegetable seeds.

In *The Little Red Ant and the Great Big Crumb*, retold by Shirley Climo, the littlest ant convinces herself that she is incredibly strong—and then is able to lift the crumb of cake she has found.

Two books, Gerald McDermott's *Musicians of the Sun* and *How Music Came to the World*, retold by Hal Ober, tell the Aztec story of how the Wind went to the Sun and brought his musicians to earth.

In McDermott's version the four musicians, each a different color, have been captured by Sun and upon their arrival the earth receives both music and color.

Ober has Quetzalcoatl, the wind god, having to negotiate a maze before he reaches the Sun and the earth awakening with the coming of the musicians.

Richard Lewis's *All of You Was Singing* is a poetic retelling of the story, which is described under Poetry and songs.

Third grade students at the Drexel Elementary School in Tucson, Arizona are the authors and illustrators of *How the Sun Was Born*. Basing their bilingual story on the Aztec concept of the sun and their illustrations on the art of the Huichol Indians, this highly original tale shows the sun as a baby dinosaur turned into a ball of fire by an erupting volcano and returning each night to its egg.

The Witch's Face, adapted by Eric A Kimmel, tells how a gentleman rescues a prospective witch, but then discovers too late that it is not her face that he loves.

Historical figures

The picture books set in Mexico include the biographies of two artists.

Diego, by Jonah Winter, depicts through paintings and a brief bilingual text the life of Diego Rivera, Mexico's well-known muralist.

Jeanette Winter's *Josefina* tells of Josefina Aguilar, who from early childhood shaped and painted clay figurines. The last portion of the book incorporates her representations of Mexican life into a counting book as she makes one sun, four flower vendors, five farmers, and ten stars.

Argentina Palacios's *Viva México!* is not only a biography of Benito Juárez, but also describes Mexico's Cinco de Mayo victory over the invading French army.

Save My Rainforest, by Monica Zak, is the true story of Omar Castillo, who as an eight-nine year old walks with his father 870 miles from Mexico City to Tuxtla Gutiérrez to persuade the governor of the state of Chiapas to save the Lacandon Rainforest. That failing, he manages to secure an audience with the President of Mexico—and then continues to pursue his efforts.

Nonfiction

Quetzalcoatl, in this case a feathered serpent, is the travel guide for a year's tour of Mexico in Robin Rector Krupp's *Let's Go Traveling in Mexico*. This book for the oldest children presents a wealth of information through text, detailed illustrations, maps, and cartoon captions.

Another introduction to Mexico, also for the oldest children, is provided in Lynn Ainsworth Olawsky's *Colors of Mexico*. The black lava of the Paricutin volcano, the gold color of the gold which attracted Cortés to Tenochtitlán (now Mexico City), and the yellow of corn tortillas are among the subjects presented.

Poetry and songs

Two bilingual books are included among the poetry books.

In *From the Bellybutton of the Moon and Other Summer Poems* Francisco X. Alarcón recalls his childhood summers when he traveled by station wagon with his family to Atoyac (in Jalisco) to visit his Mexican relatives.

Johnston's *My Mexico* presents in its poetry and accompanying illustrations a child's introduction to Mexico from the children selling iguanas in Taxco to the colorful houses and the celebration of the Day of the Dead.

A third poetry book, Richard Lewis's *All of You Was Singing*, is a lyrical presentation for older children that relates the myth of the coming of music as a part of the Aztec creation story. Two other versions of this myth are described under Fables....

Stories

Johnston's *The Iguana Brothers* features the amusing dialogue of two iguanas, who decide to change their bug diet, briefly think they are dinosaurs, and make a discovery about friendship.

Many Spanish words are introduced in Campbell Geeslin's *On Ramón's Farm*. Ramón thoroughly enjoys the unusual behavior of the six farm animals: the two sheep who love wearing ribbons, the goat who spins on a windmill, the rooster who charges his reflection, the pig who tricks Ramón into giving him more food, and the burro who dances backwards to the marketplace.

Pumpkin Fiesta, by Caryn Yacowitz, tells of Foolish Fernando, who tries to learn Old Juana's pumpkin-growing secrets by copying the extraneous things that she wears and does. This failing, he steals her three best pumpkins and takes them to the pumpkin fiesta. After Old Juana rightfully gains the fiesta crown, she teaches Foolish Fernando the real secret to growing pumpkins: hard work.

Rosalinda's lemons are stolen and her lemon tree ailing in Edith Hope Fine's *Under the Lemon Moon*. With the help of La Anciana, the Old One, the lemon tree bears fruit which Rosalinda shares with her neighbors, her grandmother—and the thief and his family.

Eve Bunting's *Going Home* describes how Carlos and his family travel to Mexico to visit his parents' old village. It is then that Carlos comes to understand both why Mexico will always be home to his parents and why they have become farm workers in the United States.

The Old Lady and the Birds by Johnston tells of an old lady who spends the entire day and night in her garden, content to be with just the birds and a cat.

Barbara Sorros's *Grandmother's Song* for older children tells of another old lady, a grandmother, who through stroking and singing to her frightened granddaughter instills in her strength, dignity, and courage. Even when as an adult her grandmother has died, the granddaughter is supported by her grandmother's spirit.

Books

Aardema, Verna, reteller. *Borreguita and the Coyote: A Tale from Ayutla, Mexico.* Illustrated by Petra Mathers. Translated by reteller. New York: Alfred A. Knopf Books for Young Readers, 1991; Random House Books for Young Readers, 1998, paperback.

Ada, Alma Flor. *Mediopollito/Half-Chicken.* Illustrated by Kim Howard. Translated by Rosalma Zubizarreta. New York: Bantam Doubleday Dell Books for Young Readers, 1995; 1997, paperback.

Alarcón, Francisco X. *From the Bellybutton of the Moon and Other Summer Poems/Del ombligo de la luna y otros poemas de verano.* Illustrated by Maya Christina Gonzales. San Francisco: Children's Book Press, 1998.

Bernhard, Emery, reteller. *The Tree That Rains: The Flood Myth of the Huichol Indians of Mexico.* Illustrated by Durga Bernhard. New York: Holiday House, 1994.

Blanco, Alberto. *Angel's Kite/La estrella de Angel.* Illustrated by Rodolfo Morales. Translated into English by Dan Bellm. San Francisco: Children's Book Press, 1998, paperback.

Bunting, Eve. *Going Home.* Illustrated by David Diaz. New York: HarperCollins Children's Books, 1996; Harper Trophy, 1998, paperback.

Burr, Claudia, Krystyna Libura, and Maria Cristina Urrutia. *When the Viceroy Came.* Designed by authors. Toronto: Groundwood Books/Douglas & McIntyre (Distributed by Publishers Group West), 1999.

Climo, Shirley, reteller. *The Little Red Ant and the Great Big Crumb: A Mexican Folktale.* Illustrated by Francisco X. Mora. New York: Clarion Books, 1999.

Coburn, Jewell Reinhart, adapter. *Domitila: A Cinderella Tale from the Mexican Tradition.* Illustrated by Connie McLennan. Auburn, CA: Shen's Books, 2000.

Corpi, Lucha. *Where Fireflies Dance/Ahí, donde bailan las luciérnagas.* Illustrated by Mira Reisberg. San Francisco: Children's Book Press, 1997.

Cruz Martinez, Alejandro. *The Woman Who Outshone the Sun: The Legend of Lucia Zenteno/La mujer que brillaba aún más que el sol: La leyenda de Lucía Zenteno.* Retold by Harriet Rohmer and David Schecter. Illustrated by Fernando Olivera. Translated into Spanish by Rosalma Zubizarreta. San Francisco: Children's Book Press, 1991; 1994, paperback.

Czernecki, Stefan, and Timothy Rhodes. *The Hummingbirds' Gift*. Illustrated by Stefan Czernecki. New York: Hyperion Books for Children, 1994.

Czernecki, Stefan, and Timothy Rhodes. *Pancho's Piñata*. Illustrated by Stefan Czernecki. New York: Hyperion Books for Children, 1992; 1999, paperback; Hyperion Paperbacks for Children, 1994, paperback.

dePaola, Tomie. *The Lady of Guadalupe*. Illustrated by author. New York: Holiday House, 1980; 1980, paperback.

dePaola, Tomie, reteller. *The Legend of the Poinsettia*. Illustrated by reteller. New York: G. P. Putnam's Sons, 1994; Paperstar, 1997, paperback.

Drexel Elementary School (Tucson, Arizona) Third Grade Students. *How the Sun Was Born/Como el sol nació*. Illustrated by authors. Translated into Spanish by Dora Recinos. Dublin, OH: PAGES Publishing Group, 1993.

Ehlert, Lois. *Cuckoo: A Mexican Folktale/Cucú; Un cuento folklórico mexicano*. Illustrated by author. Translated into Spanish by Gloria de Aragón Andújar. San Diego: Harcourt, 1997.

Estes, Kristyn Rehling. *Manuela's Gift*. Illustrated by Claire B. Cotts. San Francisco: Chronicle Books, 1999.

Ets, Marie Hall, and Aurora Labastida. *Nine Days to Christmas*. Illustrated by Marie Hall Ets. New York: Viking Children's Books, 1959; 1991, paperback; Puffin, 1991, paperback.

Fine, Edith Hope. *Under the Lemon Moon*. Illustrated by René King Moreno. New York: Lee & Low Books, 1999.

Flora, James. *The Fabulous Firework Family*. Illustrated by author. New York: Margaret K. McElderry Books, 1994.

Geeslin, Campbell. *On Ramón's Farm*. (An Anne Schwartz Book) Illustrated by Petra Mathers. New York: Simon & Schuster Children's Publishing, 1998.

Gollub, Matthew. *The Twenty-five Mixtec Cats*. Illustrated by Leovigildo Martinez. New York: Tambourine Books, 1993.

Gollub, Matthew. *Uncle Snake*. Illustrated by Leovigildo Martinez. New York: Tambourine Books, 1996.

Grossman, Patricia. *Saturday Market*. Illustrated by Enrique O. Sánchez. New York: Lothrop, Lee & Shepard Books, 1994.

Haskins, Jim. *Count Your Way through Mexico*. (Count Your Way Books) Illustrated by Helen Byers. Minneapolis: Carolrhoda Books, 1989; 1989, paperback.

Johnston, Tony. *Day of the Dead*. Illustrated by Jeanette Winter. San Diego: Harcourt, 1997.

Johnston, Tony. *The Iguana Brothers*. Illustrated by Mark Teague. New York: Blue Sky Press, 1995.

Johnston, Tony. *My Mexico/México mío*. Illustrated by F. John Sierra. New York: G. P. Putnam's Sons, 1996.

Johnston, Tony. *The Old Lady and the Birds*. Illustrated by Stephanie Garcia. San Diego: Harcourt, 1994.

Johnston, Tony. *The Tale of Rabbit and Coyote*. Illustrated by Tomie dePaola. New York: G. P. Putnam's Sons, 1994; Paperstar, 1998, paperback.

Kimmel, Eric A., adapter. *The Witch's Face: A Mexican Tale*. Illustrated by Fabricio Vanden Broeck. New York: Holiday House, 1993.

Krull, Kathleen. *Maria Molina and the Days of the Dead.* Illustrated by Enrique O. Sánchez. New York: Macmillan Books for Young Readers, 1994.

Krupp, Robin Rector. *Let's Go Traveling in Mexico.* Illustrated by author. New York: Morrow Junior Books, 1996.

Levy, Janice. *The Spirit of Tío Fernando: A Day of the Dead Story/El espíritu de tío Fernando: Una historia del Día de los Muertos.* Illustrated by Morella Fuenmayor. Spanish translation by Teresa Mlawer. Morton Grove, IL: Albert Whitman & Company, 1995; 1995, paperback.

Lewis, Richard. *All of You Was Singing.* Illustrated by Ed Young. New York: Atheneum Books for Young Readers, 1991.

Lewis, Thomas P. *Hill of Fire.* (An I CAN READ History Book) Illustrated by Joan Sandin. New York: HarperCollins Children's Books, 1971; Harper Trophy, 1983, paperback.

Lopez, Loretta. *The Birthday Swap.* Illustrated by author. New York: Lee & Low Books, 1997; 1999, paperback.

McCunney, Michelle. *Mario's Mayan Journey.* Illustrated by author. Greenvale, NY: Mondo Publishing, 1996, paperback.

McDermott, Gerald. *Musicians of the Sun.* Illustrated by author. New York: Blue Sky Press, 1994; Simon & Schuster Children's Publishing, 1997.

Madrigal, Antonio Hernández. *Erandi's Braids.* Illustrated by Tomie dePaola. New York: Putnam Publishing Group, 1999.

Mora, Pat. *Uno, Dos, Tres: One, Two, Three.* Illustrated by Barbara Lavallee. New York: Clarion Books, 1996.

Mora, Pat, and Charles Ramírez Berg. *The Gift of the Poinsettia/El regalo de la flor de nochebuena.* Illustrated by Daniel Lechón. Houston, TX: Piñata Books, 1995.

Ober, Hal, reteller. *How Music Came to the World: An Ancient Mexican Myth.* Illustrated by Carol Ober. Boston: Houghton Mifflin Company, 1994.

Olawsky, Lynn Ainsworth. *Colors of Mexico.* (Colors of the World) Illustrated by Janice Lee Porter. Minneapolis: Carolrhoda Books, 1997; 1997, paperback.

Palacios, Argentina. *Viva México!: A Story of Benito Juárez and Cinco de Mayo.* (Stories of America) Illustrated by Howard Berelson. Austin, TX: Raintree Steck-Vaughn Publishers, 1993.

Rice, James. *La Nochebuena South of the Border.* Illustrated by author. Translated by Ana Smith. Gretna, LA: Pelican Publishing Company, 1993.

Riecken, Nancy. *Today Is the Day.* Illustrated by Catherine Stock. Boston: Houghton Mifflin Company, 1996.

Sorros, Barbara. *Grandmother's Song.* Illustrated by Jackie Morris. Brooklyn, NY: Barefoot Books, 1998.

Winter, Jeanette. *Josefina.* Illustrated by author. San Diego: Harcourt, 1996.

Winter, Jonah. *Diego.* Illustrated by Jeanette Winter. Translated from English by Amy Prince. New York: Alfred A. Knopf Books for Young Readers, 1994, paperback.

Yacowitz, Caryn. *Pumpkin Fiesta.* Illustrated by Joe Cepeda. New York: HarperCollins Publishers, 1998.

Zak, Monica. *Save My Rainforest.* Illustrated by Bengt-Arne Runnerström. Translated by Nancy Schimmel. Volcano, CA: Volcano Press, 1992, paperback.

"Almost everywhere we go, calypso and reggae music plays sweetly to our ears."
—Lessac. *My Little Island.*

Montserrat

Montserrat is a British crown colony.

Frané Lessac's paintings provide a realistic setting for *My Little Island*'s story of a young boy, who returns with a friend for a visit to his native Montserrat.

Book

Lessac, Frané. *My Little Island.* Illustrated by author. New York: Lippincott Children's Books, 1985; Harper Trophy, 1987, paperback.

"Late one Saturday afternoon, three brothers left the village of Ulwas on the Coco River in Nicaragua."
—Rohmer, Chow, and Vidaure. *The Invisible Hunters.*

Nicaragua

Written in both English and Spanish, Harriet Rohmer's adaptation of the folktale, *Uncle Nacho's Hat*, tells how Uncle Nacho is so busy trying to dispose of his old hat that he fails to enjoy his new one.

In the bilingual *The Invisible Hunters* by Rohmer, Octavio Chow, and Morris Vidaure, three Miskito Indian brothers break their promise to the Dar and as a result become permanently, not temporarily, invisible. Older children may be able to grasp the historical significance of the temptations offered by the traders who come to the brothers' isolated village.

Books

Rohmer, Harriet, adapter. *Uncle Nacho's Hat/El sombrero del tío Nacho.* Illustrated by Veg Reisberg. Translated into Spanish by Rosalma Zubizarreta. San Francisco: Children's Book Press, 1989; 1993, paperback.

Rohmer, Harriet, Octavio Chow, and Morris Vidaure. *The Invisible Hunters: A Legend from the Miskito Indians of Nicaragua/Los cazadores invisibles: Una leyenda de los indios miskitos de Nicaragua.* (Stories from Central America) Illustrated by Joe Sam. Translated into Spanish by Rosalma Zubizarreta and Alma Flor Ada. San Francisco: Children's Book Press, 1987; 1993, paperback.

"The people from the country, the campesinos, brought fruit and vegetables to sell in the market."
—Palacios. *A Christmas Surprise for Chabelita.*

Panama
Republica de Panama

Family life is featured in two books set in Panama.

Even very young children should be able to share in the excitement of the little Panamanian girl whose grandmother arrives for her weekly visit in Ana Sisnett's *Grannie Jus' Come!* The rhythmic Caribbean English and the colorful pictures capture the narrator's delight in her grandmother's shoes, her straw hat, and even the touch of her skin. The story takes place in the author's hometown of Paraiso.

Another little Panamanian girl, Chabelita, lives with her grandparents in Argentina Palacios's *A Christmas Surprise for Chabelita.* Chabelita enjoys daily shopping with her grandfather and starting school, but greatly misses her mother who works in a large city.

Books

Palacios, Argentina. *A Christmas Surprise for Chabelita.* Illustrated by Lori Lohstoeter. Mahwah, New Jersey: BridgeWater Books, 1996, paperback; Troll Medallion, 1996, paperback.

Sisnett, Ana. *Grannie Jus' Come!* Illustrated by Karen Lusebrink. San Francisco: Children's Book Press, 1997.

"We left the land behind until St. Lucia was a cutout of dark hills in a lavender world of sea and sky."
—Orr. *My Grandpa and the Sea.*

Saint Lucia

My Grandpa and the Sea, by Katherine Orr, tells the story of an older fisherman who discovers a unique way to give back to the sea he loves. Full-page paintings portray the grandeur of this Caribbean island.

Book

Orr, Katherine. *My Grandpa and the Sea*. Illustrated by author. Minneapolis: Carolrhoda Books, 1991, paperback.

"Afterwards, Sugar Cane Man and me sit on de steps sucking on two sweet sugarcanes."
—Joseph. *An Island Christmas.*

Trinidad and Tobago

Children are featured in these books set on the islands of Tobago and Trinidad.

Tobago

When an American boy named Gregory visits his grandparents and cousin in Tobago, it takes him awhile to become the "cool" title character of Caroline Binch's *Gregory Cool.*

Trinidad

Vashanti Rahaman's *A Little Salmon for Witness* tells how Rajiv finally gets salmon (and more) to give as a present for his grandmother's Good Friday birthday.

Carnival day is the special day featured in *Jump Up Time*, by Lynn Joseph. Lily becomes increasingly jealous as she helps prepare her older sister's hummingbird costume, but ends up as a happy participant in the carnival.

Another book by Joseph, *An Island Christmas*, shows how Rosie enjoys the Christmas season: picking sorrel fruit, helping make black currant cake, painting the Christmas tree, and working on a Christmas gift in her tree house.

In a third book on Trinidad by Joseph, *Coconut Kind of Day*, her poems and the accompanying illustrations depict a small girl's activities on a typical day. These include racing snails at school (frowned upon by the teacher) and joining in the pulling of the fishermen's nets.

Books

Binch, Caroline. *Gregory Cool*. Illustrated by author. New York: Dial Books for Young Readers, 1994, paperback.

Joseph, Lynn. *Coconut Kind of Day: Island Poems*. Illustrated by Sandra Speidel. New York: Lothrop, Lee & Shepard Books, 1990.

Joseph, Lynn. *An Island Christmas*. Illustrated by Catherine Stock. Boston: Houghton Mifflin Company, 1996, paperback.

Joseph, Lynn. *Jump Up Time: A Trinidad Carnival Story*. Illustrated by Linda Saport. New York: Clarion Books, 1998.

Rahaman, Vashanti. *A Little Salmon for Witness: A Story from Trinidad*. Illustrated by Sandra Speidel. New York: Lodestar Books, 1997, paperback.

*"The dolphin puts his smooth, hard nose into my
father's cupped palm and off they go together, flying
beneath the waves."*
—Orr. *Story of a Dolphin.*

Turks and Caicos Islands

Turks and Caicos Islands is a British crown colony.

Based on an actual event, *Story of a Dolphin* by
Katherine Orr tells how a people-loving dolphin and the
residents of the Caribbean island of Providenciales learn to
get along with each other.

Book

Orr, Katherine. *Story of a Dolphin.* Illustrated by author.
Minneapolis: Carolrhoda Books, 1993, paperback.

<u>South America</u>

"Tree frogs and lizards appeared and then blended into the trees."
—Skolnik and Skolnik. *Emily, the Rain Forest Monkey.*

Brazil
Federative Republic of Brazil

The rain forest is featured in four picture books.

Through text and colorful, detailed paintings Lynne Cherry's *The Great Kapok Tree* tells of the many inhabitants of a kapok tree (a boa constrictor, monkeys, an anteater, a jaguar, etc.) who one by one inform a sleeping intruder of the different reasons why he should not ax down their home.

In *Emily, the Rain Forest Monkey*, by Nancy and Ashley Skolnik, a baby monkey separated from her mother in a rain forest that is being destroyed is taken back to the United States by the daughter of a television reporter. Emily then helps raise money to save the rain forests.

Miss Mallard, the ducktective of the Miss Mallard Mystery series for older children, travels to Brazil in *Lost in the Amazon* by Robert Quackenbush. After a journey in the rain forest, she discovers who has stolen the vial of Dr. Eiderstein's liquid for restoring plant life.

The captivating rhythm of Nancy Van Laan's *So Say the Little Monkeys* makes it appealing to even the youngest children. Based on an Indian tale, this story shows why the monkeys who live along the Rio Negro continue to sleep on thorns: they are too busy enjoying themselves to take time to build a home.

Pleasant DeSpain's *The Dancing Turtle* features a clever turtle, who both dances and plays the flute. This turtle tricks two children to avoid becoming turtle soup.

Older children can learn much about Brazil from *Count Your Way through Brazil* by Jim Haskins and Kathleen Benson. The items counted, in Portugese and English, include the country's five regions, seven of its ethnic groups, and eight of its animals.

Books

Cherry, Lynne. *The Great Kapok Tree: A Tale of the Amazon Rain Forest.* (A Gulliver Green Book) Illustrated by author. San Diego: Harcourt, 1990; 1998, paperback.

DeSpain, Pleasant. *The Dancing Turtle: A Folktale from Brazil.* Illustrated by David Boston. Little Rock, AR: August House, 1998.

Haskins, Jim, and Kathleen Benson. *Count Your Way through Brazil.* (Count Your Way Books) Illustrated by Liz Brenner Dodson. Minneapolis: Carolrhoda Books, 1996; 1996, paperback.

Quackenbush, Robert. *Lost in the Amazon: A Miss Mallard Mystery.* Illustrated by author. New York: Pippin Press, 1990.

Skolnik, Nancy, and Ashley Skolnik. *Emily, the Rain Forest Monkey.* Illustrated by Linda Buschke. Petaluma, CA: Skolnik Publishing, 1997.

Van Laan, Nancy. *So Say the Little Monkeys.* (An Anne Schwartz Book) Illustrated by Yumi Heo. New York: Atheneum Books for Young Readers, 1998.

"The Sea Spirit sent in waves brimful of fish, and the rock pools teemed with shrimps and crabs and seaweed."
—Pitcher. *Mariana and the Merchild.*

Chile

Mariana and the Merchild, by Caroline Pitcher, relates the story of lonely old Mariana, who finds a merchild in a crab shell. She cares for the merchild, although the sea spirit, who is the child's mermaid mother, visits her daily. When the merchild must return to her mother, Mariana's grief is eased by the merchild's morning greetings and by the village children who have become her friends.

Book

Pitcher, Caroline. *Mariana and the Merchild: A Folk Tale from Chile.* Illustrated by Jackie Morris. Grand Rapids, MI: Eerdmans Books for Young Readers, 2000.

"Far, far away, on the other side of the world, is a place like no other...a place where volcanoes released their lava to make tiny islands that are homes to many animals but few men."
—Ted Lewin. *Nilo and the Tortoise.*

Ecuador

Betsy Lewin's *Booby Hatch* tells of Pépe, a blue-footed booby who lives on one of the Galápagos Islands. As the bird grows up, he learns of the other inhabitants of his island, his feet turn blue, and he meets Tina, the booby who will be his mate.

Based on his experiences on Isabela Island, one of the Galápagos Islands, Ted Lewin's *Nilo and the Tortoise* tells of a young boy who is stranded on the island. He is frightened by a sea lion, climbs to the top of the island's volcano, sleeps next to a giant tortoise, and in the morning is guided by a hawk to his father's boat.

Books

Lewin, Betsy. *Booby Hatch*. Illustrated by author. New York: Clarion Books, 1995; 1997, paperback.

Lewin, Ted. *Nilo and the Tortoise*. Illustrated by author. New York: Scholastic, 1999.

"You are a jaguar in the night, listening to the sky roar over your head and raindrops drum on your leafy roof."
—Ryder. *Jaguar in the Rain Forest.*

French Guiana

French Guiana is an overseas department of France.

Pretend that you are a jaguar, and Joanne Ryder's *Jaguar in the Rain Forest* will transport you into the world of a French Guiana rain forest. Children can experience a day and a night in the life of a jaguar—and search the realistic paintings for other rain forest inhabitants.

Book

Ryder, Joanne. *Jaguar in the Rain Forest.* (A Just for a Day Book) Illustrated by Michael Rothman. New York: Morrow Junior Books, 1996.

"And all around, the great snow peaks of the Andes shone in the morning sun."
—Alexander. *Chaska and the Golden Doll.*

Peru

In *The First Story Ever Told*, a book by Erik Jendresen and Alberto Villoldo for older children, an explorer searching for Vilcabamba, the legendary City of Gold, hears the Inca creation story from Grandmother Fire and discovers the secret of Vilcabamba.

Illustrated with woodcuts, Jane Kurtz's *Miro in the Kingdom of the Sun* tells the story of the search for the distant lake whose water will restore the health of the ailing Inca prince who lives in Cuzco. In this folktale adaptation it is the girl Miro who, knowing how to communicate with birds, brings back the water and frees her brothers from prison.

Chaska and the Golden Doll, by Ellen Alexander, is a modern story set near Cuzco. When Chaska finds a golden Inca doll, she sells the idol to the Inca museum and uses the money for a new village schoolhouse.

How Llama Saved the Day, which is retold by Janet Palazzo-Craig, tells how a llama warned a farmer and his wife of the coming flood and then rescued them and the animals of Peru, not by building an ark, but by leading them to the top of the highest mountain.

Also set in the Peruvian mountains is Rebecca Hickox's *Zorro and Quwi*. After Quwi the guinea pig has fooled

Zorro the fox four times, the fox decides he doesn't really want to catch the guinea pig.

Peruvian-inspired collages illustrate Lois Ehlert's *Moon Rope*, which is written in English and Spanish. The book relates Fox and Mole's attempt to climb to the moon and reveals the reason moles now burrow in the ground.

For older children, *Tonight Is Carnaval*, by Arthur Dorros, is also distinctively illustrated, in this instance by photographs of arpilleras, wall hangings sewn from cloth. The arpilleras and the narrative present the everyday life of an Andean farm family, the market where they sell their potatoes, and the much-anticipated village carnival.

Peru has become known to young children as the country of origin of the popular bear, Paddington. Books about Paddington are described under England. One of them, *Paddington Bear: My Scrapbook*, includes an account of his early life in Peru.

Books

Alexander, Ellen. *Chaska and the Golden Doll*. Illustrated by author. New York: Arcade Publishing, 1994.

Dorros, Arthur. *Tonight Is Carnaval*. Illustrated by the Club de Madres Virgen del Carmen. New York: Puffin Books, 1995, paperback.

Ehlert, Lois. *Moon Rope: A Peruvian Folktale/Un lazo a la luna: Una leyenda peruana*. Illustrated by author. Translated into Spanish by Amy Price. San Diego: Harcourt, 1992; 1996.

Hickox, Rebecca. *Zorro and Quwi: Tales of a Trickster Guinea Pig*. Illustrated by Kim Howard. New York: Picture Yearling, 1998, paperback.

Jendresen, Erik, and Alberto Villoldo. *The First Story Ever Told*. Illustrated by Yoshi. New York: Simon & Schuster Books for Young Readers, 1996.

Kurtz, Jane. *Miro in the Kingdom of the Sun*. Illustrated by David Frampton. Boston: Houghton Mifflin Company, 1996.

Palazzo-Craig, Janet, reteller. *How Llama Saved the Day: A Story from Peru*. (First-Start Legends) Illustrated by Charles Reasoner. Mahwah, NJ: Troll Communications, 1996, paperback; BridgeWater, 1999, paperback.

"There were so many houses that they reached right to the top of the mountain where the lion tracks used to be."
—Kurusa. *The Streets Are Free.*

Venezuela

The Streets Are Free, by Kurusa, tells of three enterprising children in a Caracas barrio, who, failing to get a playground from the city government, successfully enlist their neighbors to build one.

In Daniel Barbot's *A Bicycle for Rosaura*, Señora Amelia has a bicycle custom-made for her hen's birthday.

Books

Barbot, Daniel. *A Bicycle for Rosaura.* (A Cranky Nell Book) Illustrated by Morella Fuenmayor. Brooklyn, NY: Kane/Miller Book Publishers, 1991; 1994, paperback.

Kurusa. *The Streets Are Free.* Illustrated by Monika Doppert. Translated from Spanish by Karen Englander. Toronto: Annick (Distributed by Firefly Books), 1995, paperback.

Resources

Bader, Barbara. "Peter Says Please." *Horn Book Magazine* 75 (March/April 1999): 119-122.

Bookbag 4: (October/November 1999)- 5 (October/November 2000).

Book Links 8 (September 1998)-10 (October/November 2000).

Borton, Terry. "The Teachings of Paddle-to-the-Sea." *Learning* 5 (January 1977): 26-30.

Butler, Dorothy. *Babies Need Books: Sharing the Joy of Books with Children from Birth to Six.* Rev. ed. Illustrated by Shirley Hughes. Portsmouth, NH: Heinemann, 1998. p. xi.

Children's Books in Print 2000. 2 vols. New Providence, NJ: R.R. Bowker, 1999.

Cianciolo, Patricia J. *Picture Books for Children.* 4th. ed. Chicago: American Library Association, 1997.

Cooper-Mullin, Alison, and Jennifer Marmaduke Coye. *Once upon a Heroine: 450 Books for Girls to Love.* Lincolnwood, IL: Contemporary Books, 1998.

Gillespie, John T., ed. *Best Books for Children: Preschool through Grade 6.* 6th ed. New Providence, NJ: R. R. Bowker, 1998.

Hamond World Atlas: Classics Edition, 1972. Maplewood, NJ: Hammond, 1971.

Hayden, Carla D., ed. *Venture into Cultures: A Resource Book of Multicultural Materials and Programs.* Chicago: American Library Association, 1992.

Herriot, James. *James Herriot's Yorkshire.* Photographs by Derry Brabbs. New York: St. Martin's Press, 1979.

Hirsch, E. D., Jr. *Cultural Literacy: What Every American Needs to Know. Includes an Appendix, "What Literate Americans Know", by E. D. Hirsch, Jr., Joseph Kett, and James Trefil.* Boston: Houghton Mifflin Company, 1987.

Holt, John. *What Do I Do Monday?* (Innovators in Education) Portsmouth, NH: Boynton/Cook Publishers-Heinemann, 1995. p. 27.

Horn Book Magazine 60 (February 1984)-76 (September/October 2000).

Hurst, Carol Otis. *Open Books: Literature in the Curriculum, Kindergarten through Grade Two*. (The Book Report & Library Talk Professional Growth Series) Worthington, OH: Linworth Publishing, 1999.

Kruse, Ginny Moore, Kathleen T. Horning, and Megan Schliesman with Tana Elias. *Multicultural Literature for Children and Young Adults: A Selected Listing of Books by and about People of Color*. Vol. 2: 1991-1996. Madison, WI: Cooperative Children's Book Center, School of Education, University of Wisconsin-Madison with The Friends of the CCBC and Wisconsin Department of Public Instruction, 1997.

Lewis, Valerie V., and Walter M. Mayes. *Valerie & Walter's Best Books for Children: A Lively, Opinionated Guide*. New York: Avon Books, 1998.

Lima, Carolyn W., and John A. Lima. *A to Zoo: Subject Access to Children's Picture Books*. 5th. ed. New Providence, NJ: R.R. Bowker, 1998.

Merriam-Webster's Biographical Dictionary. Springfield, MA: Merriam-Webster, 1995.

Merriam-Webster's Geographical Dictionary. 3d. ed. Springfield, MA: Merriam-Webster, 1997.

Miller-Lachmann, Lyn. *Our Family, Our Friends, Our World: An Annotated Guide to Significant Multicultural Books for Children and Teenagers*. New Providence, NJ: R. R. Bowker, 1992.

Montessori, Maria. *The Absorbent Mind*. (An Owl Book) New foreword by John Chattin-McNichols. New York: Henry Holt and Company, 1995. pp. 176-177.

Muse, Daphne, ed. *The New Press Guide to Multicultural Resources for Young Readers*. New York: New Press, 1997.

Odean, Kathleen. *Great Books for Boys: More than 600 Books for Boys 2 to 14*. New York: Ballantine Books, 1998.

Odean, Kathleen. *Great Books for Girls: More than 600 Books to Inspire Today's Girls and Tomorrow's Women*. New York: Ballantine Books, 1997.

Publishers Weekly 244 (January 27, 1997)- 246 (April 26, 1999).

Rands, William Brighty [Matthew Browne]. "The Child's World," st. 1. in *Familiar Quotations: A Collection of Passages, Phrases, and Proverbs Traced to Their Sources in Ancient and Modern Literature.* 16th ed., by John Bartlett, edited by Justin Kaplan. Boston: Little, Brown and Company, 1992. p. 503.

School Library Journal 30 (January 1984)-46 (October 2000).

Taylor, Judy, Joyce Irene Whalley, Anne Stevenson Hobbs, and Elizabeth M. Battrick. *Beatrix Potter 1866-1943: The Artist and Her World.* London: Frederick Warne & Co. with The National Trust, 1987.

Thomas, Rebecca L. *Connecting Cultures: A Guide to Multicultural Literature for Children.* New Providence, NJ: R.R. Bowker, 1996.

Tomlinson, Carl M., ed. *Children's Books from Other Countries. Sponsored by United States Board on Books for Young People.* Landham, MD: Scarecrow Press, 1998.

Trelease, Jim. *The Read-Aloud Handbook.* 4th ed. New York: Penguin Books, 1995. p. 58.

Destination Index

Abyssinia. *See* Ethiopia
Afghanistan, 73
Africa, 21-69
Arab Republic of Egypt. *See* Egypt
Armenia, 74-75
Asia, 71-163
Australia and Oceania, 9-10, 165-178
Australia, 9-10, 167-177
Austria, 181-182

Bahamas, 347
Basutoland. *See* Lesotho
Bechuanaland. *See* Botswana
Belarus, 183-185
Belgian Congo. *See* Democratic Republic of the Congo
Belorussian Soviet Socialist Republic. *See* Belarus
Benin, 23
Botswana, 26
Brazil, 405-406
Byelarus. *See* Belarus

Cambodia, 76-77
Cameroon, 25-27
Canada, 348-361
Ceylon. *See* Sri Lanka
Chile, 407
China, 78-105
Commonwealth of Australia. *See* Australia
Commonwealth of the Bahamas. *See* Bahamas
Congo. *See* Democratic Republic of the Congo
Costa Rica, 362-363
Cuba, 364

Dahomey. *See* Benin
Democratic People's Republic of Korea. *See* North Korea
Democratic Republic of the Congo, 28
Democratic Republic of Vietnam. *See* Vietnam
Denmark, 186. *See also* Greenland
Dominican Republic, 365

East Africa Protectorate. *See* Kenya
Ecuador, 408
Egypt, 29-34
El Salvador, 366
England, 187-219, 342-343
Estados Unidos Mexicanos. *See* Mexico
Estonia, 220
Estonian Soviet Socialist Republic. *See* Estonia
Ethiopia, 35-37
Europe, 8, 32, 179-344

Federal Republic of Germany. *See* Germany
Federal Republic of Nigeria. *See* Nigeria
Federative Republic of Brazil. *See* Brazil
Fiji Islands. *See* Fiji
Fiji, 178
France, 8, 32, 221-244. *See also* French Guiana; Martinique
French Guiana, 409
French Sudan. *See* Mali

Gambia, 38
German Democratic Republic. *See* Germany
Germany, 245-253
Ghana, 39-44
Gold Coast. *See* Ghana
Greece, 254-259
Greenland, 367
Guatemala, 368-370

Haiti, 371-373
Hashemite Kingdom of Jordan. *See* Jordan

Holland. *See* Netherlands
Hungary, 260-262

India, 106-114
Indonesia, 115-116
Irak. *See* Iraq
Iran, 117-118
Iraq, 119-120
Ireland, 263-271
Israel, 121
Italy, 272-285

Jamaica, 374-375
Japan, 122-139
Jordan, 140

Kampuchea. *See* Cambodia
Kazakh Soviet Socialist Republic. *See* Kazakhstan
Kazakhstan, 141
Kazakstan. *See* Kazakhstan
Kenia. *See* Kenya
Kenya, 45-46

Lao People's Democratic Republic. *See* Laos
Laos, 142
Lesotho, 47
Liberia, 48
Lithuania, 286
Lithuanian Soviet Socialist Republic. *See* Lithuania

Malawi, 49-50
Mali, 51
Martinique, 376
Mexico, 377-393
Mongolia, 143-144
Mongolian People's Republic. *See* Mongolia
Montserrat, 394
Morocco, 52

Namibia, 53
Netherlands Indies. *See* Indonesia
Netherlands, 287-289
Nicaragua, 395-396
Nigeria, 54-56
North America, 345-402
North Korea, 145
Norway, 290-292
Nyasaland. *See* Malawi

Outer Mongolia. *See* Mongolia

Palestine, 146
Panama, 397-398
People's Republic of China. *See* China
Persia. *See* Iran
Peru, 410-412
Philippines, 147
Poland, 293-298

Republic of Cuba. *See* Cuba
Republic of Hungary. *See* Hungary
Republic of India. *See* India
Republic of Indonesia. *See* Indonesia
Republic of Kazakhstan. *See* Kazakhstan
Republic of Korea. *See* South Korea
Republic of Poland. *See* Poland
Republic of South Africa. *See* South Africa
Republic of the Gambia. *See* Gambia
Republic of the Philippines. *See* Philippines
Republic of Vietnam. *See* Vietnam
Republica de Panama. *See* Panama
République française. *See* France
Rhodesia. *See* Zimbabwe
Romania, 299
Roumania. *See* Romania
Ruanda. *See* Rwanda
Rumania. *See* Romania

Russia, 300-318
Russian Federation. *See* Russia
Rwanda, 57

Saint Lucia, 399
Scotland, 319-324, 342-343
Siam. *See* Thailand
Socialist Republic of Vietnam. *See* Vietnam
South Africa, 58-64
South America, 403-413
South Korea, 148-153
South-West Africa. *See* Namibia
Southern Rhodesia. *See* Zimbabwe
Soviet Union. *See* Armenia, Belarus, Estonia, Kazakhstan, Lithuania,
    Russia, Ukraine
Spain, 325-327
Sri Lanka, 154
State of Israel. *See* Israel
Sudanese Republic. *See* Mali
Sweden, 328-336
Swiss Confederation. *See* Switzerland
Switzerland, 337-338

Tanganyika. *See* Tanzania
Tanzania, 65-68
Thailand, 155-156
The Bahamas. *See* Bahamas
the Bahamas. *See* Bahamas
The Gambia. *See* Gambia
The Netherlands. *See* Netherlands
the Ukraine. *See* Ukraine
Transjordan. *See* Jordan
Trinidad and Tobago, 400-401
Turkey, 157-159
Turks and Caicos Islands, 402
Tuva Autonomous Soviet Socialist Republic. *See* Tuva
Tuva, 160

Ukraine, 339-341
Ukranian Soviet Socialist Republic. *See* Ukraine
Union of South Africa. *See* South Africa
Union of Soviet Socialist Republics. *See* Armenia, Belarus, Estonia, Kazakhstan, Lithuania, Russia, Ukraine
United Arab Republic. *See* Egypt
United Kingdom of Great Britain and Northern Ireland. *See* United Kingdom
United Kingdom, 342-343. *See also* England; Montserrat; Scotland; Turks and Caicos Islands; Wales
United Republic of Tanzania. *See* Tanzania
U.S.S.R. *See* Armenia, Belarus, Estonia, Kazakhstan, Lithuania, Russia, Ukraine

Venezuela, 413
Viet Nam. *See* Vietnam
Vietnam, 161-163

Wales, 344

Zaire. *See* Democratic Republic of the Congo
Zimbabwe, 69

Author Index

Aardema, Verna, 39-40, 42, 45-46, 48, 53, 57, 65, 67, 378, 388
Ada, Alma Flor, 325-326, 378, 388
Adams, Jeanie, 174
Adinolfi, JoAnn, 31-33
Adler, David A., 287-288
Agee, Jon, 227
Aksakov, Sergei, 310, 313
Alarcon, Francisco X., 386, 389
Alderson, Brian, 203, 210
Alexander, Ellen, 410-411
Alexander, Lloyd, 25-26
Aliki, 31, 33, 228, 234, 238, 255, 258
Allen, Judy, 147, 257-258
Allen, Laura Jean, 322-323
Alphin, Elaine Marie, 366
Alvarez, Julia, 365
Andersen, Hans Christian, 97
Anderson, Lena, 332-333
Andrews, Jan, 354, 357
Angeletti, Roberta, 221, 238
Anholt, Laurence, 205-206, 210, 229, 232, 238
Appelbaum, Diana, 365
Araujo, Frank P., 35-36, 232, 326-327
Arcellana, Francisco, 147
Arenson, Roberta, 108-109, 112
Argent, Kerry, 169, 176
Argueta, Manlio, 366
Armstrong, Jennifer, 81, 87, 228, 234, 238
Arnold, Katya, 306, 313
Arnold, Marsha Diane, 110-112, 174
Asbjørnsen, P.C., 290-291
Askar, Saoussan, 356, 360

Atkins, Jeannine, 205-206, 210
Ayres, Becky Hickox, 302, 304, 313

Backstein, Karen, 109, 112
Baden, Robert, 362-363
Baker, Jeannie, 168-171, 173-175
Baker, Keith, 132, 134
Baker, Leslie, 226, 238
Balgassi, Haemi, 151
Balian, Lorna, 268-269
Balit, Christina, 256-258
Bang, Molly Garrett, 87-88, 97
Bannatyne-Cugnet, Jo, 354-355, 357
Bannerman, Helen, 111-112
Barber, Antonia, 188, 211
Barbot, Daniel, 413
Barker, Henry, 30, 33
Barsotti, Joan Barton, 45-46
Bartos-Höppner, Barbara, 247, 251
Base, Graeme, 171, 175
Bash, Barbara, 111-112
Bateman, Teresa, 264, 269
Bateson-Hill, Margaret, 93-94, 97
Behan, Brendan, 267, 269
Belafonte, Harry, 375
Bell, Lili, 132, 134
Bemelmans, Ludwig, 8, 195, 211, 222-224, 238
Beneduce, Ann Keay, 197, 201, 211
Bennett, Jill, 202, 211
Benson, Kathleen, 230, 240, 254-255, 258, 265, 270, 406
Berg, Charles Ramirez, 382, 393
Berndt, Catherine, 110, 175
Bernhard, Emery, 301, 313, 378, 389
Berry, James, 41-42
Beskow, Elsa, 329, 333
Binch, Caroline, 400-401
Bingham, Mindy, 221, 226, 239
Birch, David, 109, 112

Bishop, Claire Huchet, 89, 97
Blades, Ann, 348, 357
Blake, Robert J., 268-269.
Blanco, Alberto, 380, 389
Bodkin, Odds, 128, 134
Bodnár, Judit A., 260-261
Bognomo, Joël Eboueme, 25-26
Boholm-Olsson, Eva, 162-163
Bond, Michael, 193-195, 201, 207, 211-212
Bond, Ruskin, 107, 112
Boon, Debbie, 236, 239
Bouchard, David, 82, 97
Breckler, Rosemary, 161, 163
Brenner, Barbara, 124, 134
Bresnick-Perry, Roslyn, 183-184
Brett, Jan, 339-340
Brighton, Catherine, 205-206, 212
Brodmann, Aliana, 251
Brown, Don, 205-206, 212
Brown, Marcia, 197, 204, 212, 232, 239
Brown, Margaret Wise, 171-172, 175, 260-261
Brown, Ruth, 209-210, 212, 320, 323
Brunhoff, Laurent de, 225, 239
Bryan, Ashley, 54
Bunting, Eve, 257-258, 269, 388-389
Burgess, Lord, 375
Burr, Claudia, 377, 389
Bushey, Jeanna, 351, 358
Byrd, Robert, 265, 269

Carey, Valerie Scho, 296-297, 368-369
Carling, Amelia Lau, 368-369
Carney, Margaret, 352, 358
Carrier, Roch, 353-354, 358
Castañeda, Omar S., 368-369
Catalano, Dominic, 322-323
Cech, John, 308, 311, 313
Cecil, Laura, 279, 282

Chall, Marsha Wilson, 226, 239
Chang, Cindy, 90, 97
Chang, Margaret, 80, 86, 89, 97-98
Chang, Raymond, 80, 86, 89, 97-98
Chapman, Carol, 248, 251
Chekhov, Anton, 312, 314
Chen, Kerstin, 87, 98
Cherry, Lynne, 405-406
Chin, Charlie, 94-95, 98
Chocolate, Deborah M. Newton, 39-40, 42-43
Choi, Sook Nyul, 148, 151
Choi, Yangsook, 150, 152
Chow, Octavio, 395-396
Claire, Elizabeth, 53
Clayton, Elaine, 197, 204, 213
Clement, Gary, 294, 297
Clements, Andrew, 31, 33
Climo, Shirley, 29-30, 33, 117-118, 149, 152, 263, 266, 269, 384, 389
Coburn, Jewell Reinhart, 76-77, 378, 389
Coerr, Eleanor, 131, 134
Cole, Joanna, 305, 314
Collard, Sneed B., III, 362-363
Collier, Mary Jo, 235, 239
Collier, Peter, 235, 239
Collins, Judy, 224, 239
Conrad, Pam, 367
Cooper, Floyd, 60, 63
Cooper, Susan, 321, 323, 344
Corpi, Lucha, 381, 389
Corrin, Sara, 247-248, 251
Corrin, Stephen, 247-248, 251
Coville, Bruce, 254, 258
Cowen-Fletcher, Jane, 23
Cox, Judy, 229, 239
Craft, Charlotte, 256, 258
Croll, Carolyn, 308, 314
Cruz Martinez, Alejandro, 380, 389-390

Cushman, Doug, 32-33, 115-116
Czernecki, Stefan, 78, 98, 369-370, 379, 383, 391

Daly, Niki, 54, 56, 59, 62-64, 277, 281-282
Davol, Marguerite, 93, 98
Day, Nancy Raines, 35-36
Dee, Ruby, 41, 43, 48
Deedy, Carmen Agra, 186
Deetlefs, Rene, 62-63
DeFelice, Cynthia, 230, 239
Del Negro, Janice, 319, 321, 323
Delton, Julie, 254, 258
DeMarsh, Mary, 230, 239
Demi, 81, 86-88, 91-95, 98-99, 110, 112, 303, 314
dePaola, Tomie, 32-34, 118, 233, 239, 263, 265-267, 270, 272-276,
    278, 281-283, 377, 382-383, 390
DeSpain, Pleasant, 406
Diakité, Baba Wagué, 51
Dionetti, Michelle, 229, 232, 240
Dorros, Arthur, 411
Downing, Julie, 181-182
Drexel Elementary School (Tucson, Arizona) Third Grade Students,
    385, 390
Drummond, Allan, 96, 99
Duncan, Jane, 322-323
Dunrea, Olivier, 223, 240, 287-288
Dupasquier, Philippe, 209, 213

Early, Margaret, 337-338
Easwaran, Eknath, 106, 112
Echewa, T. Obinkaram, 55-56
Edwards, Pamela Duncan, 227, 240
Ehlert, Lois, 384, 390, 411
Eisenstein, Marilyn, 224, 240
Esterl, Arnica, 132, 134
Estes, Kristyn Rehling, 384, 390
Ets, Marie Hall, 383, 390
Eversole, Robyn, 168-169, 175

Falk, Barbara Bustetter, 313-314
Fazio, Brenda Lena, 132, 13
Fine, Edith Hope, 377, 387-388, 390
Fisher, Leonard Everett, 288, 337-338
Flack, Marjorie, 95, 99
Fleming, Candace, 228-229, 240, 277, 283
Flora, James, 382, 391
Forest, Heather, 320, 323
Fox, Mem, 9-10, 172-173, 175
Franklin, Kristine L., 312, 314
Freedman, Florence B., 294, 297
French, Vivian, 291
Furtado, Jo, 208, 213

Gage, Amy Glaser, 368, 370
Gal, Laszlo, 303, 314
Galdone, Paul, 108, 113, 249, 251
Garland, Michael, 233, 240
Garland, Sarah, 187-188, 213
Garland, Sherry, 162-163
Garrison, Christian, 133-134
Gershator, Phillis, 23
Geeslin, Campbell, 387, 391
Gelman, Rita Golden, 115-116
Gerber, Carole, 268, 270
Gerrard, Roy, 31, 34, 274-275, 283
Gerson, Mary-Joan, 55-56
Gerstein, Mordicai, 80-81, 99
Gilbert, Lisa Weedn, 328-329, 336
Gilliland, Judith Heide, 29, 34, 119-120
Ginsburg, Mirra, 149, 152, 260-261, 308, 314
Godden, Rumer, 196, 213
Goldin, Barbara Diamond, 297-298
Gollub, Matthew, 380-381, 391
Goodall, John S., 206, 213
Goode, Diane, 224, 228, 240
Gordon, Ruth, 293-294, 298
Greenberg, Melanie Hope, 372

Greene, Ellin, 260, 262, 266, 270
Gregorowski, Christopher, 58, 63
Grifalconi, Ann, 25-26
Grimes, Nikki, 66-67
Grimm, Wilhelm, 249, 252, 279, 283
Grimm, Jacob, 249, 252, 279, 283
Grossman, Patricia, 379-380, 391
Guarnieri, Paola, 280, 283

Hague, Kathleen, 290-291
Hague, Michael, 290-291
Hale, Irina, 340
Haley, Gail E., 40, 43
Hamanaka, Sheila, 127, 135
Han, Oki S., 149, 152
Han, Suzanne Crowder, 150, 152
Hanson, Regina, 374-375
Harrison, Ted, 355-356, 358
Haseley, Dennis, 235, 240
Haskins, Jim, 107-108, 113, 121, 126, 135, 151-152, 230, 240, 248,
    252, 254-255, 258, 265, 270, 277, 283, 302, 314, 355, 358, 381,
    391, 406
Hastings, Selina, 300, 303, 314
Hausman, Gerald, 374-375
Havill, Juanita, 134-135
Hedderwick, Mairi, 320-321, 323
Hedlund, Irene, 129, 135
Heide, Florence Parry, 29, 34, 119-120
Heins, Ethel, 309, 315
Henry, Marguerite, 200, 213
Heo, Yumi, 150, 152
Herriot, James, 198-200, 213-214
Heyer, Marilee, 90, 99, 325-327
Hickox, Rebecca, 119-120, 410-411
Hidaka, Masako, 133, 135
Hillman, Elizabeth, 88-89, 99
Hippely, Hilary Horder, 261-262
Hirst, Robin, 173-175

Hirst, Sally, 173-175
Ho, Minfong, 76-77, 95, 100, 155-156
Hobbs, Will, 349-350, 358
Hodges, Margaret, 129, 135, 202, 214, 233, 241, 245-246, 252, 267,
    270
Hoestlandt, Jo, 236-237, 241
Hoffman, Mary, 38, 309, 315
Hofmeyr, Dianne, 117-118
Hogrogian, Nonny, 74-75
Holling, Holling Clancy, 357-358
Holt, Daniel D., 151-152
Honda, Tetsuya, 123-124, 135
Hong, Lily Toy, 85-86, 91, 94, 100
Hooks, William H., 128, 135
Hort, Lenny, 287-288
Howard, Elizabeth Fitzgerald, 364
Hughes, Shirley, 200-201, 207-208, 214
Hutchins, Pat, 207, 209, 214
Hutton, Warwick, 157-158, 256

Ichikawa, Satomi, 237, 241
Isadora, Rachel, 58, 61-63, 181-182
Isele, Elizabeth, 306, 315

Jackson, Ellen B., 302, 315
Jaffe, Nina, 297-298
Jam, Teddy, 356, 358
James, J. Alison, 122-123, 135
James, Simon, 193, 214
Jendresen, Erik, 410, 412
Jiang, Cheng An, 94-95, 100
Jiang, Wei, 94-95, 100
Johnson, Jane, 205, 215
Johnston, Tony, 127, 135, 276, 283, 380, 382, 387-388, 391
Joosse, Barbara M., 287-289
Joseph, Lynn, 400-401

Kahn, Rosemary, 59, 63

Kajikawa, Kimiko, 124, 135
Kajpust, Melissa, 109, 113
Kalman, Maira, 124-125, 136
Kamal, Aleph, 111, 113
Keller, Holly, 162-163
Kellerhals-Stewart, Heather, 350, 359
Kellogg, Steven, 197, 201-202, 215
Keo, Ena, 128, 136
Ketcham, Sallie, 250, 252
Kherdian, David, 74-75
Killilea, Marie, 354, 359
Kimmel, Eric A., 39-40, 43, 85, 92, 100, 127, 129-130, 136, 203, 215,
    230, 243, 279, 284, 291, 293-294, 298-299, 305, 310, 315, 325,
    327, 340-341, 385, 391
Kinsey-Warnock, Natalie, 354, 359
Kintner, Judith, 245, 252
Kipling, Rudyard, 111, 113, 170, 175
Kirby, David K, 226, 241.
Kirstein, Lincoln, 231, 241
Knutson, Barbara, 58
Koscielniak, Bruce, 204-205, 215
Kroll, Virginia, 133, 136
Krudop, Walter Lyon, 155-156
Krull, Kathleen, 382, 392
Krupp, Robin Rector, 386, 392
Kudler, David, 126, 136
Kurelek, William, 349, 359
Kurtz, Christopher, 36-37
Kurtz, Jane, 35-37, 410, 412
Kurusa, 413
Kusugak, Michael, 350-351, 357, 359-360

Labistida, Aurora, 383, 390
Lake, Mary Dixon, 41, 43
Langston, Laura, 129, 136
Langton, Jane, 309, 315, 329, 333
Lattimore, Deborah Nourse, 30, 34
Lauture, Denizé, 371-372

Lawson, Julie, 80, 100, 348-349, 360
Le Guin, Ursula K., 328, 333
Le Tord, Bijou, 229, 232-233, 241
Leaf, Munro, 326-327
Lee, Jeanne M., 76-77, 90, 94-95, 100-101, 161, 163
Lemioux, Michelle, 303, 315
Lerman, Rory S., 210, 215
Lessac, Frané, 394
Lester, Alison, 171, 175
Levine, Arthur A., 127, 136, 184-185
Levinson, Riki, 79, 101
Levy, Janice, 382, 392
Lewin, Betsy, 24, 408
Lewin, Hugh, 61-64
Lewin, Ted, 52, 107, 113, 408
Lewis, J. Patrick, 245-246, 252, 306, 309, 315
Lewis, Kim, 197-198, 215
Lewis, Richard, 385, 387, 392
Lewis, Thomas P., 379, 392
Libura, Krystyna, 387, 389
Lieberman, Syd, 261-262
Lindgren, Astrid, 331-334
Lindman, Maj, 328-331, 334-336
Little, Mimi Otey, 124, 136
Littlefield, Holly, 131, 136, 250, 252
Littlesugar, Amy, 233, 241
Lobel, Arnold, 92, 101
London, Jonathan, 52, 133, 136, 353, 360
Long, Jan Freeman, 125, 136
Lopez, Loretta, 384, 390
Lottridge, Celia Barker, 301, 316
Louie, Ai-Lin, 83, 101
Luenn, Nancy, 122, 136
Lum, Darrell, 161, 163
Lunge-Larsen, Lise, 290-292
Lurie, Alison, 306, 316

Macaulay, David, 275, 284

MacDonald, Margaret Read, 203, 216
MacGill-Callahan, Sheila, 265, 267, 271, 320
MacKinnon, Christy, 350, 360
Madrigal, Antonio Hernández, 379, 392
Mahy, Margaret, 89-90, 101
Manna, Anthony L., 257-258
Manning, Mick, 206-207, 216
Manson, Ainslie, 356, 360
Mao Wall, Lina, 76-77
Marcellino, Fred, 234, 242
Mark, Jan, 158, 256
Markel, Michelle, 368, 370
Martin, Francesca, 65, 67
Martin, Rafe, 107-108, 113, 304, 316
Mathers, Petra, 246, 252
Matthews, Mary, 433-434
Mayer, Marianna, 304-305, 316
Mayo, Margaret, 272, 277, 281, 284
McCaughrean, Geraldine, 305, 316
McClintock, Barbara, 223, 241
McCully, Emily Arnold, 79, 101, 196, 215, 223, 242, 268, 270
McCunney, Michelle, 381, 392
McDermott, Gerald, 40-41, 43, 129-130, 137, 264, 266-267, 270, 384-385, 392
McKay, Lawrence, Jr., 73
McKibbon, Hugh William, 110, 113
Medearis, Angela Shelf, 42-43, 54-56
Meeks, Arone Raymond, 170, 176
Melmed, Laura Krauss, 128, 133, 137
Mennen, Ingrid, 47, 59, 63
Merrill, Jean, 125, 137
Merrill, Linda, 196, 216
Mike, Jan M., 30, 34
Mikolaycak, Charles, 306-307, 316
Millen, C. M., 264-265, 271
Milton, Nancy, 235, 242
Mitakidou, Christodoula, 257-258
Moak, Allan, 352, 360

Mochizuki, Ken, 286
Moe, J. E., 290-291
Mollel, Tololwa M., 26, 41, 44, 55-56, 65-68
Moodie, Fiona, 60, 64
Moore, Inga, 237, 242
Mora, Pat, 381-383, 392-393
Moroney, Lynn, 220
Morpurgo, Michael, 167, 172, 176
Mosel, Arlene, 88, 101, 129, 137
Munro, Roxie, 228, 242
Munsch, Robert, 352, 356-357, 360
Myers, Tim, 130, 137

Nakawatari, Harutaka, 132, 137
Namioka, Lensey, 96, 101, 127, 137
Nerlove, Miriam, 295-296, 298
Nic Leodhas, Sorche, 322-323
Nichol, Barbara, 181-182
Nivola, Claire A., 250, 253
Nomura, Takaaki, 132, 137
Nones, Eric Jon, 275-276, 284
Nye, Naomi Shihab, 146

O'Brien, Patrick, 209, 216
O'Callahan, Jan, 225, 242
O'Donnell, Elizabeth Lee, 266, 271
Oakley, Graham, 210, 216
Ober, Hal, 384-385, 393
Olaleye, Isaac, 54, 56
Olawsky, Lynn Ainsworth, 386, 393
Oppenheim, Shulamith Levey, 29, 32, 34, 257, 259, 287, 289
Oram, Hiawyn, 305, 316
Orr, Katherine, 399, 402
Oyibo, Papa, 55-56
Oyono, Éric, 26-27

Pacilio, V. J., 95, 101
Pak, Soyung, 148, 153

Palacios, Argentina, 369-370, 386, 393, 397
Palazzo-Craig, Janet, 410, 412
Pami, Louise Tchana, 25, 27
Parillo, Tony, 276, 280, 284
Park, Frances, 145
Park, Ginger, 145
Parkison, Jami, 106-107, 113
Paterson, Katherine, 127, 137
Pattison, Darcy, 86, 101
Perrault, Charles, 230-231, 242
Peterson, Julienne, 216, 284
Pitcher, Caroline, 407
Pittman, Helena Clare, 83, 101
Plume, Ilse, 246, 253, 279, 284
Plunkett, Stephanie Haboush, 149, 152
Polacco, Patricia, 228, 242, 306-307, 311, 316
Pomeranc, Marion Hess, 250-251, 253
Pomerantz, Charlotte, 374-375
Poole, Amy Lowry, 78-79, 92, 101-102
Poole, Josephine, 234, 243
Porazinska, Janina, 295, 298
Potter, Beatrix, 188-193, 216-218
Poulin, Stéphane, 353, 360-361
Prokofiev, Sergei, 303, 317
Provensen, Alice, 235-236, 243
Provensen, Martin, 235-236, 243
Pushkin, Alexander, 310, 317

Quackenbush, Robert, 81, 102, 322-324, 405-406

Radcliffe, Theresa, 110, 113
Rahaman, Vashanti, 400-401
Ransome, Arthur, 309, 317
Rappaport, Doreen, 91-92, 102
Reasoner, Charles, 148-149, 153
Reeves, James, 343
Reiser, Lynn, 362-363
Rhee, Nami, 149, 153

Rhodes, Timothy, 369-370, 379, 383, 391
Rice, James, 383, 393
Ridley, Sarah, 196, 216
Riecken, Nancy, 384, 393
Riggio, Anita, 187, 203, 218
Ringgold, Faith, 225, 243
Robbins, Ruth, 307, 317
Robertson, Bruce, 223, 243
Rodell, Susanna, 173, 176
Rohmer, Harriet, 395-396
Rojany, Lisa, 374-375
Ros, Saphan, 76-77
Roth, Susan L., 170, 176, 229, 243
Rounds, Glen, 290, 292
Rowe, John A., 125, 137
Rudolph, Marguerita, 312, 317
Rumford, James, 32, 141, 234, 243
Ryder, Joanne, 409

Sabuda, Robert, 30, 34, 203-204, 218
Sakurai, Gail, 127-128, 138
San Souci, Daniel, 150, 153
San Souci, Robert D., 74-75, 90, 102, 123, 128, 138, 202, 218, 231,
    243, 264, 271, 347, 376
Sanderson, Ruth, 279-280, 284
Sawyer, Ruth, 182
Say, Allen, 125-126, 130-131, 138
Schaefer, Carole Lexa, 96, 102
Schanzer, Rosalyn, 295, 298
Schermbrucker, Reviva, 59-60, 64
Schmidt, Gary D., 267, 271
Schroeder, Alan, 81, 102, 129, 138
Schuch, Steve, 300-301, 317
Schur, Maxine Rose, 184-185
Schwartz, Amy, 293, 298
Schwartz, David M., 332, 336
Seibert, Patty, 168, 170-171, 176
Seibold, J. Otto, 277, 284

Seuling, Barbara, 202, 218
Shank, Ned, 106, 112, 114
Shannon, Mark, 230, 243
Shea, Pegi Deitz, 155-156
Sheehan, Patty, 172, 176
Shepard, Aaron, 108, 114, 117-118, 301-302, 317
Sherman, Josepha, 311, 317
Sierra, Judy, 49, 115-116, 123, 138, 325, 327
Silverman, Erica, 296, 298
Sis, Peter, 115-116, 281, 284
Sisnett, Ana, 397-398
Sisulu, Elinor Batezat, 58-59, 64
Skolnik, Ashley, 405-406
Skolnik, Nancy, 405-406
Smucker, Barbara, 352, 361
Snyder, Dianne, 122-123, 138
Sorros, Barbara, 388, 393
Souhami, Jessica, 41, 44, 108, 114
Spagnoli, Cathy, 76-77, 142
Spalding, Andrea, 348, 357, 361
Spivak, Dawnine, 130, 138
Stanley, Diane, 274, 284
Stanley, Sanna, 58
Steptoe, John, 69
Stevens, Janet, 274, 285, 290, 292
Stewart, Dianne, 62, 64
Stewig, John Warren, 158, 256, 326-327
Stock, Catherine, 69, 254-255, 259
Stuart, Chad, 268, 271
Stuve-Bodeen, Stephanie, 67-68
Sweeney, Joan, 229, 234, 243

Taback, Simms, 296-298
Takaya, Julia, 124, 134
Takeshita, Fumiko, 132, 138
Talbott, Hudson, 263-264, 271
Talley, Carol, 277, 285
Tan, Amy, 82, 95, 102

Tarbescu, Edith, 261-262
Taylor, Alice, 268, 271
Tchana, Katrin Hyman, 25, 27
Tejima, Keizaburo, 123, 139
Temple, Frances, 374-375
Thiele, Colin, 169, 176
Thompson, Kay, 225, 243
Tildes, Phyllis Limbacher, 307, 318
Titus, Eve, 227, 244
Tolstoy, Leo, 312, 318
Tomioka, Chiyoko, 133, 139
Tompert, Ann, 89, 96, 102
Toye, William, 348, 361
Tresselt, Alvin, 339, 341
Trinca, Rod, 169, 176
Trottier, Maxine, 162-163
Tseng, Grace, 81-82, 103
Tsubakiyama, Margaret Holloway, 96, 103

Uchida, Yoshiko, 125, 129, 139
Ungerer, Tomi, 237, 244
Urrutia, Maria Cristina, 377, 389

Va, Leong, 88, 103
Valgardson, W.D., 349, 361
Van Laan, Nancy, 371-372, 405-406
Vaughan, Marcia, 122, 139, 172, 176
Vidaure, Morris, 395-396
Vigna, Judith, 281-282, 285
Villoldo, Alberto, 410, 412
Visconti, Guido, 275, 280, 285
Volkmer, Jane Anne, 369, 370

Wahl, Jan, 203, 219
Waite, Michael P., 126, 139
Walker, Barbara, 157-158
Walker, Richard, 197, 201-202, 219
Wallace, Ian, 350, 361

Wallner, Alexandra, 205, 219
Walsh, Jill Paton, 31, 34
Walsh, Vivian, 277, 284
Wang, Rosalind C., 92, 103
Ward, Leila, 45-46
Ward, Lynd, 356, 361
Watts, Bernadette, 249, 252
Weedn, Flavia, 328-329, 336
Wells, Rosemary, 183-185
Wells, Ruth, 129, 139, 256, 259, 290, 292, 342-343
Wettasinghe, Sybil, 154
Wheatley, Nadia, 167-168, 176
White, Carolyn, 321, 324
Whitfield, Susan, 78, 85, 103
Wild, Margaret, 174, 197, 248, 253
Wildsmith, Brian, 247, 253, 277, 280, 285
Willard, Nancy, 197, 205, 219
Williams, Jay, 143
Williams, Karen Lynn, 49-50, 371-372
Williams, Laura E., 128, 139
Wilson, Barbara Ker, 83, 103
Wilson-Max, Ken, 45-46, 60, 64
Winch, John, 173, 177
Winter, Jeanette, 249-250, 253, 379, 385, 393
Winter, Jonah, 385, 393
Winthrop, Elizabeth, 304-305, 318
Wisniewski, David, 133-134, 139
Wolf, Gita, 109, 114
Wolfson, Margaret Olivia, 59, 64, 178
Wolkstein, Diane, 87, 91, 103, 372-373
Wood, Douglas, 355, 361
Woodman, Allen, 226, 241
Woodruff, Elvira, 313, 318

Xiong, Blia, 142

Yacowitz, Caryn, 387, 393
Yashima, Taro, 133, 139

Ye, Ting-xing, 96, 103
Yen, Clare, 85, 103
Yep, Laurence, 80, 83, 88, 91-93, 104, 143-144
Yolen, Jane, 88, 104, 157, 159, 210, 219, 247, 253, 319, 321, 324, 347
Yorinks, Arthur, 209, 219, 224, 244
Young, Ed, 83-85, 94, 104-105
Young, Russell, 86, 105

Zak, Monica, 386, 393
Zamorano, Ana, 326-327
Zelinsky, Paul O., 274, 278-279, 285
Zemach, Harve, 181, 219, 285
Zeman, Ludmila, 355, 361

Title Index

Abuela's Weave, 368-369
Acrobat & the Angel, The, 230, 243
Alfie and the Birthday Surprise, 201, 207, 214
Alfie's 1 2 3, 200-201, 207, 214
Alfie's ABC, 200, 207, 214
Ali, Child of the Desert, 52
All about Alfie, 208, 214
All of You Was Singing, 385, 387, 392
All the Lights in the Night, 184-185
Always Room for One More, 322-323
Amazing Mallika, 106-107, 113
Ananse's Feast, 40, 44
Anansi and the Moss-Covered Rock, 39, 43
Anansi and the Talking Melon, 39, 43
Anansi Does the Impossible, 40, 42
Anansi Finds a Fool, 40, 42
Anansi Goes Fishing, 39-40, 43
Anansi the Spider, 40-41, 43
Anatole and the Cat, 227, 244
Anatole and the Toyshop, 227, 244
And Sunday Makes Seven, 362-363
Androcles and the Lion, 274, 285
Angel's Kite, 380, 389
Angkat, 76-77
Animals of the Chinese Zodiac, 78, 85, 103
Ant and the Grasshopper, The, 78-79, 101
Appley Dapply's Nursery Rhymes, 190, 216
Arctic Stories, 351, 359
Arthur and the Sword, 203-204, 218
At Grandpa's Sugar Bush, 352, 358
At the Crossroads, 62-63
At the Wish of a Fish, 309, 315

Atlantis, 256-258
Aunt Lilly's Laundromat, 372

Baba Yaga (Arnold), 306, 313
Baba Yaga (Kimmel), 305, 315
Baba Yaga and the Wise Doll, 305, 316
Baba Yaga and Vasilisa the Brave, 304-305, 316
Babar Loses His Crown, 225, 239
Baboushka and the Three Kings, 307, 317
Babushka, 306-307, 316
Babushka Baba Yaga, 306, 316
Babushka's Doll, 307, 316
Babushka's Mother Goose, 307, 316
Bach's Big Adventure, 250, 252
Badger and the Magic Fan, The, 127, 135
Ballymara Flood, The, 268, 271
Banza, The, 372-373
Baseball Bats for Christmas, 350-351, 359
Basho and the Fox, 130, 137
Bear for Miguel, A, 366
Bearhead, 310, 315
Bears' Autumn, The, 123, 139
Beast of Monsieur Racine, The, 237, 244
Beatrix Potter, 205, 219
Beautiful Butterfly, The, 325, 327
Beautiful Warrior, 79, 101
Bee and the Dragon, The, 125, 136
Beethoven Lives Upstairs, 181-182
Beggar's Magic, The, 80, 97
Bernal & Florinda, 325, 327
Beware the Brindlebeast, 187, 203, 218
Bicycle for Rosaura, A, 413
Bicycle Man, The, 125-126, 138
Big Alfie and Annie Rose Storybook, The, 208, 214
Big Alfie Out of Doors Storybook, The, 208, 214
Big Anthony, 272-273, 281-282
Big Anthony and the Magic Ring, 273, 282
Big Boy, 65-67

Big Brother, Little Sister, 55-56
Big City ABC, A, 352, 360
Biggest Bear, The, 356, 361
Biggest Frog in Australia, The, 170, 176
Bijou, Bonbon & Beau, 233, 243
Bill and Pete, 32-33
Bill and Pete Go Down the Nile, 32, 34
Bill and Pete to the Rescue, 32, 34
Billy Beg and His Bull, 266, 270
Bimwili & the Zimwi, 65, 67
Bird or Two, A, 229, 233, 241
Bird Who Was an Elephant, The, 111, 113
Birds' Gift, The, 340-341
Birthday Swap, The, 384, 392
Black Geese, The, 306, 316
Blind Men and the Elephant, The, 109, 112
Blossom Comes Home, 199, 213
Blue Butterfly, A, 229, 232, 241
Bonaparte, 226, 239
Bonjour, Lonnie, 225, 243
Bonjour, Mr. Satie, 233, 239
Bonny's Big Day, 200, 213
Bony-Legs, 305, 314
Booby Hatch, 408
Boots and His Brothers, 291
Borreguita and the Coyote, 378, 388
Bouki Dances the Kokioko, 372-373
Boundless Grace, 38
Boxing Champion, The, 353, 358
Boy Named Giotto, A, 280, 283
Boy of the Deeps, 350, 361
Boy of the Three-Year Nap, The, 122-123, 138
Boy Who Drew Cats, The, 127, 136
Boy Who Held Back the Sea, The, 287-288
Boy Who Stuck Out His Tongue, The, 261-262
Brave Highland Heart, 350, 359
Brave Janet Reachfar, 322-323
Brave Little Parrot, The, 108, 113

Brave Margaret, 264, 271
Brave Martha and the Dragon, 229, 243
Bravo, Zan Angelo!, 277, 281-282
Bremen Town Band, The, 247, 253
Bremen Town Musicians, The, 246, 253
Bringing the Rain to Kapiti Plain, 45-46
Brother Sun, Sister Moon, 272, 277, 281, 284
Butterfly, The, 228, 242

Call Me Ahnighito, 367
Camille and the Sunflowers, 229, 232, 238
Can You Catch Josephine?, 353, 360
Canary Prince, The, 275-276, 284
Caravan, 73
Carp for Kimiko, A, 133, 136
Cat and Rat, 84-85, 104
Cat and the Cook and Other Fables of Krylov, The, 309, 315
Caterina, 276, 284
Cave Painter of Lascaux, The, 221, 238
Cendrillon: A Caribbean Cinderella, 376
Chalk Doll, The, 374-375
Chanukkah Tree, The, 293-294, 298
Charlie's Checklist, 210, 215
Charlie's House, 59-60, 64
Chaska and the Golden Doll, 410-411
Cherry Tree, 107, 112
Chibi, 124, 134
Child's Treasury of Irish Rhymes, A, 268, 271
Chin Yu Min and the Ginger Cat, 81, 97
China's Bravest Girl, 94-95, 98
Chinese Mirror, The, 149, 152
Chinese Siamese Cat, The, 95, 102
Chinese Zoo, A, 86, 98
Christmas Day Kitten, The, 199, 213
Christmas Surprise for Chabelita, A, 397
Christopher and Grandma on Safari, 45-46
Chubbo's Pool, 24
Church Mice and the Ring, The, 210, 216

Cinderella, 230-231, 242
City of Dragons, The, 88, 104
Clay Boy, 308, 314
Clever Katya, 309, 315
Clever Tortoise, 65, 67
Cloudmakers, The, 141
Clown of God, The, 274, 282
Cocoa Ice, 365
Coconut Kind of Days, 401
Colors of Germany, 250, 252
Colors of Japan, 131, 136
Colors of Mexico, 386, 393
Contest, The, 74-75
Copycat, 209-210, 212
Could You Stop Josephine?, 353, 360
Count Silvernose, 279, 284
Count Your Way through Brazil, 406
Count Your Way through Canada, 355, 358
Count Your Way through France, 230, 240
Count Your Way through Germany, 248, 252
Count Your Way through Greece, 254-255, 258
Count Your Way through India, 107-108, 113
Count Your Way through Ireland, 265, 270
Count Your Way through Israel, 121
Count Your Way through Italy, 277, 283
Count Your Way through Japan, 126, 135
Count Your Way through Korea, 151-152
Count Your Way through Mexico, 381, 391
Count Your Way through Russia, 302, 314
Cows Are Going to Paris, The, 226, 241
Crane Wife, The (Bodkin), 128, 134
Crane Wife, The (Keo), 128, 136
Cricket Warrior, The, 89, 97
Cricket's Cage, The, 78, 98
Crictor, 237, 244
Croco'nile, 31, 34
Crow Boy, 133, 139
Cuckoo, 384, 390

Da Wei's Treasure, 86, 98
Dancing Pig, The, 115-116
Dancing Turtle, The, 406
Danger in Tibet, 81-82
Daniel O'Rourke, 267, 270
Day Adam Got Mad, The, 332, 333
Day Gogo Went to Vote, The, 58-59, 64
Day of Ahmed's Secret, The, 29, 34
Day of the Dead, 382, 391
Days of the Blackbird, 275, 282
Dear Fred, 173, 176
Dear Juno, 148, 153
Dick Whittington and His Cat, 197, 204, 212
Diego, 385, 393
Dinner at Magritte's, 233, 240
Dinosaur's New Clothes, The, 228, 240
Distant Talking Drum, The, 54, 56
Doctor Bird, 374-375
Dog, 268-269
Dog Came Too, A, 356, 360
Domitila, 378, 389
Don't Leave Elephant to Go and Chase a Bird, 40-41
Donkey and the Rock, The, 81, 98
Doorbell Rang, The, 209, 214
Dorobo the Dangerous, 122, 139
Dragon Kite, The, 122, 136
Dragon Kites and Dragonflies, 95, 98
Dragon New Year, The, 82, 97
Dragon Prince, The 83, 104
Dragon's Pearl, The, 80, 100
Dragon's Tale and Other Animal Fables of the Chinese Zodiac, The,
    86, 98
Dragonsong, 86, 105
Dream Eater, The, 133-134
Drums of Noto Hanto, The, 122-123, 135
Duffy and the Devil, 187, 219

Eagle, 147

Egyptian Cinderella, The, 29-30, 33
Egyptian Gods and Goddesses, 30, 33
Egyptian Polar Bear, The, 31-33
Elinda Who Danced in the Sky, 220
Elisabeth, 250, 253
Elizabeti's Doll, 67-68
Eloise in Paris, 225, 243
Elves and the Shoemaker, The (Galdone), 249, 251
Elves and the Shoemaker, The (Grimm, Watts), 249, 252
Emily, the Rain Forest Monkey, 405-406
Emma and the Silk Train, 348-349, 360
Emma's Lamb, 198, 215
Emperor and the Kite, The, 88, 104
Emperor's New Clothes, The, 92, 98
Empress and the Silkworm, The, 91, 100
Empty Pot, The, 87, 99
Enchanted Book, The, 295, 298
Enchanted Tapestry, The, 90, 102
Encounter, 347
Enora and the Black Crane, 170, 176
Erandi's Braids, 379, 392
Escaping to America, 295, 298
Everyone Knows What a Dragon Looks Like, 143

Fabulous Firework Family, The, 381, 391
Face at the Window, 374-375
Faithful Friend, The, 376
Fantastic Drawings of Danielle, The, 223, 241
Faraway Home, 36
Farmer and the Poor God, The, 129, 139
Farmer Schulz's Ducks, 169, 176
Feathers, 293-294, 298
Fiddler of the Northern Lights, The, 354, 360
Fin M'Coul, 263, 265, 270
Finn MacCoul and His Fearless Wife, 265, 269
Fire on the Mountain, 35-36
Firebird, The, 303, 314
First Red Maple Leaf, The, 355, 361

First Snow, 197, 215
First Snow, Magic Snow, 308, 313
First Song Ever Sung, The, 133, 137
First Story Ever Told, The, 410, 412
Fisherman and His Wife, The, 290, 292
Five Chinese Brothers, The, 89, 97
Five O'Clock Charlie, 200, 213
Flicka, Ricka, Dicka and the Big Red Hen, 330, 334
Flicka, Ricka, Dicka and the Little Dog, 328, 331, 334
Flicka, Ricka, Dicka and the New Dotted Dresses, 331, 334
Flicka, Ricka, Dicka and the Strawberries, 331, 335
Flicka, Ricka, Dicka and the Three Kittens, 331, 335
Flicka, Ricka, Dicka and Their New Friend, 331, 335
Flicka, Ricka, Dicka Bake a Cake, 331, 335
Flood Fish, 168, 175
Floss, 198, 215
Flowers on the Wall, 295-296, 298
Fly, Eagle, Fly!, 58, 63
Flying Tortoise, The, 55-56
Fool of the World and the Flying Ship, The, 309, 317
Forest in the Clouds, The, 362-363
Fortune-Tellers, The, 25-26
Forty Fortunes, 117-118
Fossil Girl, The, 205-206, 212
Frog Princess, The (Cecil), 279, 282
Frog Princess, The (Isele), 306, 315
Frog Princess, The (Lewis), 306, 315
Frog Went A-Courting, 322-323
From Far Away, 356, 360
From the Bellybutton of the Moon and Other Summer Poems, 386, 389
Fu-dog, 196, 213
Funny Little Woman, The, 129, 137
Furaha Means Happy, 45-46

Gabriella's Song, 277, 283
Galimoto, 49-50
Genius of Leonardo, The, 275, 280, 285
Gershon's Monster, 299

Ghost of Greyfriar's Bobby, The, 320, 323
Gift, The, 251
Gift of the Nile, 30, 34
Gift of the Poinsettia, The, 382-383, 393
Gift of the Sun, 62, 64
Gift Stone, The, 168-169, 175
Giraffe That Walked to Paris, The, 235, 242
Girl, the Fish & the Crown, The, 325, 327
Girl from the Snow Country, 133, 135
Girl Who Loved Caterpillars, The, 125, 137
Glorious Flight, The, 235-236, 243
Gods and Goddesses of Olympus, The, 255, 258
Going for Oysters, 174
Going Home, 388-389
Golden Bracelet, The, 74-75
Golden Sandal, The, 119-120
Golden Slipper, The, 161, 163
Gollo and the Lion, 26-27
Gracias, Rosa, 368-370
Grain of Rice, A, 93, 101
Grandfather Tang's Story, 96, 102
Grandfather's Dream, 162-163
Grandfather's Journey, 130, 138
Grandfather's Story, 132, 134
Grandma Chickenlegs, 305, 316
Grandma's Hat, 59, 63
Grandmother's Song, 388-389
Grandpa's Town, 132, 137
Grannie Jus' Come!, 397-398
Grass Sandals, 130, 138
Great Kapok Tree, The, 405-406
Greatest of All, The, 127, 129-130, 136
Greatest Treasure, The, 93, 99
Green Frogs, The, 150, 152
Gregory Cool, 400-401
Grey Neck, 312, 317
Grusha, 312, 314

Halala Means Welcome!, 60, 64

Hand-Me-Down Horse, The, 250-251, 253
Happy New Year's Day, A, 354, 358
Harry and Lulu, 224, 244
Hat Seller and the Monkeys, The, 51
Have You Seen Josephine?, 353, 361
Hear, Hear, Mr. Shakespeare, 200, 204-205, 215
Heart of a Tiger, 110-112
Hero of Bremen, The, 245-246, 252
Hidden Forest, The, 169, 174
Hill of Fire, 379, 392
Hobyahs, The, 202, 218
Honk!, 227, 240
Horses with Wings, 235, 240
House in the Sky, The, 347
House of Wisdom, The, 119-120
How Llama Saved the Day, 410, 412
How Music Came to the World, 384-385, 393
How Snowhare Rescued the Sun, 301, 313
How the Ox Star Fell from Heaven, 85-86, 100
How the Rooster Got His Crown, 92, 102
How the Sun Was Born, 385, 390
Howling Hill, 349-350, 358
Hummingbird King, The, 369-370
Hummingbirds' Gift, The, 379, 391
Hundredth Name, The, 29, 32, 34
Hush! (Gerber), 268, 270
Hush! (Ho), 155-156

I, Crocodile, 234, 242
I Am Eyes/Ni Macho, 45, 46
I Have an Olive Tree, 257-258
Iguana Brothers, The, 387, 391
Impossible Riddle, The, 302, 315
In the Heart of the Village, 111-112
In the Month of Kislev, 297-298
In the Moonlight Mist, 150, 153
Incredible Painting of Felix Clousseau, The, 227, 238
Inside-Outside Book of Paris, The, 228, 242
Invisible Hunters, The, 395-396

Irish Cinderlad, The, 263, 266, 269
Iron Hans, 279, 283
Is It Far to Zanzibar?, 66-67
Island Christmas, An, 400-401
Island in the Sun, 375
Island Summer, 254-255, 259
It Happened in Chelm, 294, 297
It Takes a Village, 23

Jack and the Beanstalk (Beneduce), 197, 201, 211
Jack and the Beanstalk (Kellogg), 197, 201-202, 215
Jack and the Beanstalk (Walker), 197, 201-202, 219
Jack the Dog, 125, 137
Jackal's Flying Lesson, 53
Jade Horse, the Cricket, and the Peach Stone, The, 89, 102
Jafta, 61, 63
Jafta—The Homecoming, 62-63
Jafta—The Journey, 61, 64
Jafta—The Town, 61, 64
Jafta and the Wedding, 61, 64
Jafta's Father, 61, 64
Jafta's Mother, 61, 64
Jaguar in the Rain Forest, 409
Jamela's Dress, 62-63
Jamie O'Rourke and the Big Potato, 266, 270
Jamie O'Rourke and the Pooka, 266, 270
Jingle, the Christmas Clown, 278, 282
Joan of Arc (Hodges), 233, 241
Joan of Arc (Poole), 234, 243
Jojofu, 126, 139
Josefina, 379, 385, 393
Joseph Had a Little Overcoat, 296-298
Judge Rabbit and the Tree Spirit, 76-77
Jump Up Time, 400-401
Junior Thunder Lord, The, 91, 104
Just Enough Is Plenty, 297-298
Just like Floss, 198, 215
Just Stay Put, 294, 297

Kashtanka, 312, 314
Katie Morag and the New Pier, 320-321, 323
Kele's Secret, 66-67
Kente Colors, 42
Khan's Daughter, The, 143-144
Kinderdike, 288
King and the Tortoise, The, 26
King Midas, 158, 256
King Midas and the Golden Touch, 256, 258
King of Ireland's Son, The, 267, 269
King of Magic, Man of Glass, 248, 252
King's Chessboard, The, 109, 112
King's Day, The, 228, 234, 238
King's Giraffe, The, 235, 239
Kisses from Rosa, 246, 252
Kites, 94, 99
Koala Lou, 9, 172, 176
Koi and the Kola Nuts, 48
Komodo!, 115-116
Kongi and Potgi, 149, 152
Korean Cinderella, The, 149, 152
Kylie's Song, 172, 176

Lady of Guadulupe, The, 377, 390
Language of Birds, The, 304, 316
Lao Lao of Dragon Mountain, 93-94, 97
Lassie Come-Home, 342-343
Last Snake in Ireland, The, 267, 271, 320
Last Train, The, 198, 215
Laziest Boy in the World, The, 96, 101
Leaving for America, 183-184
Legend of Mu Lan, The, 94-95, 100
Legend of Old Befana, The, 278, 282
Legend of the Milky Way, 90, 100
Legend of the Persian Carpet, The, 118
Legend of the Poinsettia, The, 382-383, 390
Leon and Bob, 193, 214
Leopard's Drum, The, 41, 44

Leprechauns Never Lie, 268-269
Let the Celebrations Begin!, 247, 253
Let's Eat, 326-327
Let's Go Traveling in Mexico, 386, 392
Letter to the King, A, 88, 103
Liang and the Magic Paintbrush, 87-88, 99
Lily and the Wooden Bowl, 129, 138
Lily Cupboard, The, 287, 289
Ling Cho and His Three Friends, 95, 101
Lion's Whiskers, The, 35-36
Little Golden Lamb, The, 260, 262
Little Humpbacked Horse, The, 304, 318
Little Johnny Buttermilk, 203, 219
Little Kit, 196, 215
Little Mouse & Elephant, 157, 159
Little Oh, 128, 137
Little Red Ant and the Great Big Crumb, The, 384, 389
Little Salmon for Witness, A, 400-401
Little Salt Lick and the Sun King, 228, 234, 238
Little Snowgirl, The, 308, 314
Lon Po Po, 83-84, 104
Long Silk Strand, The, 128, 139
Long-Haired Girl, The, 91-92, 102
Longest Home Run, The, 353-354, 358
Loon's Necklace, The, 348, 361
Lord of the Cranes, 87, 98
Lost Horse, The, 84, 104
Lost in the Amazon, 405-406
Lotta's Bike, 331-332, 334
Lotta's Christmas Surprise, 332, 334
Lotta's Easter Surprise, 332, 334
Lotus Seed, The, 162-163
Loyal Cat, The, 127, 137
Lucy & Tom's 1.2.3., 201, 214
Lucy Dove, 319, 321, 323

Madame LaGrande and Her So High, to the Sky, Uproarious
    Pompadour, 227-228, 240

Madeline, 8, 222, 238
Madeline and the Bad Hat, 222, 238
Madeline and the Gypsies, 222-223, 238
Madeline in London, 195, 211, 223
Madeline's Christmas, 222, 239
Madeline's Rescue, 222, 239
Madoulina, 25-26
Magic Amber, The, 148-149, 153
Magic Babushka, The, 307, 318
Magic Cap, The, 328-329, 336
Magic Dogs of the Volcanoes, 366
Magic Ear, The, 129, 136
Magic Fan, The 132, 134
Magic Feather, The, 374-375
Magic Purse, The, 125, 139
Magic Spring, 149, 153
Magic Tapestry, The, 91, 99
Magic Tree, The, 55-56
Magic Wings, The, 87, 103
Magid Fasts for Ramadan, 33-34
Making of a Knight, The, 209, 216
Mama & Papa Have a Store, 368-369
Mama Elizabeti, 67-68
Mama Rocks, Papa Sings, 371-372
Mama's Perfect Present, 224, 240
Man Who Caught Fish, The, 155-156
Man Who Kept House, The (Asbjørnsen, Moe), 290-291
Man Who Kept House, The (Hague, Hague), 290-291
Man Who Tricked a Ghost, The, 92-93, 104
Mandela, 60, 63
Manu and the Talking Fish, 108-109, 112
Manuela's Gift, 384, 390
Maples in the Mist, 95, 100
Marguerite Makes a Book, 223, 243
Maria Molina and the Days of the Dead, 382, 392
Mariana and the Merchild, 407
Marie in Fourth Position, 233, 243
Mario's Mayan Journey, 381, 392

Market Day, 269
Market Square Dog, The, 199, 213
Marriage of the Rain Goddess, 59, 64
Mary Anning and the Sea Dragon, 205-206, 210
Mary of Mile 18, 348, 357
Matreshka, 302, 304, 313
Mats, The, 147
Max & Ruby's First Greek Myth, 256, 259
Max & Ruby's Midas, 256, 259
Maya, Tiger Cub, 110, 113
Me and Mr. Mah, 348, 357, 361
Mean Hyena, The, 49
Mediopollito, 378, 388
Memory Coat, The, 313, 318
Mei-Mei Loves the Morning, 96, 103
Merry Christmas, Strega Nona, 273, 282
Michelangelo's Surprise, 276, 280, 284
Midas Touch, The, 158, 256
Mighty Mountain and the Three Strong Women, 129, 135
Min-Yo and the Moon Dragon, 88-89, 99
Ming Lo Moves the Mountain, 92, 103
Minou, 221, 226, 239
Mirette on the High Wire, 223, 242
Miro in the Kingdom of the Sun, 410, 412
Mitten, The (Brett), 339-340
Mitten, The (Tresselt), 339, 341
Mole's Daughter, The, 150
Monkey and the Crocodile, The, 108, 113
Monkey and the Mango, The, 106, 112
Monkey Bridge, The, 107, 113
Monkey Sunday, 28
Moon Lady, The, 82, 102
Moon Rope, 411
Morning Chair, The, 287-289
Moses the Kitten, 199, 213
Moshi Moshi, 133, 136
Mountains of Tibet, The, 80-81, 99
Mouse Match, 84, 94, 104

Mousehole Cat, The, 188, 211
Mozart Tonight, 181-182
Mr. Horrax and the Gratch, 343
Mr. Lunch Borrows a Canoe, 277, 284
Mr. Seminola-Seminolus, 257-258
Mufaro's Beautiful Daughters, 69
Mummies Made in Egypt, 31, 33
Music for the Tsar of the Sea, 301, 316
Musicians of Bremen, The, 247, 253
Musicians of the Sun, 384-385, 392
My Arctic 1, 2, 3, 351, 359
My Dear Noel, 205, 215
My Farm, 171, 175
My Father, 224, 239
My Father's Boat, 162-163
My Gran, 236, 239
My Grandma Lived in Gooliguch, 171, 175
My Grandmother's Journey, 311, 313
My Grandpa and the Sea, 399
My Little Island, 394
My Mexico, 387, 391
My Place, 167-168, 176
My Place in Space, 173-175
My Rows and Piles of Coins, 66-67
My Uncle Nikos, 254, 258
Mysterious Giant of Barletta, The, 276, 282
Mystery of King Karfu, The, 32-33
Mystery of the Monkey's Maze, The, 115-116

Nabulela, 60, 64
Naughty Crow, The, 340
Nekane, the Lamiña & the Bear, 232, 326-327
Newf, 354, 359
Night of the Goat Children, 245-246, 252
Night Visitors, 84, 105
Nightingale, The, 86-87, 97
Nilo and the Tortoise, 408
Nine Days to Christmas, 383, 390

Nine-in-One, Grr! Grr!, 142
No Dinner!, 108, 114
Nochebuena South of the Border, La, 383, 393
Nora's Castle, 237, 241
Nora's Roses, 237, 241
Northern Alphabet, A, 355, 358
Northern Lights, 351, 359
Not So Fast, Songololo, 62-63

O Canada, 356, 358
O'Sullivan Stew, 263-264, 271
Oh Brother, 209, 219
Oh, Kojo! How Could You!, 140, 142
Oh, No, Toto!, 25, 27
Okino and the Whales, 132, 134
Old Lady and the Birds, The, 388, 391
Old Man Who Loved to Sing, The, 173, 177
Old Woman and Her Pig, The, 203, 215
Old Woman Who Lived in a Vinegar Bottle, The, 203, 216
Old Woman Who Loved to Read, The, 173, 177
On Christmas Day in the Morning, 207, 216
On Ramon's Farm, 387, 391
Once upon a Lily Pad, 229, 234, 243
One Eye, Two Eyes, Three Eyes, 340-341
One Fine Day, 75
One Grain of Rice, 110, 112
One Round Moon and a Star for Me, 47
One Woolly Wombat, 169, 176
Only a Pigeon, 36-37
Only One Cowry, 23
Only One Woof, 199, 213
Oscar, Cat-about-Town, 199, 213
Our Home Is the Sea, 79, 101
Over the Green Hills, 58, 63

Paddington Bear, 193-194, 211
Paddington Bear: My Scrapbook, 194, 211, 411
Paddington Bear All Day Long, 195, 207, 211

Paddington Bear and the Busy Bee Carnival, 194, 211
Paddington Bear and the Christmas Surprise, 194, 211
Paddington Bear Goes to Market, 195, 207, 211
Paddington Meets the Queen, 194, 211
Paddington Rides On!, 194, 211
Paddington's ABC, 185, 201, 212
Paddington's Colors, 195, 212
Paddington's First Word Book, 195, 201, 212
Paddington's 123, 195, 201, 212
Paddington's Opposites, 195, 212
Paddle-to-the-Sea, 357-358
Pages of Music, 276, 283
Painted Dreams, 371-372
Painter Who Loved Chickens, The, 287-288
Painting the Wind, 229, 232, 240
Pancho's Pinata, 383, 390
Papa Gatto, 279-280, 284
Papa Piccolo, 277, 285
Papa Tells Chita a Story, 364
Paper Dragon, The, 93, 98
Paris Cat, 226, 238
Park Bench, The, 132, 138
Pascual's Magic Pictures, 368, 370
Passage to Freedom, 286
Patrick, 267, 270
Patrick's Day, 266, 271
Peacebound Trains, 151
Peach Boy (Hooks), 128, 135
Peach Boy (Sakurai), 127-128, 138
Peacock's Pride, The, 109, 113
Peddler's Gift, The, 184-185
Pelle's New Suit, 329, 333
Pepi and the Secret Names, 31, 34
Perfect Orange, The, 35-36
Periwinkle Isn't Paris, 224, 240
Persian Cinderella, The, 117-118
Peter and the Wolf (Hastings), 300, 303, 314
Peter and the Wolf (Lemieux), 303, 315

Peter and the Wolf (Prokofiev), 303, 317
Peter in Blueberry Land, 329, 333
Petrosinella, 274, 284
Pheasant and Kingfisher, 170, 175
Picture Book of Anne Frank, A, 287-288
Pied Piper of Hamelin, The (Bartos-Höppner), 247, 251
Pied Piper of Hamelin, The (Corrin, Corrin), 247-248, 251
Piggins, 210, 219
Pippi Longstocking's After-Christmas Party, 332, 334
Pirate Queen, The, 268, 270
Possum Magic, 9-10, 172-173, 175
Prairie Alphabet, A, 354-355, 357
Prairie Boy's Summer, A, 349, 359
Prairie Boy's Winter, A, 349, 359
Prince Ivan and the Firebird, 303, 314
Princess and the Peacocks, The, 196, 216
Princess Florecita and the Iron Shoes, 326-327
Promise Is a Promise, A, 357, 360
Pulling the Lion's Tail, 35-36
Pumpkin Fiesta, 387, 393
Pumpkin Runner, The, 174
Puss in Boots (Kirstein), 231, 241
Puss in Boots (Perrault, Lunelli), 231, 242
Puss in Boots (Perrault, Marcellino), 231, 242

Queen's Necklace, The, 329, 333

Rabbit and the Moon, 355, 361
Rabbit Pirates, 229, 239
Rabbit's Escape, The, 150, 152
Rabbit's Judgment, The, 150, 152
Rabbit's Tail, The, 150, 152
Raisel's Riddle, 296, 298
Rama and the Demon King, 108, 114
Rapunzel, 274, 278-279, 285
Rare Treasure, 205-206, 212
Rechenka's Eggs, 307, 316
Remarkable Christmas of the Cobbler's Song, The, 182

Return of Freddy Le-Grand, The, 236, 238
Rhymes for Annie Rose, 207, 214
Rice Is Life, 115-116
Ride on the Red Mare's Back, A, 328, 333
Rikki-Tikki-Tavi (Kipling, Davis), 111, 113
Rikki-Tikki-Tavi (Kipling, Pinkney), 111, 113
Ring of Truth, The, 264, 269
Rise and Shine, Mariko-chan!, 133, 139
River Dragon, The, 86, 101
Rollo and Tweedy and the Ghost of Dougal Castle, 322-323
Roman Twins, The, 274-275, 283
Rome Antics, 275, 284
Rooster's Antlers, The, 85, 100
Royal Bee, The, 145
Royal Drum, The, 41, 43
Ruined House, A, 206-207, 216
Running the Road to ABC, 371-372

Sacred River, 107, 113
Sadako, 131, 134
Saint Ciaran, 267, 271
Saint Francis, 279-280, 285
Saint Patrick and the Peddler, 267, 270
Salt, 309, 315
Samurai's Daughter, The, 123, 138
Sanyasin's First Day, The, 106, 112, 114
Sato and the Elephants, 134-135
Saturday Market, 379-380, 391
Save My Rainforest, 386, 393
Savitri, 108, 114
Sayonara, Mrs. Kackleman, 124-125, 136
Scarlet Flower, The, 310, 313
Screen of Frogs, 127, 135
Sea and I, The, 132, 137
Sea King's Daughter, The, 301-302, 317
Sea Maidens of Japan, The, 132, 134
Seal, 257-258
Sebastian, 249-250, 253

Sebgugugu the Glutton, 57
Secret Footprints, The, 365
Seeing Red, 187-188, 213
Seeker of Knowledge, 32, 234, 243
Selina and the Bear Paw Quilt, 352, 361
Selina and the Shoo-Fly Pie, 352, 361
Seven Chinese Brothers, The, 89-90, 101
Seven Gods of Luck, The, 126, 136
Seventh Sister, The, 90, 97
Shadow Dance, 65, 67
Shell Woman & the King, The, 91, 104
Shepherd Boy, The, 197, 215
Shoemaker and the Elves, The, 279, 284
Shoemaker Martin, 312, 318
Silent Lotus, 76-79
Silent Observer, 350, 360
Silver Cow, The, 344
Sing-Song of Old Man Kangaroo, The, 170, 175
Singing Man, The, 54-56
Sitti's Secrets, 146
Sled Dog for Moshi, A, 351, 358
Sleeping Bread, The, 369-370
Smudge, the Little Lost Lamb, 199, 214
Snap!, 172, 176
Snipp, Snapp, Snurr and the Big Farm, 330, 335
Snipp, Snapp, Snurr and the Big Surprise, 330, 335
Snipp, Snapp, Snurr and the Buttered Bread, 330, 335
Snipp, Snapp, Snurr and the Gingerbread, 329-330, 335
Snipp, Snapp, Snurr and the Magic Horse, 330, 335
Snipp, Snapp, Snurr and the Red Shoes, 329, 335
Snipp, Snapp, Snurr and the Reindeer, 330, 336
Snipp, Snapp, Snurr and the Seven Dogs, 330, 336
Snipp, Snapp, Snurr and the Yellow Sled, 330, 336
Snipp, Snapp, Snurr Learn to Swim, 330, 336
Snow White, 249, 252
Snow White and the Seven Dwarfs, 249, 252
Snow Wife, The, 128, 138
So Say the Little Monkeys, 405-406

Soldier and Tsar in the Forest, 309-310, 317
Somewhere in Africa, 59, 63
Song for Lena, A, 261-262
Song of Mu Lan, The, 94-95, 101
Song of Six Birds, The, 62-63
Song of the Chirimia, 369-370
Sorry, Miss Folio!, 208, 214
South African Night, A, 61, 63
Spider and the Sky God, 30-40, 43
Spirit of Tio Fernando, The, 382, 392
Squash It!, 325, 327
Squiggle, The, 96, 102
Stairway to Doom, 322-324
Star of Fear, Star of Hope, 236-237, 241
Starry Messenger, 281, 284
Stina, 332-333
Stone, The, 117-118
Stone Girl, Bone Girl, 205-206, 210
Stone Lion, The, 81, 102
Stone Soup, 232, 239
Stonecutter, The (Demi), 94, 99
Stonecutter, The (McDermott), 129-130, 137
Story about Ping, The, 95, 99
Story of a Dolphin, 402
Story of a Main Street, The, 206, 213
Story of Ferdinand, The, 326-327
Story of Lightning & Thunder, The, 54, 56
Story of Little Babaji, The, 111-112
Story of Rosy Dock, The, 170-171, 175
Story, A Story, A, 40, 43
Storytellers, The, 52
Streets Are Free, The, 413
Streets of Gold, 183-185
Strega Nona, 272-273, 283
Strega Nona: Her Story, 272, 283
Strega Nona Meets Her Match, 273, 283
Strega Nona Takes a Vacation, 273, 283
Strega Nona's Magic Lessons, 273, 283

Subira Subira, 66, 68
Sugaring-Off Party, The, 353, 360
Sun, the Wind, and Tashira, The, 53
Sun Girl and the Moon Boy, The, 150, 152
Sunday with Grandpa, A, 209, 213
Sundiata, 51
Supergrandpa, 332, 336
Sweet Dried Apples, 161, 163
Symphony for the Sheep, A, 264-265, 271
Symphony of Whales, A, 300-301, 317

Tailor of Gloucester, The, 193, 216
Tale of Benjamin Bunny, The, 189, 216
Tale of Ginger and Pickles, The, 191, 217
Tale of Hilda Louise, The, 223, 240
Tale of Jemima Puddle-duck, The, 190, 217
Tale of Johnny Town-mouse, The, 192, 217
Tale of Little Pig Robinson, The, 192-193, 217
Tale of Mr. Jeremy Fisher, The, 191, 217
Tale of Mr. Tod, The, 189, 217
Tale of Mrs. Tiggy-winkle, The, 191, 217
Tale of Mrs. Tittlemouse, The, 189-190, 217
Tale of Neshka the Kvetch, The, 248, 251
Tale of Peter Rabbit, The, 188-189, 217
Tale of Pigling Bland, The, 192, 217
Tale of Rabbit and Coyote, The, 380, 391
Tale of Samuel Whiskers, The, 190, 218
Tale of Squirrel Nutkin, The, 192, 218
Tale of the Flopsy Bunnies, The, 189, 218
Tale of the Mandarin Ducks, The, 127, 137
Tale of the Pie and the Patty-pan, The, 190-191, 218
Tale of the Turnip, The, 203, 210
Tale of Tom Kitten, The, 190, 218
Tale of Tsar Saltan, The, 310, 317
Tale of Two Bad Mice, The, 191,218
Tales of Trotter Street, 208, 214
Tam Lin (Cooper), 321, 323
Tam Lin (Yolen), 319, 321, 324

Tangerine Tree, The, 374-375
Tap-Tap, 371-372
Tasty Baby Belly Buttons, 123, 138
Tea with Milk, 130-131, 138
Teeny Tiny, 202, 211
Teeny Tiny Woman, The, 202, 218
Temple Cat, 31, 33
Ten Suns, 92, 100
Thank You, Santa, 174, 177
Three Billy Goats Gruff (Rounds), 290, 292
Three Billy Goats Gruff (Stevens), 290, 292
Three Golden Oranges, The, 325-326
Three Perfect Peaches, 230, 239
Three Sacks of Truth, 230, 243
Tiger Soup, 374-375
Tiger Woman, 80, 104
Tigers, Frogs, and Rice Cakes, 151-152
Tikki Tikki Tembo, 88, 101
Tim O'Toole and the Wee Folk, 264, 270
To Capture the Wind, 265, 271
Toad Is the Uncle of Heaven, 161, 163
Toad Overload, 168, 170-171, 176
Today Is the Day, 384, 393
Token Gift, The, 110, 113
Tomten, The, 333-334
Tomten and the Fox, The, 333-334
Tonight Is Carnaval, 411
Tony's Bread, 275, 283
Too Much Talk, 42-43
Tortillas and Lullabies, 362-363
Tower to Heaven, 41, 43
Treasure Chest, The, 92, 103
Tree of Cranes, 131, 138
Tree That Rains, The, 378-379, 389
Trojan Horse, The, 157-158, 256
Troll with No Heart in His Body and Other Tales of Trolls from
    Norway, The, 290-292
Truffle Hunter, The, 237, 242

Tsugele's Broom, 296-297
Tuan, 162-163
Tulips, 225, 242
Turnip, The, 308, 318
Turtle Songs, 178
Tutankhamen's Gift, 30, 34
Twenty-Five Mixtec Cats, The, 380-381, 391
Two Brothers, The, 76-77
Two Greedy Bears, 260-261
Two of Everything, 94, 100
Two Ways to Count to Ten, 48
Tye May and the Magic Brush, 87-88, 97

Umbrella Thief, The, 154
Uncle Alfred's Zoo, 281-282, 285
Uncle Nacho's Hat, 395
Uncle Snake, 380, 391
Under the Lemon Moon, 377, 387-388, 390
Uno, Dos, Tres, 381, 392
Up the Chimney, 202, 214

Vasilissa the Beautiful, 304-305, 318
Vassilisa the Wise, 311, 317
Very Hungry Lion, The, 109, 114
Very Last First Time, 354, 357
Village of Round and Square Houses, The, 25-26
Visit to William Blake's Inn, A, 197, 205, 219
Viva Mexico!, 386, 393

Wagonload of Fish, A, 260-261
Walking Stick, The, 162-163
Warrior and the Wise Man, The, 133-134, 139
Watermelons, Walnuts, and the Wisdom of Allah, 157-158
Wave, The, 129, 135
Weave of Words, A, 74-75
Weaving of a Dream, The, 90, 99
Weighing the Elephant, 96, 103
Wheel on the Chimney, 260-261

Wheels on the Bus, 236, 244
When Africa Was Home, 49-50
When the Viceroy Came, 377, 389
Where Are You Going, Manyoni?, 69
Where Fireflies Dance, 381, 389
Where Is Gah-Ning?, 352, 360
Where the Forest Meets the Sea, 168, 175
Where's Our Mama?, 224, 240
Whispering Cloth, The, 155-156
White Cat, The, 232, 243
White Tiger, Blue Serpent, 81-82, 103
White Wave, 91, 103
Whuppity Stoorie, 321, 324
Why Rat Comes First, 88, 103
Why the Crab Has No Head, 28
Why the Sea Is Salt, 291
Why the Sky Is Far Away, 55-56
Why the Sun & Moon Live in the Sky, 54, 56
Wild Horse Winter, 123-124, 135
Wilderness Cat, 354, 359
William Shakespeare's A Midsummer Night's Dream, 254, 258
William Tell (Early), 337-338
William Tell (Fisher), 337-338
Willow Pattern Story, The, 96, 99
Wind Blew, The, 207, 214
Window, 173, 175
Winged Cat, The, 30, 34
Winter Rescue, 349, 361
Wise Old Woman, The, 129, 139
Wise Shoemaker of Studena, 261-262
Wishbones, 83, 103
Witch's Face, The, 385, 391
Wolfhound, The, 312, 314
Woman Who Flummoxed the Fairies, The, 320, 323
Woman Who Outshone the Sun, The, 380, 389-390
Wombat Goes Walkabout, 167, 172, 176
Wombat Stew, 172, 176

Yanni Rubbish, 257, 259

Year of Fire, The, 356, 358

Yeh-Shen, 83, 101

Yellow Star, The, 186

Yeoman's Daring Daughter and the Princes in the Tower, The, 197, 204, 213

Yoshi's Feast, 124, 135

Yoshiko and the Foreigner, 124, 136

Yossel Zissel and the Wisdom of Chelm, 293, 298

Young Kangaroo, 171-172, 175

Young Mozart, 181-182

Yunmi and Halmoni's Trip, 148, 151

Zorro and Quwi, 410-411